Napoleon Recaptures Paris

Napóleon Recaptures Paris

❋ *March 20, 1815* ❋

by

CLAUDE MANCERON

translated from the French by

GEORGE UNWIN

W·W·Norton & Company · Inc ·

NEW YORK

à Janine Montupet, l'amie inséparable
des cent jours qui ont fait ce livre

❉ *Contents* ❉

MARCH 14th

MARCH 15th

MARCH 16th

MARCH 17th

Contents

MARCH 18th

THE FORTY HOURS OF MARCH 20th

✳ *Illustrations* ✳

between pages 164 and 165

With the exception of Nos. 6 and 7 the illustrations were provided by
the Mansell collection.

* *March* *14th* *

'Forget the past!' say the royalists.

So, the French must be made to forget their women violated, their properties laid waste, and France her glory destroyed, her name dishonoured by the Bourbons? The people must be made to forget that the wolves are in the place of the shepherd and his dogs?

NAPOLEON

(Note in the margin of the *Mémoires* of F. de Chaboulon)

1

Not quite a spring . . .

On March 20, 1815, Napoleon began again. If one prefers, another Napoleon began. For the first time in her history France, or at least the majority of the nation, triumphantly 'elected' her ruler and installed him in the Palace of the Tuileries. The man of the Fontainebleau good-byes, whose race was run, the megalomaniac of the broken dream of universal empire, 'recaptured' that Paris from which treason and his own mistakes had driven him less than a year earlier. And he showed Europe an unknown face: that of 'the repentance of a great man'. He had become—at least in appearance—a tribune of the people, a liberal monarch, shunning war and dictatorship. The workers called him on that day 'the great entrepreneur'. Sparked off by the army, a movement emanating from the depths reconsecrated him Emperor, more authentically than the anointing by the Pope and the complicity of the business world, by which he had reigned for ten years. It was Sisteron, Gap, Grenoble, Lyons, Mâcon and Auxerre that led him on to Paris.

Hour by hour, we shall try to relive the last days of this little revolution. It is the most unappreciated in the history of France, because the catastrophe of Waterloo three months later crushed all the seeds of progress that it contained. And because those obsessed with the Napoleonic legend, by putting all the interest of the event on the actions and conduct of the Emperor, have thrust into the shadows the vast tragi-comedy, French and European, which might yet have changed the face of the world. What happened on March 20th was much more than the return from the island of Elba, much more than one of those startling

19

episodes in an exceptional life. It was a challenge thrown down by France, once again, to false necessity, and it was history hesitating at the edge of the interminable morass of the Holy Alliance and the Established Order. The year 1815 was a replay of 1789 and 1793 at double or quits. Humanity, that year, might have advanced by a century. Perhaps the matter is worth considering a little more closely.

Rather than describe the classic step which Napoleon and his little army took at Porto Ferraio and follow them all the way to Paris, it seemed to me preferable to come at once to the decisive week from March 14th to 20th, when the news of Napoleon's landing ceased to be confidential, or unreal, and became a fact in face of which every man in France had to take sides . . . or changed sides. On March 14th, the Emperor moved on from Mâcon to Chalon; the King, at last aware of the danger, placed all his hopes in the army which Marshal Ney was leading to bar the way to him. Ney, precisely, proceeded at midday to rally to Napoleon, and to make of that day the day which was to render March 20th possible. But that same morning, in Vienna, Talleyrand could breathe at last: by a Declaration of the Allied Powers, the 'disturber of the peace of the world' was outlawed from humanity, and March 14th thus prepared that other day when, at Waterloo, June 18th would cancel out March 20th.

Let us forget all that blood upon the corn. Let us go back to March 14th. Let us start from there. Not a shot has been fired yet. And under the shrinking patches of snow in the bare fields, breaking through here and there, are the first violets of a spring which might, indeed, have become that of Europe.

2

We've all done some foolish things

On the morning of Tuesday, March 14, 1815, Mâcon presented the very picture of France, convulsed by the return from the island of Elba. The people were amazed, the notables at a loss, and soldiers emerged from every corner. Seven or eight thousand gunners, infantry and cavalry had slept where they could, amongst the inhabitants, at the inns or on the pavements, causing the population of the main township of the Saône-et-Loire to be almost doubled. These were the troops of General Brayer, who since Lyons had been escorting 'the Emperor Napoleon back into his Estates'. On the walls of the town, notices still quite fresh had been posted three days earlier. They enjoined the Mâconnais, as all Frenchmen, to 'fall upon Napoleon Buonaparte, declared a traitor and rebel for having introduced himself by force into the department of the Var, to apprehend him and convey him forthwith before a military tribunal'.

It was a matter of an 'ordinance of the King containing general security measures' which Louis, 'by the grace of God, King of France and of Navarre', had given out at the Château des Tuileries on March 6, 1815, 'in the twentieth year of his reign'.

The fine and biting rain which was falling over northern and central France—for winter lingered on—had not had time to blur these notices, round which a sullen mob had congregated for three days, emerging from the narrow streets, dark, dirty and tortuous, which made up the essential Mâcon and the reverse side of the splendid scene laid out by its embankment on the Saône, where everything was only a proud façade: the town hall, the theatre, the public baths and a few inns for rich travellers. It was the most sumptuous of these that Napoleon had chosen in which to spend the night: the Auberge du Sauvage.

For he was at Mâcon. Buonaparte? The Emperor? The Usurper? The legitimate sovereign? The Ogre? The bloody Corsican? His Majesty? A little plebiscite settled the matter, for Mâcon at least, when soldiers of the 4th Artillery Regiment came at dawn to cover the King's notices with the proclamation in which Napoleon exclaimed:

'Frenchmen, in my exile I heard your laments and your prayers; you demanded that government of your choice which alone is legitimate. You blamed my long sleep, you reproached me for sacrificing to my repose the great concerns of our motherland. I have crossed the seas amid perils of every kind, I arrive amongst you to resume my rights, which are your own.'

March 14th

With the posting of this appeal, issued at Golfe-Juan on March 1st by 'Napoleon, by the grace of God and the constitution of the State, Emperor of the French, etc., etc., etc.,'[1] blazing bonfires and repeated cheering bore witness to the popular revelry. Like Sisteron, Digne, Gap, Grenoble, Lyons and Villefranche, Mâcon 're-enthroned' Napoleon.

The 'lower orders', at least, that is to say seven or eight thousand of the town's 11,000 inhabitants: the vine-tenders, the boatmen of the Saône, the workers in the tanneries and factories. For the notables, it was another matter. The magistrates, the 'proprietors' (in 1815 this was a 'profession' often proclaimed) and the officials who ruled undivided over the town, and disposed of all commissions, all employments and all revenue, had absolutely no idea any more to which ruler to give their allegiance. On March 14th, the weathercocks of Mâcon were at dead centre and provided, here again, a perfect picture of the hesitation waltz to which the French middle classes were to be a prey that week.

Napoleon had slept at the Auberge du Sauvage because the Prefect, Germain, had beat a retreat the day before, after having issued against him 'an offensive proclamation in the form of a libel'. The Emperor had shrugged his shoulders:

'Yet I made him, formerly, a count and chamberlain, for no very good reason. This little Germain thought he had to run away from me? He'll come back to us.'[2]

It had been impossible, however, with a numerous retinue, to put up in the ungracious buildings of the old archepiscopal residence (transformed into a prefecture after the Revolution), not out of regard for Germain, but because when the Prefect left he had locked everything up and taken his staff with him. Where would one have found linen and dishes? Napoleon was welcomed therefore at the Sauvage, where the cooks, beside themselves with joy, roasted 200 birds and offered the Emperor the delights of Mâcon: that celebrated preserve which is known

[1] These three *etcs.* replaced, at all events, the sonorous titles of the Great Empire: King of Italy, Protector of the Swiss Confederation, Mediator of the Confederation of the Rhine.

[2] Auguste-Jean Germain de Montfort, born 1786, had become a chamberlain at twenty and then one of Napoleon's aides-de-camp. His alacrity in adhering to the King had opened up a prefectorial career to him.

there as *cotignac* but which Parisians, for some reason, have rechristened *raisiné*. Napoleon tasted very little of it, but called several times for his favourite wine, Chambertin.

He rose very early and in a rather gloomy mood, in spite of the cheering of the mob, which had begun in the middle of the night beneath his windows. He was tired, depressed by a heavy cold and disappointed by the Prefect's flight, which made him fear that the notables of Burgundy, into which he was now about to plunge, would prove more reticent than those of the Lyonnais. Would he once again have to deceive, discuss, coax and lie, as he had done between the Golfe de Juan and Grenoble? Hardly awake, he enquired after the Mayor, a certain Bonne, naturally a wine merchant, who had fled in the Prefect's tracks. In the end, for want of anything better, about a third of the municipal staff were pushed into the Emperor's room, led by a deputy-mayor, Brunet, who spluttered his way through 'a long rigmarole', so ill-contrived that a faint smile returned to Napoleon's pale lips. He enjoyed raising the poor man to the peak of embarrassment by asking him point-blank:

'Tell me, you have received the Bourbons very well in this town? Especially the Duchess of Angoulême, from what I've been told?'

'Sire . . . I . . . we . . . the circumstances . . . '

'But you acted very well, Monsieur; the Duchess of Angoulême is my cousin, isn't she? . . . '

And in the silence of the bewildered dignitaries, Napoleon added:

'My wife's at least, the Empress, whom you will be seeing again shortly.'

Then, finding Brunet a good chap, he asked him:

'My landing really surprised you then?'

'Ah, my word! Yes, Your Majesty! When I knew you had landed I said to everyone: "The man must be mad; he'll never get away with it".'

This time Napoleon laughed heartily, but resumed his gloom when a secretary brought him the local gazette, in which a royalist editor had rather cleverly managed to slip into an account of the events at Lyons a lachrymose panegyric on Louis XVIII, 'this king too good to rule over the French'. Terrified, the secretary tried in vain to get the paper away from the Emperor, who muttered:

'Have this journalist replaced, he's a fool.'

So, towards nine in the morning, it was an austere and querulous little man whom the Mâconnais saw appear on the balcony of the Auberge du Sauvage, and who greeted with a few brusque gestures the numerous crowd massed on the embankment, in front of the wooded island that divided the river in two, at the boundary between Burgundy and Bresse. In the foreground, a few men, all abashed, stood to attention, like a class of great boys caught red-handed: these were the officers of the National Guard, whom the Emperor suddenly took it into his head to call to account:

'How was it that you surrendered your town last year to a squad of fifteen Austrian Uhlans? Mâconnais, you have not upheld the honour of Burgundy. Couldn't you have fought and held out, as the brave men of Tournus and Chalon did for more than a month after you?'

These few words were hard on the poor men, crushed for three years by much misfortune: conscription, the death of the best young men in Russia and Germany, two bad harvests one after the other and suddenly, in a terrible winter, the appearance of the Uhlans, and then Cossacks, who for long weeks after the fighting had still 'pillaged, violated, robbed, smashed and burned', as was borne out by hundreds of reports collected by the prefecture. No one ventured to point out to the Emperor that they too, perhaps, might have had some questions to put concerning the collapse of the Empire. Timidly, the worthy Brunet merely dared to observe:

'It was not our fault, Sire, we were badly governed. You gave us a poor mayor.'

This was that Louis Bonne, who had just scampered off before the eagle and the three colours, but who had welcomed the Allies the previous year with open arms in order to sell them his wine, and whose 'total lack of character bordered on cowardice'. Napoleon relented and dismissed all these memories with the back of his hand:

'It may be so! We have all done some foolish things; they must be forgotten. The welfare and safety of France, that, from now on, is the sole object with which we must concern ourselves.'[1]

He went back into the inn, and as he took a hasty breakfast he received some officers who had arrived from Paris at full gallop, and whom the royalist police along the way had allowed to pass 'as through a strainer'. The Emperor heard them all the more attentively since he knew nothing of what had happened in the capital since the first defensive measures taken against him by the Bourbons. At Lyons he had learned with much amusement of the famous ordinance enjoining all to *fall upon* him, and of the departure of Count d'Artois to bar the way to him. But since then? Now that the King knew the full extent of the danger, and that his advisers were taking the matter seriously, what would they do?

'The National Guard of Paris, Sire, seems determined to defend the King. The population of the better districts of Paris is against you. As for Louis XVIII, he swears by all the gods that he will not leave the Tuileries.'

'If he is able to wait for me there, I agree, but I very much doubt it. He is letting himself be lulled by the émigrés' fanfares, and when I'm fifty miles from Paris they'll abandon him, as the nobility of Lyons abandoned Count d'Artois. What would he be able to do anyway, with the old puppets who surround him? A single one of our grenadiers would settle a hundred of them with the butt of his musket!'

He rose, threw his napkin to the table and ordered his horses. Already, for an hour, regimental drums had announced that the army of the new revolution had begun to move off to the north. On the threshold, Napoleon turned to remark further:

'As for the National Guard, they are crying out from afar. When I'm at the gates they'll be still. Their job is not to wage civil war, but to maintain order and peace. There's nothing wrong with them but a few officers. I'll have them dismissed. Go back to Paris. Tell my friends not to compromise themselves, and that within ten days my grenadiers will be on guard at the Tuileries.'

---

[1] According to his own version, Napoleon is supposed himself to have said: 'Let us mutually forget our mistakes.'

Towards eleven o'clock, four or five carriages, each yoked to six horses, set off at high speed, escorted by a few French and Polish cavalry. Not only all the inhabitants of Mâcon but several thousand peasants from the vicinity thronged their passing, and ran as long as they could to escort the barouche in which the Emperor greeted them, with impatient little gestures 'as if he were swatting flies'. The carriages followed the left bank of the Saône and took the 'first route from Lyons to Paris', known as the 'Burgundy' route, that which crosses the Morvan range through Chalon, Autun and Avallon and reaches Fontainebleau via Auxerre and Sens; the second route, known as the 'Bourbonnais', passing much further to the west through Moulins, Nevers and Montargis.[1]

The rain increased; the piercing cold made it turn to snow. Several witnesses noticed the Emperor's glum appearance, at this nevertheless triumphant moment. Was it because of the coarseness of the cries from the mob, which were interspersed occasionally, at Mâcon as at Lyons, beneath the innumerable '*Vive l'Empereurs*', by outbursts far less orthodox: '*Down with the priests!*', '*Lynch the émigrés!*', and even these strange cries down by the river: '*Long live death! Down with virtue! Down with God!*'?

Was it not rather because news received during the night had confirmed that one of the most popular leaders in the whole army, Marshal Ney, was hurrying a complete division towards him in order to bar his way between Besançon and Lons-le-Saunier? The man who, more than all the others, had forced him into the abdication at Fontainebleau was one of the only men capable of ordering fire against him. In Napoleon's mind, at the end of that morning, there were thus two masses, each of about ten thousand men, rolling towards each other across Burgundy, and their impact could unleash civil war.

A secretary heard him sigh.

'There's still Paris!'

---

[1] See the map, pp. 14-15: Route Nationale 6 today follows to a great extent the line of the first route which, however, makes a big detour at Autun, while Nationale 7 follows the second. This map, drawn up in 1812, is taken from the *Description routière et géographique de l'Empire français*, issued in 1813, 'chez Potey, libraire, rue du Bac à Paris'.

Measures have been taken
between Lyons and Paris

What a strange Paris it was, on March 14th! The great city was inscrutable. Many people were silent; 'a million mutes with eyes aflame', but not with the same fire: hope, joy, fear, terror. Order reigned in the city and even in the outskirts, not by coercion, but through a kind of instinctive prudence: for the first time since July 14, 1789, the French debate was going on outside Paris, somewhere between Lyons, Besançon, Auxerre and Orleans. The people made no move; they did not know, they did not 'feel' what they should do. Neither did the great mass of the middle classes: they waited. To be sure, there were mobs standing in front of the King's proclamations.

But they read them in silence. No one knew his neighbour. This happening, this return from the island of Elba, was the intervention of the unprecedented and the unexpected in the collective life, and in each private life. For a quarter of a century, God knows, things had happened in France! . . . But at least it had been possible to anticipate them or dread them a few days in advance, and build up an attitude, whether it were the fall of Robespierre or the abdication at Fontainebleau! Whereas this had caught history napping; this sudden breaking of France in two, because Napoleon had grounded at Golfe-Juan, forced on every citizen a decisive choice in the depths of his being. At least he would rather not broadcast it. On March 14th, the Parisian crowd kept its secret, and at Tortoni's, at the Café Anglais, and along the promenades, where late revellers still prowled, they talked with affectation of Talma's latest successes —a brilliant season—or of the failure of that poor Mlle Georges at the Comédiens Français, why did she persist in roles that did not suit her? . . .

The irrepressibles had their meeting-place, nevertheless: a little whirlpool of humanity formed each morning between the terrace of the Tuileries and the great hall of the palace, where the King was cooped up on the first floor. There, those unable to contain themselves for rage or delight came for news. As the days went by, fine fellows in dark redingotes and collared cloaks were to be seen infiltrating more and more the groups of rabid royalists, who paraded in glossy pumps and knee-breeches, with the jabot, three-cornered hat and horizontal sword of the emigration period.

The following scene was observed by a journalist that morning word for word: an officer on half-pay, that is to say unemployed and miserable, was standing silently amongst a group of powdered old periwigs who were vying with each other, jabbering about 'a great victory which the Duke of Orleans was supposed to have secured in the neighbourhood of Bourgoing over *the enemy*'. He had a woman on his arm, young and pretty, who suddenly let out a piercing cry: a soldier of the King's light infantry, with huge epaulettes, had just trodden very heavily on her little foot. The half-pay officer reacted courteously at first:

'Monsieur! You might have been more careful! . . . '

The other was up in arms at once:

'What's that, Monsieur? How? What? Long live the King, Monsieur!'

'Monsieur, it is not a matter of that, but of my companion's foot! You . . . '

'Long live the King, Monsieur! Long live the King!'

'But, once again, I should like to point out . . . '

'Long live the King! I tell you, long live the King!'

'Bah! That's all you can say! Very well! Long live the Emperor! Long live the Emperor! . . . ' the officer burst out, and with a stroke of his riding-whip demolished one of the two 'pigeon's wings', i.e., one of the flaps of the high, turned-up collar which protected the lout's ears.

A rash gesture in that place. The half-pay officer disappeared quickly through the knots of people and reached the gardens, bearing his limping *grisette* with him. The incident was soon forgotten, for the general mood of the courtiers that morning was set fair: the *Moniteur*, the *Débats* and the *Quotidienne* had 'digested' the defections of Grenoble and Lyons, the arrival of the Usurper in France's second city. Today, the papers quietly explained that 'opinion cannot be misled as to the effects of the rapidity of the enemy's advance; by hastening it, he weakens himself; at no point does he present any real forces; nothing indicates that the troops by whom he is followed have increased, and, in order to stop him, ours are arriving in all commands at the various points that have been assigned to them.'

And again:

'A large number of dispatches, which have arrived today addressed to the Minister of War by various senior officers, provide testimony to the unshakable attachment of the troops to the person of the King and the cause of our motherland.'

These were not just words: it was known since the day before that an army mutiny hatched in the north by some officers who wanted to march their regiments on Paris, in conjunction, everyone was certain, with Napoleon's attempt, had broken abruptly before the firmness of the generals loyal to the King. Was this not proof that Bonaparte's success in the south-east was nothing but a soap bubble, which would burst in the same way at the first real obstacle?

Towards eleven o'clock, the Chamber of Representatives met in secret session. Sixty deputies sat the benches, highly perturbed for their part, for the little official world of 'well-informed' people, two or three hundred at most, consisting of the ministers, the King's familiars, the peers, the representatives and . . . the telegraph employees, were far from sharing the optimism of the press.

The Abbé de Montesquiou, Minister of the Interior, took the rostrum in an attempt to raise their spirits a little. He had no need to pretend; the Abbé floated in optimism, whatever the circumstances might be, and his doleful features, pale and wan above his little collar, shone with the conviction of a prompt revenge. In a great silence, the deputies strained their ears to catch his thread of voice, rendered even less audible by his strange way of not pronouncing S's. He threw out as food for thought a name of magic properties:

'Gentlemen, the most recent piece of news which we have to communicate to you is that Marshal Ney, who is very satisfied

29

with the good spirits of the troops under his command, is advancing on Lyons through Lons-le-Saunier.'

From that moment, then, Hope was called Ney for the enheartened royalists. To this the Abbé de Montesquiou added some considerable reinforcements:

'Count Dupont,[1] who is also heading towards Lyons through Montargis, is equally well pleased with his army corps. The officers of the regiments which are at Blois give no less satisfactory accounts of these corps. Marshal Oudinot has received orders to advance towards Paris,[2] with the Old Guard, to whom is reserved the glory of being the model and pattern of all armies. . . . '

So the Guard, in exile in the east since the Restoration, was marching on Paris? Not one representative thought of asking the Minister why, in that case, it had been stationed so far from the Sovereign whom it had always had the mission, in theory, of guarding. This was the first time the King had deigned to recall its existence. And many royalists saw it approach with mixed feelings: these learned gentlemen were well acquainted with the story of the Trojan horse.

From the King himself, who had never drafted so many appeals and messages as in the last ten days, there came that day an anxious proclamation dated forty-eight hours earlier:

'The moment has come to set a great example. We are counting on the vigour of a nation free and brave; she will find Us ever ready to direct her in this enterprise to which is attached the well-being of France. Measures have been taken to halt the enemy between Lyons and Paris. Our means will suffice, if the nation sets before him the invincible obstacle of its devotion and courage. France will never be defeated in this struggle of liberty against tyranny, of loyalty against treason, of Louis XVIII against Bonaparte . . . '

The text, like the others, was 'given at the Château des Tuileries, on March 12, 1815, and of our reign the twentieth

[1] Defeated at Baylen.
[2] From Metz, where he was in command of the military area.

. . . '. It was followed, comically, by a royal ordinance conveying that 'the law of the 4th Nivôse, Year IV will continue to be applied in accordance with its form and purport and that in consequence anyone who recruits for the enemy or for the rebels will be punished with death'. Louis XVIII thus made use of a law of the Convention passed against the recruiters of Koblentz and the Chouans.

So Paris went its way, between two showers of sleet. There was a crowd as always at Pancouke's, the great bookseller, where the wits were buying up the *Almanach des Muses*, and the new work which everyone was talking about: *The Sentimental Nights of a Young Recluse*, the work of a M. Varrot, whom the critics were calling a moralist 'greater than La Rochefoucauld, La Bruyère, Montaigne and Montesquieu'.

There was one inhabitant of Paris at least whose feelings were clear: this was a poor devil called Dautun, who had had the unhappy notion of butchering his aunt and his cousin. Condemned to death on February 23rd, he was awaiting the executioner. But it would be some time before the King had the leisure to examine his appeal-file. Dautun prayed for Napoleon with all his heart: he was not unaware that Louis XVIII had resumed the wholesome tradition of Louis XVI and Louis XV: the last Bourbons were not fond of reprieves.

4

We are on the eve of a great revolution

Lons-le-Saunier, the night of March 13 to 14, 1815. The 'Red Lion' slept at the Golden Apple. This was what the soldiers still called Marshal Ney, Duke of Elchingen, Prince of the Moskwa. But they had also christened him *le Rougeaud* ('Red Face'), 'the Brave of the Brave', and 'Michel the Fearless'. Of all the marshals of the Empire, he was the one who had kept the greatest personal ascendancy over the herd: his feats of arms in Germany, Poland, Spain, and above all, Russia, had made him a knight of modern times whose name was a synonym for courage and stubbornness.

He had arrived two days earlier, at three in the morning, in the little town of the Jura, almost alone, having come from Besançon, where the headquarters of his area command were located. His carriage had sped at the gallop through the main street, lined with picturesque arcades, and then crossed the Place d'Armes, before pulling up in front of the large hostelry of the Golden Apple, a vast collection of buildings, courts and gardens, where his arrival had immediately caused a mustering of land-lord and servants. After that, Ney had not gone out again, but had passed from his room to his salon, dictating letters, receiving officers and notables of the district, walking up and down and dis-coursing at random, or wrapping himself up in profound reveries.

Four o'clock in the morning. A carriage drove into the court-yard of the inn. It had run through a town half awake: four battalions of infantry and six squadrons of cavalry had arrived two days previously and were encamped, after a fashion, in the squares and the outskirts. The inhabitants, dismayed for the most part, knew that it had to do with the 'spearhead' of the little army which Ney was endeavouring to lead towards the Usurper on behalf of the King, in order to confront the rising tide head on and bring about an ebb. After the fall of Lyons, and the defection of the eight to ten thousand men already set before Napoleon, there remained only one real hope any more for the King: that Ney would fire the first shots without hesitating, and unleash civil war.

Alighting from the carriage was Baron Cappelle, Prefect of the Ain, a devoted royalist, driven from Bourg by the revolt of the town. With him, General Count de Bourmont, Ney's deputy. He had not hesitated to conduct the Prefect to him at once, because of the news he brought. A former leader of the Vendée, Bourmont kept an eye on Ney as much as he served him, and had given himself the officious job of keeping him on the right path.

The two men talked casually in low voices, while the aide-de-camp, Levavasseur, his eyes red with fatigue, woke the Marshal. Cappelle was uneasy, as yet without good reason, about the Marshal's loyalty. Bourmont reassured him in all sincerity: for two days, Ney had been preparing a real war; he had recalled all available troops for fifty miles around, he had had a hundred thousand cartridges sent from Besançon, and he had despatched more than thirty letters to the generals commanding adjacent sub-divisions, to galvanize resistance at Auxonne, Chalon, Mâcon, etc. Receiving the sub-prefect and the officers, he had renewed his peremptory declarations:

'We'll be fewer in number, but we'll give them a drubbing.'

'I shall take a musket, I shall fire the first shot, and everyone will advance.'

'Nothing will be lacking to me when I am in a state to take the offensive.'

And finally to the sub-prefect, M. de Bourcia:

'Bonaparte is a wild beast, a mad dog on whom one must throw oneself in order to avoid its bite. If I have the good fortune to stop him, I certainly hope to take him alive to Paris, in an iron cage.'

He had made the same declaration to Louis XVIII, a week earlier, as he kissed the royal hand swollen with gout, and the old King, blasé as he was, had not repressed a start:

'It's a rare little canary he'll be bringing me,' he had sighed, 'we don't require that much of him.'"

One letter, however, might have caused Bourmont some alarm: the one Ney had just written to Suchet, his 'neighbour', who commanded the Strasbourg sub-division, where he was hard put to keep his men obedient:

'We are on the eve of a great revolution. It is only by cutting the evil at the root that one can still hope to avoid it. Everyone is astonished at this rapidity, and unfortunately the popular classes have contributed to it[1] at several places along its way: the contagion is to be feared also for the soldier. I trust, my dear friend, that we shall soon see the end of this mad venture, above all if we put plenty of speed and unanimity into the advance of the troops.'

That was the point: up till then, Ney had shown a fierce determination to *fall upon Buonaparte*. So Bourmont was quite unperturbed when he entered the vast room, where the fire glowed and where hastily lighted candles lit up the bed, still

[1] Marshal Ney was a cooper's son from Sarrelouis.

33

made, on to which the Marshal had thrown himself fully dressed, without even drawing the alcove curtains. There he was, on his feet before them, in shirt-sleeves and wearing boots he had not taken off for three days. Ill-shaven, his movements jerky, like those of a somnambulist, Ney still overflowed with a superabundance of barely contained energy. He was of the same age as Napoleon, but had never let himself be overtaken by obesity, nor by baldness: a powerful chest, a face carved as from wood, dominated by an abundant shock of hair with coppery tints, which was continued very low by two handsome side-whiskers, he was still the hussar of '93, the commander of the free corps of the army of Sambre-et-Meuse, who had scarcely known how to write at twenty and had somehow or other insinuated his athletic frame into the trappings of a Marshal and Prince of the Empire. His chin between his hands, his eyes blank, he listened, without showing anything at first, to poor Cappelle telling him of his misfortunes:

'Monsieur le Maréchal, from Bourg to Lons-le-Saunier, there's nothing but disorder and violence. I saw the revolutionary madness springing up again everywhere amongst the dregs of the people, and amongst the soldiers. All this reminded me of the first period of the Revolution.'

Ney listened to him attentively, and then waxed indignant at the incompetence of officials and the negligence of princes:

'It is unheard of that I myself should be left without news and without orders since leaving Paris. The King, Monsieur, the Minister for War, everybody is leaving me to flounder . . . I don't even know where my regiments are. In the old days, it was quite different; when I had ordered horses to be sent to such and such a place, I was at ease, I slept at night. Where do you think Napoleon may have got to now? What is his strength?'

'His advance guard at least is now at Mâcon. On leaving Lyons, he already had 5,000 men at his disposal, but the 76th Regiment of the Line has just defected, so too probably have other bodies of troops. Bonaparte can't have less than 12,000 men now.'

A long silence, crowded with the thousand sounds of the little town in a state of siege: the hooves of restless horses, the calls of sentries, and a muffled clamour of mobs quickly dispersed.

34

Then Cappelle and Bourmont heard Ney murmur, as if to himself:

'What do you expect? I can't stop the sea with my hands!'

Thinking to hearten him, Baron Cappelle committed a blunder significant of the royalists' state of mind during those days:

'But Marshal, don't forget that we can still count on the Swiss. They are ready to move off to join the defenders of the royal cause.'

At this Ney was on his feet in a fury:

'Monsieur, if foreigners set foot on French soil, all France will be for Napoleon! There's nothing left for the King, for his part, but to place himself at the head of his troops, to have himself borne on a litter, so as to fire the soldiers and resolve them to fight!'

Flushed now, and in the grip of a kind of trance, he showed the two men to the door, carrying on a monologue in which he spoke of the effect produced abroad by the return from the island of Elba. 'This will reverberate all the way to Kamchatka!'

And now the Prefect began to be no longer quite sure where he was with him; he took Bourmont's arm on the great wooden staircase, amongst the bright copper, and whispered in a low voice:

'General, do you still count on the Marshal's loyalty?'

'I *think* one can be sure of it; I am relying on his good faith.'

But was it the hour? Was it tiredness? M. de Bourmont was green.

5

The desolation of the proprietors

Where, in fact, did France stand on March 14th?

The north, the west, the south-west, the Ile-de-France and the east remained under the authority of the King. This left him four-fifths of the country still; even more, since to this must be added Provence, where it is true the Duke d'Angoulême and Masséna had kept the white flag flying along the coast, wherever the little army of the Island of Elba had passed like a flash.

The south-east interior, on the other hand, with the two key towns of Lyons and Grenoble, lived under the Imperial regime as if Napoleon had never ceased to rule : prefects kept on or nominated by him, corporations made up of the most humble officials, all awaited his orders.

Finally, the central region between the Saône and the Loire, with an extension to the east towards the Jura and to the south towards the Bourbonnais, formed a sort of 'storm-front', where the two currents came into collision; there, everything would be played out, according to how the dynamism of the one or the other would sweep it along. Napoleon, however, held a master card : his own person. It was he who dashed into Burgundy, while the King stayed in his palace. Hence a crushing modification of the political geography of France, brought about above all by the events that marked out 'the flight of the Eagle'.

Hence too those multiple cracks that on March 14th tested the royalist ice still lying heavy over almost all the land : at Saint-Brieuc, some fishermen and labourers slashed the royal ordinances, to the cry of '*Vive l'Empereur*'; at Lille, General Dufour, anxious about the riotous gatherings, suggested to the Minister of War that English troops should be brought into the town from Belgium; and at Nancy, the students distributed numerous handwritten copies of a song composed by Mme Azaïs, the wife of the superintendent of the town library, a philosopher, eminent and woolly, but a rabid Bonapartist :

> Come back ! Come back ! the cry of France goes,
> To end her disgrace and all her woes . . .

On the same day, they cried '*Vive l'Empereur*' and trampled the white cockades in the barracks of Sarreguemines, Mézières, Amiens, Le Havre, Brest and Auch. Finally, an event far more serious than the outcries, between March 10th and 13th, five regiments of infantry and the 3rd Hussars, drawn up in echelon from Moulins to Bourg, had revolted, hoisted eagles hidden in the N.C.O.s' kit-bags, and marched off towards Mâcon, two of them overthrowing their Colonel on the way, in order to join *le Petit Tondu*.

In the 'storm-front' the events were repeated. Dijon was in complete insurrection; there the spark had been struck three

36

days previously by a group of six young men, one of whom, the son of a blacksmith and already recipient of a Prix de Rome for sculpture, was called François Rude. Perched on the debris of a building-site in the Saint Étienne square, they had cried 'Vive l'Empereur' as two squadrons of light cavalry went by who were moving down towards Lyons, with surly resignation, to resist Napoleon. Taken up again by the third platoon, the cry had then spread from one end of the column to the other among all the troopers, who decided to stop there and then and 'Bonapartize' the town, already rumbling. The common people tore up the paving stones, and the citizens' National Guard fell in with the movement, which seized Beaune and the whole of the Côte d'Or department. The Prefect fled; General Veaux, the area commander, 'proclaimed' the Emperor, who had already been proclaimed on all sides by his soldiers, and then rode post-haste to Avallon in order to take full credit for the operation with the returned exile. This gave rise on that day to the following account in the Paris papers:

'Bonaparte, reckoning up the small number of men who surround him, and realizing the inadequacy of his means to assure himself of the troops who follow him, and to make up for his real weakness, proceeds to look for support in the system of anarchy, disorganization and terror to which we owed the most frightful years of the Revolution. His scouts, or rather his emissaries, have succeeded in rousing at Mâcon, Tournus and Chalon that scum of the populace to whom it is only necessary to give occasion for plunder for it to be carried to the worst excesses. The same events took place at Dijon, at the same time and always by the same insurrectionary means. M. Terray, Prefect of the Côte d'Or, found himself helpless, in no state to resist the rebellion, and made for Châtillon-sur-Seine. We repeat that the lowest classes of the people alone took part in these criminal acts. They have struck terror and desolation into the hearts of all persons of property.'

In Saône-et-Loire, the Prefect Germain, driven first from Mâcon and then from Chalon by the 'scum of the populace', found a hasty refuge at Autun, where all the eddies that stirred Burgundy seemed to meet on the morning of March 14th. Two

37

days previously, as in all the neighbouring towns, the labourers and half-pay officers had taken over the streets since the Sunday morning. Under the impetus of two daring young men, Antoine Duvault-Pichard, a clerk of the court, and François Vial, a draper, multifarious bands had invaded the chamber of the municipal council and carried off the flag of the National Guard, in order to tear the embroidered fleurs-de-lys from it. At the cathedral, Duvault-Pichard and his friends had burst in during high mass, invaded the sacristy, climbed the ladder inside the belfry, and fixed a tricolour flag to the gallery outside the great spire. An old gendarme, Philippe Brossard, had corrupted the representatives of order and persuaded the gendarmerie lieutenant Tugnot to 'seize authority'. The gendarmes themselves were at that time pulling down the fleurs-de-lys and the white flags on the barracks of the Champ-de-Mars and the Rue-aux-Rats. One column, made up of tannery workers, gendarmes and old soldiers, had triumphantly paraded the bust of Napoleon, before carrying it on to the balcony of the town hall, from which the mayor and his councillors had been unceremoniously ejected.

That had been too much! Exasperated by this scene that reminded them so much of the time of the goddess Reason, the councillors and some royalist officers had met again by night at the house of the mayor, M. Pignot, an octogenarian full of vigour. On the morning of the 13th they carried out a surprise reoccupation of the town hall, where there reigned, moreover, the most benevolent muddle, and the indignant old man, appearing on the balcony with a fleur-de-lys flag, summoned the officers of the National Guard. The latter were uneasy; here and there the rioters had broken café windows and had even ruffled a few petticoats. After a day of complete confusion, when the tricolour had fluttered over the cathedral and the white flag on the trees of the broad terraced walk, it was the National Guard that again decided the struggle for the time being,[1] by reoccupy-

[1] The National Guard, moreover, was to be the arbiter of delicate situations in France for a good part of the century. Wherever there was no contingent of soldiers in garrison, the real power belonged to these citizens of sufficient means to buy themselves a uniform and arms, which they kept in their homes, and in the handling of which they trained regularly. Faced with their guns, of what account were the fists or sticks of the 'lower orders'.

ing the whole town on March 14th at midday. The Bonapartists, bearing away with them the gendarmes, highly chastened by their adventure, took refuge at the gates, in the direction of Chalon, where they awaited Napoleon's army. They established their headquarters in the old seminary, a magnificent seventeenth century edifice, secularized by the Revolution, where the nuns had recently set up a 'linen and cotton manufactory'. The pious women had fled from these Jacobins, who camped there, did justice to the excellent wines of the country and swore vengeance in no uncertain terms. All night long the citizens of Autun, appalled by their own victory, heard them singing and shouting, five hundred yards from the toll-gates: 'To the gallows with the Mayor! To the firing-squad with the town-guard!' . . . In the meantime, royalist Autun, isolated amid the complete insurrection of Burgundy, was nevertheless placing a bolt across the road that Napoleon had elected to take. M. le Préfet of Saône-et-Loire would at least be able to sleep there for a couple of nights.

6

Rejected by all mankind

On March 14th Vienna lay under a mantle of snow, which gave a false air of Christmas to the nocturnal bustle in her streets: all those palaces and hotels lit up far into the night, all those coaches, escorted by torchbearers in glittering livery . . . But it was an appearance only, and the loiterers were not deceived: they knew that at last, for the past week, the Congress had no longer been playing. In evidence were the frigid features of the Czar, the red and indignant face of the King of Prussia, who was always hard to distinguish from his guards, the set smile of the King of Denmark, and the gloomy countenance perched on high over the long frame of the Grand-Duke of Baden; and one caught on the wing some of the carter's oaths with which the King of Bavaria decorated his shifts of bulk. As for the Emperor of Austria, very popular here among the common people, he was not to be seen: he shut himself up in his closet, where Prince

Metternich went to join him, to 'receive instructions' . . . which he respectfully suggested to His Apostolic Majesty to give to him. Sovereigns and ministers, moreover, were all in a bad mood, because of the ructions which the news of the return from Elba was occasioning in their daily lives, as well as from fear or anxiety about the approaching war. The latter, at bottom, was coming in the nick of time to reconcile them, superficially at least. The Congress had been going badly. The Austrians, British and French on the one side, and the Prussians and Russians on the other, had been in danger of ending by coming to blows over Saxony, Poland, indemnities . . . They were going to fight, but all together, in order to bring the people of France to their senses. So the disputes were shelved. But this work, these conferences, the packing to be done, the orders to dispatch, the mistresses to dismiss hastily, at the very moment when one might doze off!

Today, however, a change could be noted in the rhythm of the comings and goings. Emperors, Kings, Highnesses and Excellencies had slept late, for the first time since that morning of March 7th when they had had the impudence to awaken Prince Metternich at six o'clock, in order to hand him an urgent dispatch from the Royal and Imperial Austrian Consulate at Genoa :

'The British Commissioner for the island of Elba, Sir [Neil] Campbell, has just put into the port to enquire whether Napoleon has been seen in Genoa, as he has disappeared from the island of Elba.'

There had followed a fine confusion throughout the city! More than twenty-five couriers needed to inform the sovereigns, the ministers and the chiefs of staff! But the Chancellor, for once, had not wasted time. At eight o'clock he was with his Emperor, who immediately sent him to warn the King of Prussia and the Czar. At ten o'clock, Metternich, this double commission fulfilled, had returned to the chancellery, received the commander-in-chief, Prince Schwarzenberg, and then assembled in his cabinet the ministers of the High Powers. At the same time, aides-de-camp left in every direction to carry to the army corps that were on their way home the order to stop. 'War was declared in less than an hour.'[1] Without the least problem, without the least hesitation. Nothing bears greater witness to the awareness the Allies had of their military might that spring than such rapidity of decision, coming from cabinets generally renowned for their dilatoriness. And nothing, either, to the crushing development effected in the character of the Courts by the basic principles of the Holy Alliance: conservatism and the reign of divine right. In one winter Europe had slipped back a century into the past, to the extent that its masters had become more aware of the mortal danger that the French Revolution, and then its personal incarnation, Buonaparte, had conveyed to their system. A year earlier, they had still forced Louis XVIII to promulgate a Charter of liberal hue, the Marshals of the Empire were consulted, the opinion of Paris was sounded: 'Would you prefer a Regency? Bernadotte?'

This time, among these princes full of mutual detestation and jealousy, agreement came of its own. Bonaparte, by returning from the island of Elba, had touched their deepest chord, that which released a panic reflex. His landing was 'something that wasn't done'. Was it not said that the band of his little army was playing the *Marching Song for the Army of the Rhine* as it made its way to Paris, like that horde of bandits from Marseilles who, twenty-three years earlier, had followed almost the same route on their way to dethrone Louis XVI? In one elemental bound, they rose to chase the intruders from the European salon.

Still necessary was to give form to the decision taken and to proclaim the Crusade. For this, there was at Vienna an unsurpassable talent. From March 7th to 13th they had been able to place full confidence in M. de Talleyrand.

* * *

The Prince of Benevento had slept until ten o'clock, that morning of March 14th. He was, moreover, the only diplomat present in Vienna who had never given up his late mornings. It was now the hour of his little levee, in the sumptuous Kaunitz Hotel, placed at his disposal by the Austrians. A small group of intimates witnessed the ceremony, which seemed to have retained a liturgical reflection of the time when he had been a

[1] Metternich's *Mémoires*.

bishop, thirty years earlier. Enveloped in a muslin dressing-gown, pleated and crimped, Talleyrand was committing his abundant locks to two hairdressers. His face, weary and shrewd, suggested more years than he had. His sixty-first birthday had just been celebrated, but he seemed almost a septuagenarian, with numerous wrinkles, sallow complexion, and those folds dropping from the corners of his lips. His eyes still sparkled with a lively fire and their play made up for the oracular silence in which he encased himself, through fatigue, and affectation. A strange gentleness came into them when they rested upon his niece, the young and beautiful Countess Edmond de Périgord. It was she whom he had commandeered for a few days in order to draft the Declaration, which the plenipotentiaries of the eight powers had signed the day before. He had not even required the services on this occasion of La Besnardière, his secretary, his shadow and devoted slave. Making a fresh start several times, he had forced the young woman to 'wage war upon words', as he said. Patiently, he had weighed the expressions, corrected, deleted, begun again. This short text of one page was to cost the poor Countess two balls; she had trembled occasionally from nervous tension.

Talleyrand asked for it to be read over to him once again, while his barber-cum-bath-attendant enveloped him in a cloud of powder and rubbed his crippled leg with *eau de Barèges*:

'The sovereigns of Europe declare that if, contrary to all expectation, there should result from this occurrence any danger whatsoever, they would be ready to give the King of France and the French nation the assistance necessary to restore peace.

' . . . The Powers declare that by breaking the agreement which had established him on the island of Elba, Napoleon has destroyed the sole legal title to which his existence was bound; that by reappearing in France, he has placed himself beyond civic and social relations, and that, as an enemy and disturber of the peace of the world, he has delivered himself up to public vengeance.'

A smile, 'almost malicious', appeared on the Prince's thin lips.

Was he remembering at that moment the celebrated humiliation which the disturber of the peace of the world had inflicted upon him in 1809, in front of the whole Imperial Court? 'Talleyrand, you're nothing but a shit in silk stockings.' The reply was coming six years after, signed by Britain, Austria, Spain, Portugal, Prussia, Russia, Sweden . . . and France, for whom his hand had held the pen.

Last of all, it was the *valet de chambre* who officiated, to knot the huge cravat in which his chin would be buried. But before that, Talleyrand was concerned:

'Have they sent off my letter for the Princess de Courland?'

. . . An old friend, among many others.

'It is still open, Uncle. You wanted to add a few words in sending her the text of the Declaration.'

A little table was pushed over to Talleyrand; he was handed paper, pens, sand and seals. And while the snow began to fall once more on Vienna, he cheerfully set down this postscript: 'I do not believe, my dear, there has appeared a document like the one I am sending you. History furnishes no example of a similar rejection by all mankind.'

To the King, he added a copy of a piece printed by order that morning in all the papers of Vienna, a 'Notice to the Nations', the first line of which gave the assurance that 'Bonaparte is no longer coming to reign except for the benefit of the Jacobins'.

7

As in 1790

Lons-le-Saunier, March 14th, half-past twelve. The town was vibrant with the rolling of drums and the sound of bugles: it was the call to arms so dreaded by soldiers. Marshal Ney was to harangue the troops. The infantrymen of the 60th and 77th Regiments of the Line, the troopers of the 8th Regiment of Light Cavalry and of the 5th Dragoons left their camp to the east of the town, in the water-meadows, and drew up near the first houses. For their part, the inhabitants thronged the streets and ran towards the place of assembly. There were only mutterings and grumblings: here, eight men out of ten, among the troops and among the people, were for Napoleon. Now up to the present, Ney had had no communication except with the dignitaries and had published no order of the day. A diffuse hope existed among the common people: hope of a complicity between *le Rougeaud* and *le Petit Tondu*. The local papers had indeed published the incredible appeals against the Emperor by his old lieutenants, and especially that of Soult:

'Bonaparte thinks so poorly of us that he believes we can abandon a sovereign, legitimate and well-loved, in order to share the fate of a man who is no more than an adventurer. He believes it, the madman! And his latest act of lunacy shows it completely.'

But there were also the imprecations of Victor, Augereau, Suchet, Jourdan and Moncey, who provided a chorus. As for them, the people were hardly surprised. They knew that for the past year they had rallied to the Bourbons, with their titles, their annuities and their estates.

But the Red Lion? The man who had taken Magdeburg and 20,000 Prussians with a platoon of cavalry? The man who, all on his own, had saved hundreds of brave men during the last station of the way of the Cross from Russia? It was well known that he had no love for the Bourbons and that they had none for him. He had been playing the peasant for months on his estate of *les Coudreaux*. Would he join his voice to the cries of the pack? Would he by doing so become its leader and confound, to the depths of their being, the thousands of honest men who refused to believe that he was just like the rest?

A weak sun lit up the glittering procession coming from the inn of the Golden Apple, through the Rue Saint-Désiré, the Place d'Armes and the Rue du Jura. Riding alone in his full-dress uniform, in front of his staff officers, Ney advanced in silence, followed by Generals Bourmont and Lecourbe, visibly perturbed. He had just had a two-hour conference with them, about which nobody as yet knew anything. As the gleaming party approached the troops, the crowd, silent and tense, pressed more and more closely about them. All the young people of Lons, their pockets full of tricolour cockades, had played truant and were filtering into the ranks. One of them, Jean-Louis Bidot, suddenly found himself right between the legs of Ney's horse.

The Prince of the Moskwa, whose anxious air struck one witness, arrived, very pale, and more moved than he had ever been in battle, before the first of the troops forming a square. He took up a place in the middle, while the drums solemnly rolled. It was then noticed that his dress hat of a Marshal of France no longer bore a cockade, either white or tricolour. What did that mean?

The drums stopped. Suddenly, the silence was unbearable. Marshal Ney then drew a sheet of paper from his pocket, and with a flash, unsheathed his sword:

'I call the senior officers to the centre!'

The voice was stentorian, the best produced of the whole French army, the one that had been heard, at Elchingen, from one bank of the Danube to the other. The officers, in a few paces, formed a star around him. Some were manifestly afraid: 'The most sombre silence preserved by the thousands of soldiers was as terrible as that of a storm, before the tornado. A sort of electric quiver ran through the ranks, where elbows were feverishly pressed.' All the conditions for a mutiny, military and popular, were brought together at that moment. One of the officers, Colonel de Préchamps, who was expecting an appeal in favour of the King, anticipated at the time 'a great catastrophe; it was possible to believe that, as in 1790, the officers were going to be driven out or massacred by the men'.

'Officers, non-commissioned officers and men, *the Bourbon cause is lost for ever!*'

Ney was unable to continue. In defiance of all discipline, a thunder of frenzied cheering interrupted him. Two thousand men, yelling with delight, experienced the finest moment of their lives.

8

A bas les rats!

At that moment Napoleon was arriving at Tournus. Shortly after leaving Mâcon, he had fallen into the restoring semi-somnolence customary to him on carriage journeys for several years, during which he often 'recuperated' more than at fixed halts, where he worked as soon as he was settled in. He had not even looked up when his companions had pointed out to each other the still imposing shell of the chateau of Senosan, burnt during the Revolution; its avenue, planted with beautiful trees, seemed to bring this tragic memory to the very edge of the road.

But the Emperor had been obliged to show his face at the window and salute a little further on, passing through Saint-Albin, where the officers of his suite exclaimed at a charming sight: the women and girls of the little market town wearing 'the prettiest country costume it would be possible to see': little round discs of hats, placed lightly on the head and tilted with abandon over one ear or the other, like those of shepherdesses in the theatre. The rest of the costume was in keeping; one would have thought one was in the Valais. And all these people crowded round the barouche like a living bouquet. But they were not stopping before Tournus, where the population, usually of five thousand souls, seemed to have increased fivefold. People were coming in from all directions. They were packed tight on the wooden bridge where the road to Lons-le-Saunier, through Louhans, began.

'By the way, is there any news of Ney?'

'No, Sire, not yet.'

The Emperor delayed 'the moment for refreshment and relaying', almost to the feet of the flesh-pink towers of Saint-Philibert, one of the most venerable Romanesque abbeys of Europe. He was not to give it a glance; his artistic sense was limited, and his vast culture entirely political. He had had Cluny demolished, not far from there, because its repair would have cost too much. Why waste money on old stones? Saint-Philibert, in 1815, was a huge agglomeration of ruins. Grain was stored beneath its crumbling arches, where jackdaws nested. Napoleon had the notables form a circle, congratulated them on their courage the previous year, and decreed that his party was to whip on immediately; he would lunch on the wing of a bird in his carriage. He wanted to avoid too great an accession of people obstructing his way. 'Every minute', one of his companions noted, 'there were platoons of soldiers, on foot or on horse, commanded by N.C.O.s, who came to offer their services and join the army, and the further we went the more considerable did the Emperor's escort become. These were soldiers of every arm who had abandoned their corps in order to have the happiness of regaining their father and of accompanying him on his triumphal journey.' This aspect, of a peripatetic triumph, would be found again in Napoleon's recollections, dictated at St Helena:

'At Tournus, and in all the towns along the route, a huge crowd had gathered. Everywhere, the same sentiments, expressed in every way by the people: there was *Père la Violette*, who had come to deliver France; there was abuse against the enemies of the nation. The oldest soldiers expressed their affection for their *Caporal*. In Burgundy, as in Dauphiné, the tunes were different, but the ideas on which they turned were the same. Sometimes, to these exclamations were added the cries: "Down with the excisemen, *à bas les rats!*" '[1]

At Tournus, again, two incidents contrived to give the day its tone: a sapper with a Jove-like beard overturned all in his path and got to the Emperor, whom he almost lifted from the ground as he embraced him. He then transferred himself from his own commander to the escort, from which there would be no question of removing him before Paris. All along the way, the spectators outdid each other in hoots of laughter at this giant, whose bushy beard seemed to be a direct continuation of his bearskin. At another point, Napoleon had a slight access of calculated ill-humour: a peasant shouted out as he went by:

'No more collected dues!' In other words, no more indirect taxes.

'No,' replied the Emperor curtly, raising his voice to make himself well heard. 'No! This would be to return among you like a rebel. We must have sacrifices and money in order to maintain the national honour in the present crisis.'

A sharp check to demagogy, which he had not been so loath to use a week earlier, at Sisteron and Grenoble. But he had never liked the common herd at over-close quarters, and the sapper's rough hug had completed his irritation. They moved off again in that amiable confusion which helped to exasperate him, a

[1] *Rat de cave* = exciseman who visits cellars holding wines and spirits [trs.].

regular hurly-burly of vehicles and riders of every rank, still by the same road, sticking close to the Saône, and crossing a fertile plain transformed during those days into a sponge by the equinoctial rains.

9

The Bourbon cause is lost for ever

Ney had to break off for a long moment, his face suddenly drained of all blood by the violent emotion which he was experiencing. Around him, in that wide waste ground between the fields and the town of Lons, there was 'a thunder of cheering, the frenzied acclamation of a whole army who, in a transport of delirium, forgot all discipline'. As soon as quiet was restored, he began to read, and this time without a break, the rest of his proclamation:[1]

'The legitimate dynasty which the French nation has adopted is about to reascend the throne: it is the Emperor Napoleon alone to whom the duty belongs of ruling over our fair land.

'Whether the Bourbons and their nobility exile themselves, or whether they consent to live in our midst, of what matter is that to us? The sacred cause of our liberty and our independence will suffer no longer from their baneful influence. They have sought to debase, to wipe out, our military glory, but have they been able to do so? No, this glory acquired at the cost of our blood and by the most noble labours, this glory which is still fresh to us, can have left behind only the most honourable memories for You. The times are no more when nations were

[1] We give here the exact text, the one that Ney spoke that day, word for word, and not the somewhat 'arranged' text, perhaps by Napoleon himself, published three days later. This, the true text, was found among the Marshal's papers, written entirely by hand. At the same time, it gives the lie to the version according to which Ney is supposed to have confined himself to reading a prefabricated text which the Emperor had sent him. It really is a matter of a proclamation written and conceived by Ney alone. It is enough, moreover, to analyse the heavy and clumsy style of this text to deny its authorship to Napoleon.

governed by the most ridiculous prejudices, when the rights of
the people were ignored and stifled. Liberty is triumphing at
last, and Napoleon, our august Emperor, is about to establish it
for ever.

'May this noble cause henceforth be ours and that of all
Frenchmen, and may all the brave men whom I have the honour
to command be imbued with these sentiments which animate
me. Officers, non-commissioned officers, men! I have often led
you to victory. Follow me! I would take you to that immortal
host which will march with the Emperor Napoleon to Paris:
you will see him there within a few days. There, at last, will be
realised our dearest wishes and all our hopes.'

The acclamations were resumed and broke in a deafening
wave. The acclamation, rather: a fundamental surge coming
from the depths of the heart, from the lives of all those men
who suddenly found themselves once more in harmony with the
world about them. It was a very great moment in French history,
through the intensity which was released in it. The mediation
of one of the 'great', of a 'Prince', a man with a chateau, with a
plume and a carriage, suddenly brought the 'little' people the
transition from dream to reality, and the feeling of having been
right. Napoleon regained, the three colours, equality, opportunity open once again to the Dubois, the Martins, and the lads
of the village. An end to the time of lies and resentment; the
curés would come back to the churches and the nobles leave
once more for Koblenz. All those men, from the Marshal, Prince
of the Moskwa, to the latest conscript, felt the same dizziness at
the prospect of a life in harmony with their deep desire, and this
intoxication which arose from brotherhood, sharper than that
of wine, conquered once again.

Ney threw himself from his horse, reeling just as if he were
drunk, and rushed into his officers' arms. He ran over to the men,
mingled with the crowd and went through the ranks, but there
were ranks no longer. There was nothing any longer but simple
good fellows in tears, spluttering and dancing on the spot, who
all sought to touch *le Rougeaud*. The Marshal embraced the
very pipers and drummers: he regained in them his twenty-year-
old self. In that moment he had wiped from his life the burdens,

the compromises, the search for wealth; he regained the happiness and the pride which had assailed him on the 8th Prairial, Year II, when the officers, N.C.O.s and men of the Colonel-in-Chief of Hussars at Metz had testified in a certificate that 'Citizen Ney, promoted to the rank of captain by the voice of election, has, since the Revolution, given constant proofs of the most unblemished patriotism and the most inviolable devotion to the cause of liberty'.

'*Vive l'Empereur!* Down with the white rag!'

One witness noticed that this cry recurred the most frequently on the lips of the soldiers, all busy tearing the white cockades from their shakos and the fleurs de lys from the revers of their uniform. In the same movement they had 'downed' haversacks and taken out the tricolour cockades, religiously hidden there for a year. The *vivandières* mingled with them and entered the fray, their little kegs of brandy over their shoulders: they were no longer selling it, they were giving it away. A couple of paces from Marshal Ney, a group of men held up a cask to them for refilling, to which they stretched out hands that were bleeding from a few quick scratches. Drinking the brandy mixed with their blood, they swore to spill it to the last drop for Napoleon.

How long did the scene last? Nobody was able to say. It was one of those moments that go unreckoned and fill a lifetime by themselves alone. The first to recover his wits was Ney, through the force of circumstances; having returned from the midst of the whirlpool, he found himself rudely disillusioned by a little gathering of sad figures. The few officers of his staff who had not succumbed to the collective spell had assembled around Generals Lecorbe and de Bourmont. They formed a sort of unmeltable ice-flow at the heart of the break-up. One word, one alone, divided them from the rest for ever: *the oath*. They had taken it to the King and were unable to forget it. An old colonel, Count de Grivel, commander of the National Guard of Lons-le-Saunier, stood in Ney's path and broke his sword across his knee, saying:

'Prince, this sword cannot and must not serve any but the descendants of Saint-Louis!'[1]

---

[1] Louis IX, 1215-70. The Royal and Military Order of Saint-Louis was created by Louis XIV in 1693, suppressed in 1790, and re-established from 1815 to 1830 [trs.].

A worthy N.C.O. bent down and picked up a piece of it, muttering:

'I'm a soldier of the Emperor myself, but upon my word, this was the sword of a gallant man. I'll keep a bit of it, it'll bring me luck.'

Then it was Dubalen, Colonel of the 64th regiment of the line, who came forward:

'Prince, I judge no one, but I consider myself bound by my oath. I request you for permission to return home.'

Ney turned on him a face still lit up.

'I do not accept your resignation, but you are free to leave. Go quickly, and above all don't let yourself be illtreated by your men.'

It was necessary to re-form the ranks and catch the frightened horses, who were galloping across the countryside. It was necessary, above all, to restore order in Lons-le-Saunier. The military revelling had become a brawl; the people rushed to destroy coats of arms, signs, flags, emblems and portraits of the monarchy. The riot converged on the café *Bourbon*, the customary rendezvous for royalists, of which it was related that the proprietress, Mme Rodet, 'had sworn to wash her hands in the soldiers' blood'. A dragoon ascended the front steps on horseback, and still mounted entered the café, where he went through the two rooms, overturning everything in his path. The café would be completely devastated before nightfall. Having hastily taken refuge in his office at the prefecture, where he was besieged because he had kept a white ribbon in his buttonhole, the Prefect, M. de Vaulchier, sent a laconic dispatch to Paris: 'Anarchy is triumphant'.

10

You really are the son of Alexander Dumas?

Villers-Cotterêts, the afternoon of March 14th. Everything was going badly for the Bonapartists in the north. It was all up with the military conspirators, who for a week had been trying to concert a seditious movement against Paris more or less with the

51

return from the island of Elba. In the little town of the department of the Aisne, an important road junction on the vital artery leading from Paris to Mézières through Soissons and Laon, everybody was out in the squares. They were besieging the diligences, the couriers, the carriages; by bribing the travellers they elicited news not to be found in the papers. It was in this way that the inhabitants of Villers-Cotterêts had learned of Bonaparte's landing and his entry into Lyons, but above all they had followed with mounting anxiety events that were in danger of affecting them on their doorstep: on March 8th, Count Drouet d'Erlon had raised the garrison at Lille, which he had set in motion towards Paris, while General Lefebvre-Desnöettes had marched on La Fère, with the light cavalry of the Guard, in order to seize the arsenal, thanks to the complicity of two brothers, Generals François and Henri Lallemand, both fanatically devoted to the Emperor.

To the extent that the Dauphiné had taken fire from one end to the other as soon as Napoleon appeared, so, in the north, all had quickly subsided into the royalist order, for want of his presence, and for want of co-ordination and intelligence among the conspirators. At Lille, the unexpected return of Marshal Mortier, who was commander-in-chief of the 16th military division, had been enough to cause the garrison to go back to their quarters. At La Fère, General Aboville and his officers had kept their soldiers in hand and forced Lefebvre-Desnöettes' *chasseurs* to an irksome wandering from town to town. The unfortunate regiment had gone from La Fère to Chauny, Noyon, and then Compiègne, destroying fleur-de-lys signs on their way but without collecting a single partisan. Finally, on March 12th, Lefebvre-Desnöettes' officers had given in and made their regiment return to the fold. Dressed in civilian clothes, Lefebvre-Desnöettes and the Lallemand brothers had made a haphazard attempt at flight, but all the gendarmes of the area had been set on their heels and left them little hope.

On March 14th, Drouet d'Erlon was in prison at Lille, Lefebvre-Desnöettes was in hiding at a friend's house, and the Lallemand brothers had been arrested, exhausted and dying, near the little village of Mareuil. This was the news that the population of Villers-Cotterêts had been talking about on that rainy afternoon, when a great commotion began to be heard, towards three o'clock, at the end of the main street, so long and so straight that one could see from a good way off the approach of two cabriolets escorted by a picket of gendarmerie.

In each of these vehicles one of the Lallemand brothers was seated between two gendarmes. Lost in the crowd stood a great lad of thirteen, in height already quite a young man, with frizzy hair above a face heavy of feature : this was the young Alexander Dumas. He observed the scene as he was to observe all things, with his eyes wide open to the world and its comedy. It was thus that he saw, not without disgust, the crowd forming a pack round the prisoners to cries of 'Vive le Roi', and a termagant, who had come out of a hat shop, jump on to the footboard of one vehicle in order to spit in the face of General Henri Lallemand.

The latter made a movement of withdrawal deeper into the chaise, and asked 'in a voice that held more pity than anger' : 'Who is this poor wretch?'

The very excess of the abuse calmed the mob. The coachmen whipped up and the vehicles disappeared towards Soissons, where the prisoners were to spend the night. It was at that moment that a hand was laid on Alexander Dumas' shoulder and a voice said in his ear :

'Come on; we're going to Soissons.'

It was his mother's voice. By no means a Bonapartist, she had been unable to tolerate, as the widow herself of a general of the Empire, the treatment inflicted on these. There were the two accomplices, then, mother and son, passing the iron portcullises and the ramparts of the old martial town, still riddled everywhere by the bullets, Russian and Prussian, of the previous year. They stopped 'their little mongrel vehicle, which was halfway between a cabriolet and a tilbury', before the entrance to the Three Maids hotel, towards five o'clock. They made anxious enquiries about the place where the Lallemand brothers were to be imprisoned : a military gaol or a civil one? If it were the former, they were powerless; if it were the latter . . .

It was the latter. In Soissons, a Bonapartist town, because it was military, the captives were treated with good will and they were accommodated in a gaol that was more like a lodging-house than a prison. There, Alexander Dumas was about to have his

53

first adventure and the door to living history opened to him for ever. The son of the prison *concierge* was his play-fellow. The friendship between the two families, and the sympathy which the guards themselves showed to their prisoners, would allow the young Alexander to find his way in to one of the two, in order to hand him two pistols and a roll of fifty louis.

He was to remember all his life the distinguished gentleman, sitting sadly on the edge of a camp-bed, quite moved suddenly to see, coming from out of the night and advancing towards him, the son of a brother in arms, dead eight years previously.

'You really are the son of Alexander Dumas? What do you want with me, my boy?'

'General, I am charged, by my mother and some friends of yours, to deliver you a pair of double-barrelled pistols, loaded, and a roll of fifty louis. I have them in my pockets. Do you want them?'

For a moment the General remained without speaking; then he brought his face close to the youngster's.

'No, thank you, my friend,' he said, embracing him. 'The Emperor will be in Paris before we can be tried . . .'

Half an hour later, his mother came in search of the boy :
'What did he say?'

'He said the Emperor would be in Paris before they could have him shot, him and his companions.'

'God let it be so!'[1]

11

All I see there is a rabble

The large town of Chalon, at the heart of the Saône-et-Loire, had been awaiting the Emperor since noon with growing impatience. Having remained Bonapartist after its brave conduct the pre-

[1] Thirty years later, Alexander Dumas, at the start of his fame, was to meet General Lallemand for a second time. It was at a grand dinner at the house of a duke and compeer of King Louis-Philippe. 'The man's hair had whitened, the boy's hair had greyed.'
'General, do you remember March 14, 1815?'
A moment later, the two men fell into each other's arms.

vious year, and the vexations it had endured at the hands of the Allied troops, the National Guard had risen as soon as the first detachments of the Imperial advance guard arrived. Everybody was gathered, as on one of the famous fair-days that swelled the town, in February, June and October, with a great human tide. Since noon, people had been coming in from Charolles, from Paray-le-Monial, from all the surrounding country, rich in cattle and vines. Work had stopped everywhere. In the streets, ten thousand inhabitants, half of whom were destitute, but proud, 20,000 peasants in their Sunday best, and the mounting flood of soldiers, more difficult to billet hour by hour: those who were coming 'up' from Lyons, in order or disorder, in the van of *Père la Violette*, and those who were coming 'down' from Paris, in order or disorder, sent to bar him the way, but who were about to make it smooth for him. All this was to make his entry into Chalon so glorious that later Napoleon would even be mistaken about the weather. 'There was brilliant sunshine', he was to maintain, whereas a dozen observers bore witness to the sleety rain that continued to play havoc, though nobody, it is true, paid any attention to it.

The sun, at any rate, had already set. It was the twilight hour when proportions and distances can no longer be distinguished. The final leagues had been tiring for the Emperor and his suite, forced to make frequent stops by the people who came in crowds. And the jolting road was unending, with its incomprehensible meanderings in such a straight plain, in order to avoid the marshes. But at last, towards seven o'clock, there could no longer be any mistake; the whole town outside the town was welcoming its Emperor, whose carriage no longer moved at more than a walk. A kind of encampment had been improvised, before even the outskirts, where several thousand men and women, their clothes all steamy, stood around some upended carts parked in the fields. They shouted their heads off, '*Vive l'Empereur*'; their outcry announced to the others the arrival of the great man, whom hardly anyone actually saw.

But before the gates of the town, he ordered a halt and demanded: 'What's that over there?'

He pointed to the dark shapes lined up at right angles to the road, crouching little monsters that threw off sudden gleams as they reflected the torches. A score of voices hastened to inform him: 'They're the guns that were sent from Paris to fire on you, Sire! We confiscated them for you, good and proper!'

It was a convoy of artillery sent to Lyons from the central depot at Auxonne on the imprudent orders of Count d'Artois; it was their arrival here that had set off the revolt two days earlier. The Chalonnais, furious, had decided to keep the cannon for the Emperor. Vine-tenders, tradesmen and bleak-fishers had themselves unharnessed the horses and detached the limbers, at the same time as the white flag on the hospital, the highest building in the town, had been torn down, in order to hoist the tricolour there. 'Upon my word, all I could do was save myself . . . ' concluded the gallant General Rouelle, commander of the convoy, in his report.

The Emperor smiled and tried to make himself heard, at least to those nearest. He was still hoarse, though much less so than at Lyons, from the effects of the unpleasant 'cold in the chest' which he had caught among the snows of the mule-tracks, in the first days of his mad escapade. He was forced therefore to speak only to the spectators in the front ranks, during the innumerable harangues that he had to produce so prodigally. He knew that his words were immediately repeated, taken up again, enlarged upon, and carried to all corners of the towns and provinces, like the shreds of his proclamations scattered to the four winds.

'That's right, my boys! You always were good citizens! I have not forgotten that you held out against the enemy for forty days and valiantly defended the crossing of the Saône. If every Frenchman had had your patriotism and your courage, not a single foreigner would have left France alive!'

These words worked through the crowd and, in contrast to the cold shoulder he had shown the Mâconnais, would carry the exaltation of Chalon to its highest pitch. All those brave men at last had the feeling that they had not fought for nothing in 1814. And it was as if they had won the lost war.

After that, the entry of the Emperor unfolded as in a picture by Rembrandt: a trail of torches through a crowd of shadows. The night, the rain, the multitude, the cries, the stamping of horses, the orders, the trumpet-calls. . . . The Emperor's barouche was able to go at a good pace, because the National Guard had cleared the streets down to the embankment, where one of the most celebrated inns of France, the Hôtel du Parc, with forty windows adorned with little multi-coloured lights, had been selected for the overnight stop. One black spot did indeed remain, here as at Mâcon: the reticence of the authorities. The Prefect, Germain, who had tried to harangue the Mâconnais on his way through, had all but had himself cut down in the main square near the canal, at the foot of an obelisk erected in honour of Napoleon six years earlier. He had taken refuge at Autun. But the Mayor had barricaded himself in his house. This persistent abstention of the notables was enough to make him gloomy when he appeared on the balcony of the Hôtel du Parc, torn from his supper and the couriers by the violence of the acclamations. Ten thousand men showed their adoration at the tops of their voices, but a hundred were lacking to him, those he considered essential, and his vexation grew on hearing the clamour further off, which ran along the two banks of the Saône: some gangs of ruffians, intoxicated with joy and the barrels on tap in front of every café, were pouring into the streets and throwing stones at any window not lit up. Napoleon waved his hands vigorously, saluted, bowed to right and left, and the 'Vive l'Empereurs' redoubled. Never, perhaps, had he been so wildly acclaimed, even at Lyons.

'Those are not cries,' he murmured to himself. 'That's frenzy. All I see there is a rabble.'

A very unfair reflection on the citizen guard of Chalon. Back in his room, he at once had his boots pulled off and hastily went to bed, his nervous energy exhausted. He ordered Bertrand to draw him up a list of the troops he would have at his disposal the following day, and the Grand Marshal was to spend the whole night enumerating the effectives. Napoleon did not want to rely on the rabble alone.

12

Monsieur le Maréchal, you are lost!

In the evening of March 14th, the proprietor of the Golden

57

Apple Hotel at Lons-le-Saunier served up a feast that would long be remembered. Marshal Ney gave a supper for his general staff and the senior officers present in the town. They were brought oxtail, cooked over embers for five whole hours and basted with vintage Chablis, calf's tongue on the spit accompanied by Côte-de-Pitoy, and an innumerable profusion of partridge, fat pullets *aux cornichons, coqs au vin,* cold pies *en terrine* and '*gâteaux de viande*'. The guests, fifteen men in the full prime of life, all more or less seamed with scars collected in one corner or another of Europe, appeared somewhat ill at ease; they remained in a strained silence, little in keeping with the bubbling joy of the town, which beat at the windows of the inn. Like the majority of those officers, Ney for three days had been full of injunctions of loyalty to the Bourbons and zeal for their cause. The previous day still, at the same hour, he had harshly reprimanded those of them who had failed to show much enthusiasm at the idea of shooting Napoleon . . .

At the heart of the festivity, therefore, was this meal, unfestive and without heart: the top brass 'no longer believed in it' and celebrated their agape like priests who had lost their faith. The rite would be respected, however, to the very end. The punch was brought in, drawn from the oldest keg, shipped from the Islands; everyone stood up, and the blue flame rising raw cruelly emphasized the puffiness in Ney's face: a week of moral agony and twenty-four hours of delirium had made it a mask of the damned. But now, at last, he was seeing it through to the end.

'Gentlemen, the Emperor!'

'The Emperor!'

The meal came to a close in this artificial atmosphere, well in retreat from the enthusiasm of midday. Since his return to the Golden Apple, intercepted afresh by the crowd and his soldiers, Ney had faced in formal mufti the formal men of note, hesitant, divided, indignant.

A hard end to the afternoon! Immediately after dispatching aides-de-camp to Napoleon, Oudinot and Suchet, to inform them of his decision, he had received the Prefect of the Jura, and that had been a good beginning!

'*Monsieur le Maréchal,* I was delegated by the King and I cannot serve two masters.'

Then it was General Mermet, reminding him that only the day before Ney had called upon him 'to devote himself entirely to the well-being of the King'. The Marshal had begun to get angry:

'Go to Besançon at once, to make my proclamation known there and to take command as senior officer; if not I shall have you arrested! . . . '

Mermet had left, indeed, but to return home. After him, General Delort declined the military command of the Jura.

'In whose name are you offering it to me, *monsieur le Maréchal*, in the name of the King who sent you here, or in the name of the Emperor whom you have just proclaimed?'

Ney had also to suffer the reproach in the agitated face that Baron Cappelle, his last nocturnal visitor, turned toward him.

'You told me this very morning, *monsieur le Maréchal* . . . '

'Baron, we must seek the general good of the country, before defending a lost cause. Don't be alarmed. Napoleon is coming with the best intentions in the world. He wants to forget all the past, reconcile the interests, save France, in short! Go to your post and resume the prefecture of the Ain!'

Cappelle had fled, boiling with indignation, while Ney called after him: 'I would a thousand times rather be pounded in a mortar by Bonaparte than be humiliated by people who have never made war!'

There still remained, in a corner of the room, the faithful aide-de-camp Levavasseur, who had the right to say what he felt and not hold back. He had been almost in tears since the scene of the rallying. On the way there, had he not assured his comrades that Ney was about to make a proclamation in favour of the King? . . .

'*Monsieur le Maréchal*, you are lost Why tarnish so much glory in one day? Why not withdraw quite simply to Besançon, in order to await events there?'

'I couldn't do that. I didn't want to spark off the civil war!'

'Bonaparte will never forgive you your conduct at Fontainebleau.'

'In that matter I was thinking more of France than of him. I told him so. If he is still counting on leading us into Poland, he is mistaken!'

And, as Levavasseur continued, he added: 'That's enough! You are no longer my aide-de-camp!'

How could Ney have been in a good mood at supper after that? Deep within him, he still did not know what welcome the Emperor would reserve for him, and knew the fear of having betrayed for nothing perhaps. For he had betrayed, that was a fact, and above all he had betrayed himself, a man of position carried to the forefront of events more by his own outburst than by chance. He had just become, with singular excess, the embodiment of the 'weathercock' behaviour that was to make the French notables of 1815 the laughing-stock of history. How was he to begin to explain his attitude to Eglé, his wife, the daughter of a lady's maid to Marie-Antoinette? And what was he to say the next day to the other marshals, to his friends, and the day after that to his children? To explain, to explain himself, to become his own interminable advocate, was this to be the fate from now on of the man of Elchingen and the Moskwa? That dismal evening of one of the finest days of his life ushered Marshal Ney for ever into a Shakespearean world, where all was a contrast of light and shade. Before letting him go to his fate, the historian owes it to himself—and to him—to emphasize that the documents establish that there had not at any rate been the least calculation in him, and that he cannot be accused of premeditation (though he did, alas, boast clumsily before Napoleon).

But what, after all, did come over him?

Ney's reversal is no longer an enigma of history; it is an example of a *conversion* in the proper sense of the word. If there is a secret here, it is that of a heart which reopened, and the only external agent whom one can denounce beyond question for having played his part in it is Napoleon, by the magic of his words. Why, and how did it happen, at that place and at that precise moment, Lons-le-Saunier on the night of the 13th to 14th? Because the internal pressure born of the conflict between his present and his past suddenly became unendurable for Ney, by favour of a long sleepless night during which news reached him every hour. Did he, towards midnight, receive a visit from official emissaries of the Emperor, some officers disguised in mufti, bringing him a final appeal to rally? It is certain that Bertrand sent him emissaries, but what became of them is not known. And it has never been possible to establish the names of these 'men of the night'. What has been confirmed, on the other hand, is that Ney received the decisive blow on the evening of the 12th, shortly after his arrival at Lons, when Boulongue, a linen-draper arriving from Lyons completely dazed, handed him the proclamations dated from Golfe-Juan. Ney had put them in his pocket at first, shrugging his shoulders, but as soon as the merchant had withdrawn, he read, re-read and devoured them, and then rushed to the Prefect's house to show them to him, saying:

'No one writes like this any more! This is how the King should write. This is how one talks to soldiers . . . '

And he had inflicted on M. de Vaulchier a reading of the famous proclamation to the army; it is undoubtedly the finest text to come from Napoleon's pen. In subverting Ney's soul, these phrases attained their maximum effectiveness:

'At Golfe-Juan, 1st March, 1815.
'Soldiers!

'We were not defeated: two men risen from our ranks betrayed our laurels, their country, their prince, their benefactor.[1]

'Those whom we saw, for twenty-five years, scouring all Europe to raise enemies against us, who spent their lives fighting against us in the ranks of foreign armies, execrating our fair France, would they claim to command and enchain our eagles, they who could never withstand their gaze? Must we endure that they should inherit the fruit of our glorious labours, that they should seize our honours, our goods, that they should traduce our glory? If their reign should last, all will be lost, even the memory of those immortal days! With what rancour they denature them! And if there still remain any to uphold our glory, it is among those very enemies whom we fought on the field of battle!

'Soldiers! in my exile I heard your voice! I have come through all the obstacles and all the perils! Your general, called to the throne by the choice of the people, and raised to high

[1] An accusation against Marmont, who had been disloyal at Essonnes, and Augereau, who had surrendered Lyons to the Austrians.

61

renown, has returned to you; come and join him! . . .

'Tear off those colours which the nation proscribed, and which served for twenty-five years to rally all the enemies of France! Put up that tricolour cockade! you wore it in our great battles.

'We must forget that we were the masters of the nations! but we must not endure that anyone should interfere in our affairs!

'Who would claim to be master among us? Who would have the power to be so? Take up again those eagles which you had at Ulm, at Austerlitz, at Jena, at Eylau, at Friedland, at Tudela, at Eckmühl, at Esslingen, at Wagram, at Smolensk, at the Moskwa, at Lützen, at Wurzen and at Montmirail! Do you think this handful of arrogant Frenchmen can withstand the sight of them? They will go back to where they come from, and there, if they so wish, they can reign, as they claim to have reigned for nineteen years.

'Your goods, your ranks, your glory, the goods, the ranks and the glory of your children, have no greater enemies than these princes whom the foreigners imposed upon us. They are the enemies of our glory, since the recital of so many heroic actions, which gave lustre to the people of France, fighting against them to escape their yoke, is their condemnation.

'The veterans of Sambre-et-Meuse, of the Rhine, of Italy, of Egypt, of the West, of the Grand Army are humiliated. Their honourable scars are sullied. Their successes become crimes, these brave men become rebels if, as the enemies of the people claim, the legitimate sovereigns were in the midst of the foreign armies.

'The honours, the rewards, the affections are for those who served them against our motherland and us.

'Soldiers! Come and place yourselves under the flags of your leader; his life is composed only of yours; his rights are only those of the people and yours; his interest, his honour, his glory, are no other than your interest, your honour and your glory. *Victory will advance at the charge; the eagle, with the national colours, will fly from steeple to steeple all the way to the towers of Notre-Dame.* Then you will be able to show your scars with honour, then you will be able to boast of what you have done; *you will be the liberators of the motherland.*

'In your old age, surrounded and esteemed by your fellow-citizens, they will listen to you with respect as you tell of your great deeds; you will be able to say with pride: "And I too, I was a part of that Grand Army which twice entered the walls of Vienna, of Rome, of Berlin, of Madrid, of Moscow, which delivered Paris from the stain which treason and the presence of the enemy imprinted there." [1]

'Honour to these brave soldiers, the glory of the motherland! and eternal shame to the criminal Frenchmen, into whatever class fortune may have had them born, who fought for twenty-five years with the foreigner to rend the bosom of the mother-land. NAPOLEON'

'Victory will advance at the charge! Victory will advance at the charge! . . . '

The Marshal had repeated this phrase several times, under the nose of the royalist Prefect, as he himself advanced with long strides through the salon of the prefecture of Lons. From that moment, the deepest chord had been touched in him. He had then had to struggle in vain for two days, to vituperate afresh 'in fiery phrases' against 'the misfortunes that Bonaparte is bringing back to the motherland'; the very violence of his agitation testified that it was a matter once again of one of those rearguard actions that had been his speciality, but conducted by him this time against his own self, and lost in advance. It will have lasted until the visit of Baron Cappelle, whose royalist zeal and clumsy words precipitated the Marshal's evolution.

Shortly after the departure of Cappelle, at first light, he had summoned his three lieutenants: Bourmont, Lecourbe and Mermet, and after a few incoherent words, he had thrown himself neck and crop into the lie, as of old he had crossed the Danube under a hail of fire:

'Gentlemen, the matter is settled. The King has already had to leave Paris. Up to the present I have had to pretend, even with you, but, like me, you have read the Emperor's proclamations. They are well done. The words "Victory will advance at the

---

[1] A sublime text. Truth, however, compels it to be recalled that this procedure — legitimate, but demagogic — of 'And I too' is traditional in Napoleonic proclamations.

charge" will have a great effect. Come! I can say it to you now: it is three months since we were all in agreement. If you had been in Paris, you would have known it, like me. Besides, Bonaparte has grown wiser. Austria facilitated his return. He has promised to make no more wars . . . '

Thunderstruck, Bourmont had neither moved nor spoken, only his nervous habit of looking furtively to right and left had become more pronounced. As for Lecourbe, he had exploded. He was a completely straightforward man with the manners of a peasant, whose mottled face turned purple under the influence of indignation.

'After all, you did agree to fight Bonaparte, didn't you? As for me, how do you expect me to serve a chap like that? He has done me nothing but harm, and the King has done me nothing but good! And then, I am in the King's service, what, and you know, *monsieur le Maréchal*, I do have my honour!'

'And I too have some honour!' Ney had roared. 'That's why I don't want to be humiliated. I don't want my wife coming home to me with tears in her eyes from the humiliations she has suffered at the Tuileries. The King wants none of us, that's clear. *It's only from a man of the army, like Bonaparte, that the army will be able to get any consideration.*'

He had then showed the generals a paper that lay on the table, already completely written, the fruit of that night of inner struggle, his hardest battle, which in the end would make the historic day of March 20th possible, thanks to the decisive weight which Ney threw into the scales on March 14th:

'Here's what I intend to read to the troops: *The Bourbon cause is lost for ever.*'

✳ *March 15th* ✳

13

To our last breath

There were a lot of idle people, on March 15th, loitering in the streets of Auxerre. On the bridge that crossed the Yonne, to the south, the crowd was beginning to wait for Napoleon's advent, 'as if he were going to descend in a chariot of fire, like the prophet Elijah . . . ' a clerk at the prefecture observed derisively. However, travellers declared that he had not even reached Autun yet, and that this last town, transformed into a royalist stronghold, was going to defend itself vigorously. Citizens who had been driven from the streets by the icy drizzle found a smoky and noisy refuge in the Café Milon, provided they did not display a white cockade there, and that they discreetly showed the waiters a tricolour one, all ready in the depths of their pockets. Among the habitués was a sturdy little man, spick and span in the dark uniform of a captain on half-pay : M. Coignet, who had a sharp eye for the girls and a prompt tongue for reeling off interminable tales of his campaigns as soon as he was poured a fresh mug of wine. He had begun to set them down in a close-written hand in a dozen large exercise-books, which were later to make his name famous. But he had written nothing for several days. He was waiting. 'I expected to see my Emperor arrive by now.' He muttered in his moustache against the desolation which the majority of the middle-class citizens of Auxerre had shown from the very first at the news of the return from Elba.

A further source of irritation to him that morning : the great to-do in the streets, the rolling of drums which came and went. The Commissioner of Police, Sotiveau de Richebourg, was going about the town with an address of the municipal council to the King, reading it in a loud voice and posting it up :

'Sire, at the news of the insane attempt by Napoleon Bonaparte, the municipal council and all the inhabitants of the town of Auxerre were filled with the most profound indignation. For eleven months, France has breathed under the tutelary and paternal rule of her legitimate sovereign. The misfortunes of twenty-five years were almost effaced . . . and the spirit of good appeared to have mastered the spirit of evil.

'What, therefore, can be the hopes of this perjurer who appears suddenly in our midst, a sword in one hand and a torch in the other? . . . No, the people and the army will never waver between the man who caused so many tears and so much blood to flow and a King who marks each of his days with fresh benefits . . .

' . . . As for us, Sire, unalterably attached to the august family of the Bourbons by the respect and the obedience which we owe to the law, attached to your sacred person by the bond, more powerful still, of gratitude and love, we swear to defend your crown to our last breath . . . '

It was signed—the detail would have its piquancy two days later—by the Mayor, Robinet de Malleville, the deputy-mayor, Sochet, Colonel Thierrat de Millerelle, 'an officer of distinction', the councillor for the prefecture Edme-Marie Hay, the advocate Boniface Paradis, the engineer-in-chief for the department Sutil, the judge Claude Lesseré, the notary Deschamps de Saint-Bris, Messrs Escalier, Heuvrard, Crété de la Barcelle, Cottin . . . and the commissioner Sotiveau de Richebourg.

Drafted by the municipal council three days earlier, it had been printed and posted a little too late . . . The people were silent now as they read those fine phrases. Coignet, without cause for alarm, could shrug his shoulders and spit all the juice from his quid of tobacco at the foot of the notices. Alongside that of the civic dignitaries, a proclamation by the Prefect of the Yonne, M. Gamot, made an appeal to all men of good will for 'the safety of the motherland and the protection of the throne'. General Boudin, in command of the department of the Yonne, doubled the posts of gendarmes and N.C.O.s on guard at the gateways: he ordered that 'all citizens whose papers were not in order' should be brought before him. Perhaps he expected Napoleon to be seized by the scruff of the neck?

On the same day, to the right and left of Auxerre, France continued to break out in the 'Jacobin colours'. But beyond, the royalist reaction asserted itself wherever it could rely on deep roots, especially in the traditionally godly areas of Normandy, Vendée and Anjou. After Dijon, the same scene had been enacted at Beaune, Dôle, Poligny and Auxonne, where the whole artillery depot passed into the Emperor's service. First, palliasses flying through the air in the barrack-rooms: the military rising; then, flurries in the streets: the popular rising; and finally, the National Guard, already under arms, by a simple change of cockade, bore witness to the rallying of the local bourgeoisie, and at a stroke put a brake on popular excesses. At the top, the movement ended in the comic gesticulations of the notables, forced to be its embodiment at the front of the stage, and to employ the same declamatory vigour in the proclamation for the Emperor as they had in the one they signed two days earlier for the King.

At Clamecy, the crowd swelled, threatening, in the square by the town hall and tore up the ordinances of Louis XVIII. A man suddenly sprang out of it, in the brown and shabby redingote that was, in this revolution, what the Phyrgian cap had been in '93: a uniform, a sign. It was General Allix. In a stentorian voice he read the proclamations from Golfe-Juan to bursts of frenzied cheering. Summoned by the Mayor to intervene, the lieutenant of the gendarmerie approached him with his little battalion of twelve men, muskets in hand. The representatives of the King climbed the steps and surrounded Allix. The latter let them come, a smile on his lips. He took off his large spectacles, calmly shook hands with the flabbergasted lieutenant, and then continued in a voice of thunder:

'In the name of the Emperor, I assume command of the town of Clamecy! All of you, present here, I call upon you to put up the national cockade immediately, and to regard as enemies those who do not wear it!'

A thousand pairs of eyes were levelled at the gendarmes' headdress; the latter looked to their lieutenant, who, with dignity, ordered a strategic retreat to the barracks.

At the same hour, a rising that had broken out at dawn made itself mistress of Nevers. Thus the whole centre of France proved to be ready for the insurrection. And it could not be claimed, this time, that it was the work of emissaries who had come from Elba: Napoleon had no officers to waste in any direction other than his immediate route. From March 15th, in ten or fifteen towns variously situated geographically and socially, the Bonapartists—and in a more general way, the malcontents—

deliberately became accessories to the return and acted spontaneously as if they had received orders from the Emperor.

14

A puff from the people,
without any effort

At Chalon, well before dawn on March 15, Napoleon was already at work. He had become incapable of sleeping for more than four or five hours at a stretch—but he often made up for this, it is true, by dozing during the day. In the Hôtel du Parc, full of men deep in slumber, rolled up in their cloaks on chests and tables, the first to stir, therefore, were the Emperor on the first floor and the scullions round the fires.

'Well, Bertrand? How do we stand?'

'The regular army at Your Majesty's disposal this morning consists of more than twenty thousand men. We have sixty pieces of artillery, harnessed and supplied. Besides this, we have succeeded in gathering all the isolated men who have come forward since Cannes into six battalions of officers, invalided out or on half-pay, from colonels down to second lieutenants. They were scarcely armed for the most part except for their swords. They have been issued with muskets and cartridges. Finally, in Burgundy as in Dauphiné, the towns are offering their National Guards, not to speak of the bands of peasants who throng the sides of the roads. Should Your Majesty wish to double his forces, he has only to say a word.'

A brisk gesture from Napoleon brushed this prospect aside.

'I want nothing unorganized around me, you know that very well, Bertrand. Do you see me arriving in Paris with a million peasants? Even the National Guards; I want them to organize themselves, but to stay where they are to secure order. Do you think I haven't heard in my path for a week this excessive and continual railing against the chateaux? Bertrand, write!'

Pacing rapidly up and down, he delivered at full speed, as usual, a tangle of words, the most emphatic of which Bertrand caught on the wing. This yielded:

'My friends, do not be alarmed. No French soldier will fire on my grey cloak. As soon as they see it, the schemes of the enemies of the nation will be frustrated. It will be the rallying point for all true Frenchmen. That which treason and six hundred thousand enemies from all the nations of Europe have set up with so much trouble, a puff from the people will have destroyed without any effort . . . '

After that, Napoleon called for his valet de chambre, some eau de Cologne and some hot tea. It was seven o'clock. The whole house was now astir from top to bottom, and a long line of vehicles was already waiting in front of the inn.

'Who is seeking audience, at the moment?'

'General Veaux, Sire, come post-haste from Dijon, brings you the town's submission. The members of the courts, civil and commercial. The mayors of the neighbouring districts. The officers of the National Guard.'

'The prefect, Germain? Still in flight?'

'Still, Sire.'

'But the sub-prefect, Simonnot?'

' "Confined to his bed by a slight indisposition . . . " '

'I see. I'll get rid of him. Have them put forward a man of ability to succeed him. And the Mayor of Chalon? I didn't see him yesterday evening.'

'He has barricaded himself in his house, Sire. And without the least pretence, this time.'

'I like that better. With men who are frank one can come to an understanding. Monsieur de Chaboulon!'

'Sire?'

For two days this new secretary had been frisking around unceasingly in a corner of the Imperial apartment, in search of some mission or other to make himself important.

'Go and see this mayor. It was I who appointed him, but he is siding with a bygone family and is bound to have some scruples. If he counters you with his oaths, tell him that I release him from them, and make him feel that he'll have to wait a long time if he's relying on Louis XVIII to free him from them.'

There followed a trying hour of talk between Fleury de Chaboulon and this M. Royer, Mayor of Chalon, wholly characteristic of the dialogue that developed in France that day between those who sided with Napoleon at the time they were resuming authority and those who hesitated, sometimes sincerely bound in conscience to the King, and always tortured by the fact that nothing was settled all the time the Emperor was not at the Tuileries.

'I greatly admired Napoleon, but I swore to be loyal to Louis XVIII, and I believe I am bound to observe this oath until such time as I am released from it.'

'I had my answer ready in advance,' wrote Fleury de Chaboulon. This young man had the century in his blood :

'Consider : since '89 the French have sworn in turn to be loyal to the Royalty, to the Republic, to the Directory, to the Consulate, to the Empire and to the Charter. If, to satisfy their conscience, they had chosen to resist the setting up of each succeeding regime, into what a state of despair and anarchy, into what a deluge of evils and blood would they not have plunged our unhappy motherland? Our sole guide must be the national will.'

This was very fine, but the Mayor let slip his real concern :

'We find ourselves faced with an exceptional case, unknown until today : at each change, the new government seized *all* authority *at once*. But here, the royal government remains in being !'

In other words, this was the first time that every Frenchman had been forced to take sides *before* or *during* but not *after* the change.

Fleury de Chaboulon ended by finding the decisive argument :

'I have read in all our publicists that one owes obedience to the *de facto* government, and since the Emperor has resumed power *de facto* in your town, I believe that the best thing you can do is to submit yourself to his rule.'

'Very well, Monsieur, I surrender to your observations !' . . . (It was ten o'clock.) 'Please present me to his Majesty.'

Meanwhile, Napoleon had put in a further appearance on the balcony, to receive the homage of a crowd more civilized, more select, than on the previous day. In the front ranks, nothing but middle-class citizens and some military men. The rabble had been relegated to the right and left of the quay, between the public baths and the warehouses.

'Last year, my brave men, who was the most brave, during your forty days of resistance?'

A worthy fellow was thrust before Napoleon, all gnarled and sprouting an enormous nose. This was the mayor of Saint-Jean-de-Losne. He simpered and spluttered today like a little girl, but the year before had planted his pitchfork right in the belly of the Uhlans. If the latter had not hanged him, it was because the whole of his village had contrived to hide him for three months, under stacks in barns and in press-houses.

'I shall decorate him. It is for brave men like him and like you that I instituted the Légion d'Honneur, and not for the émigrés pensioned by our enemies. The towns of Chalon, Tournus and Saint-Jean-de-Losne will henceforward bear in their arms the Eagle of the Légion.'

A cheer ran down the whole length of the embankment and redoubled round the Emperor, who had performed this last scene standing by the door of his coach, ready to leave between ten and eleven o'clock. The Mayor of Chalon arrived at that moment, too late, crestfallen, and with a right to only a very brief nod. He should have been there the previous evening, or, if absolutely necessary, have rushed back with Fleury de Chaboulon without requiring much persuasion. M. Royer would be dismissed the following day.

Escorted as far as the gates by one of the battalions formed of officers without troops, the Emperor's carriage set off on a solid road of local limestone; it travelled through fields in which there were no longer oxen, but horses pulling the plough. By way of Bourgneuf, Saint-Léger and Saint-Émilon, it would reach 'the hill of Autun', on which the soldiers of the King had still been encamped the previous evening.

But there things had changed. The first platoons of cavalry, sent in advance along the Emperor's route, had given an account of the situation the previous evening to General Brayer. This last, a military man without dash, but a good organizer, and one who had stayed close to the men, had been assistant to Count d'Artois when the latter had rushed down from Paris to Lyons to stop Napoleon. No sooner arrived, Brayer had let his Bonapartist sentiments emerge, had done all he could to sabotage the defensive measures taken by the Prince and Macdonald, and quickly

73

thrown off the mask. By taking the head of the military revolt, he had helped to discipline the rising of the silkweavers and the workers of the Guillotière. After Bédoyère (at Grenoble), Brayer had thus been the second senior officer to transform the anarchic impulse which was flinging the soldiers of France towards the Emperor into a rally with traditional leaders at its head. Napoleon, in gratitude, and from policy, had relieved Cambronne of the command of his advance guard (leaving him only control of the battalion of the Old Guard), in order to entrust it to General Brayer. The publicity given to this measure was to complete the unsettling of the leaders sent against him by the King, by dangling before their eyes the glittering prospect of converting their mission as gendarmes into that of triumphal heralds.

Brayer, therefore, had been advancing since Lyons with half a day's start on Napoleon, at the head of the 13th regiment of dragoons, which had gone over at the same time as he. He had phlegmatically put in hand the 'retaking' of Autun, which unfolded in the morning of March 15th with neither preliminaries nor hesitations; the 'Jacobins', who had taken refuge in the seminary, had been asked to lie low. And the posts of the royalist National Guard had suddenly seen swooping down on them, at the grey hour of reveille, six hundred troopers at the gallop, sabres in hand. Brayer had followed, close behind the dragoons. Happily, maddened by the profusion of white flags, the stories of the Bonapartists and the haughty attitude of the old Mayor, the soldiers had begun to set about the latter and his supporters with the flats of their sabres. Brayer had locked up these defenders of the *ancien régime* in the abbey of Saint-Martin, where they were to remain with the tomb of Brunehaut, 'the most wicked of queens'.

15

If one must despair of France

From Autun to Paris, the behaviour of the 13th regiment of dragoons was seen through a distorting glass. As was, moreover, the attitude of Marshal Ney. Why should the Parisians torment themselves? On March 15th, along with their breakfast or *petit déjeuner* (which was still called *déjeuner* plain and simply), they could savour the following news, distilled by the papers:

'Letters from Lyons declare that as soon as he had been informed of Marshal Ney's advance, Buonaparte hurriedly withdrew his outposts from the region of Mâcon and had them fall back on Lyons. Marshal Ney is on the march at the head of a corps of about ten thousand men, of troops of the line and National Guards, regularly trained in the garrison-towns of Franche-Comté; these troops are animated by an excellent spirit, of that vigour and courage which Marshal Ney could not fail to impart to them.

'The same letters make it known that the greatest part of the 13th regiment of dragoons, who had been carried away for an instant by the allurements of the enemy, felt the full enormity of their position, and that, preferring even the most severe punishment to armed treason against the motherland, they had ranged themselves on the side of Marshal Ney, who had received the soldiers like men led astray for a moment, in whom sincere repentance merits leniency.

'The last event has made the most lively impression on Buonaparte's band. From that moment they appear, even more than before, anxious, uncertain and dismayed; defections, too, have already been numerous among them.'

Everything seemed for the best, therefore, in the best of worlds. Napoleon was in the process of dissolving like a lump of sugar somewhere between Lyons and Mâcon. But if this were really so, why on that same day did the *Journal des Débats* publish an appeal, betraying anguish in its frenzy?

'A great epoch has arrived. The fate of France is about to be decided, and it is France who will decide it. If she accepts slavery, she will deliver up her name to the opprobrium of the nations. *The subjects of Buonaparte will no longer be Frenchmen.*[1] They

---

[1] I have intentionally underlined some passages in this article. They are characteristic of a certain 'ultra' spirit which excluded wrong-thinkers from the national community, and which was to perpetuate itself in a direct line down to the men of Versailles who allied themselves with Bismarck to crush the Communards, and to Maurras and his friends, who were delighted by the 'heavenly surprise' of 1940.

75

will have to adopt another name, out of respect for their country.

'Louis XVIII has given us peace, the Constitution and liberty. What is Buonaparte bringing us? *A civil war so indispensable that it would perhaps be shameful if it did not break out on the day of his triumph* . . .

'Frenchmen! In leaving Fontainebleau Buonaparte said *that Robespierre was the only man who had known how to govern you.*[1] And this is the sovereign who is being offered you by a handful of rebels tainted with their brothers' blood.

'Frenchmen! Be Frenchmen! At least die Frenchmen, if one must despair of France . . .'

' . . . if one must despair of France' (which in the language of these people always meant: 'If the French give themselves other rulers than us'), at least the *Journal des Débats* did not despair of the foreigner. In the same issue, sentiments of calculated perfidy seemed to have been dictated from Vienna by Talley-rand:

'It is confidently asserted that several foreign ministers[2] have said to the King: "Sire, we will not conceal from Your Majesty that we have given our courts an account of what is taking place in France, and that should this state of affairs be at all prolonged, their response will be *the entry into France of our sovereigns' troops.*" And so here, Frenchmen, is one of the benefits which Buonaparte is bringing us: a foreign war that could bring the Cossacks back to the gates of Paris! And yet should we not arm ourselves to repulse this man, who does not fear to plunge us into the horrors of a civil and foreign war in order to glut his odious ambition? What!—we would hesitate between a King who alone with his pacifying hand holds back beyond our frontiers two hundred thousand British, Russians

---

[1] Words which Napoleon certainly never uttered in this form. But certain confidences, reported by the *Journal de Bertrand* on Saint Helena, bear witness to the permanence of his respect, indeed his admiration, for Robespierre's qualities as orator and statesman. It is possible that the scribbler of the *Débats* had picked up an anecdote with some such sally. His reaction, there again, is evidence of the assimilation which the royalists made in March 1815 of Napoleon to the men of '93.

[2] In other words, the ambassadors of the Allied Powers.

and Prussians, and a tyrant whose presence is about to bring them among us?'

On reading these lines, the opposition did not forbear to observe that 'the pacifying hand' of Louis XVIII seemed far rather to be giving the foreign troops the sign to come in than to be holding them back at the frontiers. One other piece of news was officially announced on March 15th: 'His Majesty has decided to re-establish the office of Prefect of Police of Paris.[1] He appoints to this office Monsieur de Bourrienne, chargé d'affaires at Hamburg.'

The individual in question was a noble of good pedigree. His blood was also the one and only trace of nobility that could be remarked in the man's appearance and career. Louis-Antoine Fauvelet de Charbonnière de Bourrienne was born at Lens in the same year as Napoleon [1769], whose friendship he had culti- vated so successfully at Brienne that he had become his first secretary in the Italian campaign under the Consulate. Only under the Consulate. . . . For Napoleon did not tolerate thieves (not in his own immediate entourage, at least) and still less braggarts. But M. de Bourrienne[2] had proved to be full of vices and intrigues. His dossier turns, from 1802, into a police dossier, which hardly marked him out for the post of prefect: speculator, embezzler, swindler, adventurer. He trafficked in State secrets in exchange for millions, which were immediately lost in gambling. Many another would have ended up at Vincennes when Napoleon's eyes were opened. But their youthful friend- ship had commuted the penalty into a post as plenipotentiary at Hamburg, where for ten years Bourrienne had been swindled by the Russians, the British and the Germans, until he rallied spectacularly to the King in 1814. His distinctive features were a pronounced squint, a glib tongue, a great deal of intuition, if not of education, and a remarkable memory. He had abandoned the mists of Hamburg for the banks of the Seine since the

[1] Abolished at the Restoration. This was the 'director-general of the police of the realm' (one no longer said 'the minister of police') who after ten months was assuming the functions of prefect of police.

[2] Perhaps driven already by the first manifestations of that disordered mind which was to cause him to die in the asylum at Charenton.

change of regime, and he had patiently haunted the anterooms, waiting for someone to throw him a bone to gnaw. It happened, at the moment when he was no longer expecting it. Why Bourrienne as Prefect of Police on March 15th? Because a better nark could not have been found anywhere. For in those hours when the whole apparatus, built up brick by brick from a mixture of personnel of the Empire and of the Monarchy, was collapsing around the princes; when the latter were distrustful of a Soult and had begun to rely on a Ney no longer, the King found himself in need of one of those rare men with a thorough knowledge—such at least was their claim—of all the men of the Bonapartist party, their resources and their connections. If anyone could sort the wheat from the tares, it was Bourrienne.

In the meantime, the ministers had at least one consolation : supporters of the King were coming forward and organizing more than in the preceding days. Recruits had been canvassed for the *Volontaires royaux* for several days, without much idea, moreover, of what would be done with them, but they had hardly been jostling each other in the halls of the lifeguards, on the ground floor of the Tuileries. This morning they were arriving from all directions : old aristocrats coming back to life to relive August 10th, but also a certain number of young people, all enrolled, it is true, by their schools. The pupils of Stanislas College, with shocks of hair marked with the tonsure of the good fathers since the age of ten, a thousand students of law, some students of medicine, some pupils of the École Normale—towards noon the flow was such that it became necessary to put up tables in the Carrousel courtyard, with what protection was possible from the rain and the wind, in order to enter the names and addresses of the volunteers. Certain onlookers were surprised too : why such a mobilization against an enemy who was coming with a few hundred men?

Those enrolled were divided into four battalions, grouped as far as possible according to age. The young ones were rigged out in comic-opera costumes, in the style of Henry IV; they were supplied with a flag, embroidered in haste by the ladies of the Faubourg Saint-Germain, and an octogenarian commanding officer, General de Vioménil. And since it was very necessary to occupy them, they were sent on a hazardous expedition : a march-past beyond the barriers of right-thinking Paris, into the somewhat uncertain areas of the Faubourg Saint-Antoine, from which had come, twenty-five years earlier, the eruption that had taken the Bastille. A little surprised at their own audacity, the King's Volunteers went to show themselves to the workers. And the latter said not a word. It even appears that a few bravos had broken out here and there. The following day, the *Moniteur* recorded this success:

'The officers and volunteers who had enrolled themselves to march in the common defence, under the princes and the Counts of Vioménil and la Tour-Maubourg, assembled today at the appointed place. Preceded by drums and a band, they passed through the town and the Faubourg Saint-Antoine, to cries of *Vive le Roi*, repeated by a huge crowd which thronged their route and by the numerous spectators who, ranged at the windows, gave the same tokens of satisfaction and encouragement.

'The volunteers betook themselves to Vincennes, where the population of the vicinity had preceded them and foregathered. They were inspected by Generals de Vioménil and de la Tour-Maubourg, accompanied by a numerous concourse of general and senior officers. These brave young people gave themselves up, with all the ardour and all the effusion of the French character, to the expression of the sentiments that filled them. Confidence and courage were imprinted on every face. They were at once happy and proud of their self-sacrifice. Next Friday, they will assemble again in order to complete their organization and to receive their arms.'

In the heat of that glorious action, the young men of the Medical School drafted a highly warlike address to the King. The scalpels were turning into bayonets.

'Sire,
'The Medical School, too, can offer you some brave men devoted to the defence of the throne and the motherland. They have just sworn at Your Majesty's feet to defend to the death their motherland, their King, their liberty; they have asked you for arms: let their valour be directed, and France will see that

the same hand that can save the life of a useful citizen, can also mete out death to a base sedition-monger, to a rebellious traitor.'

16

Dialogue among the shades

On March 15th, M. de Marsilly, lieutenant in the corps of one hundred Swiss Guards that protected the King, noted in his diary: 'At nine o'clock I was with the captain of the lifeguards, where numerous officers were to be found. The spirit at the chateau is good; would to God that it animated all the troops! One thing is certain, that the conspiracies which had arisen in the north are discovered. The King received the deputations of the department of the Cher, the town of Dunkirk and the department of Seine-et-Oise.' At the lifeguards, he fell into the arms of a tall bean-stick of a man, all aquiver with rage and antiquity, M. de Gobineau, whom he was meeting again after twenty-five years of separation. Marsilly was sixty-three, quite young for this place. Gobineau was seventy-eight. Both had served in the lifeguards of Louis XV, and then Louis XVI. Gobineau had saved his head by emigrating, and Marsilly, who had remained in Reims under the Terror, had saved his by playing the horn in a theatre orchestra. He had spent the whole of the Empire in a provincial retreat detesting Napoleon, but not destitute of philosophy: 'I managed to keep myself occupied and the days went by all too fast. I stayed in my room, I read, I wrote a diary of little interest, but in which I gave an account of the day. At half-past nine I had breakfast, warmed by two fires, the sun and the fire in my chimney. A book in hand, I enjoyed a glass of wine, accompanied perhaps by a piece of pie, or some other dish.'

The Allied invasion, in 1814, had plucked this epicurean from the backwaters of his life, and although he longed for the downfall of the Empire with all his heart, his first move had been patriotic. Faced with the panic of the Reims authorities, 'I put into execution', he recounted, 'the plan that I had conceived in myself, which was that at the first hint of the approach of

80

enemies, *Papa l'ingambe* would take up his old carbine and his three-cornered hat! . . . I went along to the town hall and had myself enrolled in the National Guard . . . ' But that had been the full extent of his heroism: the carbine had remained silent when 150 Cossacks had sufficed to cause the municipal council of Reims to capitulate, and M. de Marsilly had then welcomed the Russian and Prussian officers very amiably, especially that dear Major-General de Warmsdorff, whom he had known so well in the old days . . . He had found himself once more among men of the world, after having had to abandon the stage for a quarter of a century to those soldiers sprung from the gutter, the Lannes, the Murats, the Buonapartes.

As soon as he learned of the King's return and the re-estab-lishment of the old companies of lifeguards, M. de Marsilly had rushed to Paris by diligence to resume his place in the Swiss Guards; he had managed to do so, but not without difficulty, for there had been nearly a thousand such phantoms as he to con-tend for those hundred places, and their commanding officer, the Duke de Mortemart, a brat of twenty-seven (late aide-de-camp to Napoleon), had made desperate efforts to keep the number of sexagenarians, indeed septuagenarians, as small as possible. For-getting his grudge against émigrés, he embraced his senior, M. de Gobineau, in brotherly fashion:

'Well now, my friend, what have you been doing since the King's return? How is it we've not seen you at Court?'

There they both were in a window-recess, telling each other their stories. Gobineau had a good deal on his mind; misfortune had overtaken him in trying his luck in business.

'Eh! I wasted the whole summer looking for a lucrative post that would suit me at Court! Finally, I was forced to take up with the plebeians. A fellow from Bordeaux called Pailhès came to see me with the proposal that I should obtain the privi-lege, going half shares with him, of supplying the wines for the Royal Household . . . He was to procure the capital; I was to get the agreement of the Court. There would certainly have been a vast fortune to be made there. But, my poor friend, the stirring up he had to do, of people, opportunities, intrigues and promises, it would fill a volume!'

'But where have you just come from now, Monsieur de Gobineau?'

81

He had abandoned his trading and his endless discussions with wily dealers on the price of Burgundies or Bordeaux, and like the rest, had just regained his fervour of 1792, when he had sharpened his dagger to defend the good Louis XVI.

'You know, of course, that in each legion of the National Guard volunteers were asked for, to march against Buonaparte? I came forward, this morning. They mustered us in the Horse-guards. And I have just taken part there in the most ridiculous and most deplorable scene. There were about three hundred of us at the riding-school of Count de Sourdis. All of us, with one voice, were begging to march. Immediately, a discussion broke out between the Marquis de Castries and M. de Sourdis, as to which of the two was in command. The first made play with the title of Superintendent, the other replied that he was head of the legion. They appealed to us in the matter! They said pretty harsh and offensive things to each other! . . . which are best left unmentioned, for they were not honourable. Tired of this scandal, I brought it to an end by crying out that I would give my vote to whichever of the two should be the first to get on his horse to lead us to the enemy!'

'Very good! And then? . . . '

'Everybody there agreed with me, but the two of them left. I still haven't got a commanding officer . . . '

'Excuse me, my friend, but I have to be on duty.'

One hurried along by the other, the two old bundles of bones reached the doors of the Pavillon de Flore, where the King lived. Nobody took much notice of them; at this time the Tuileries saw thousands of such encounters between the moribund. We shall be meeting these two again later: they kept their diaries to the end.

17

I am expecting a great deal of Marshal Ney

Nothing was more dreary than the Royal apartments, on the first floor of the Tuileries, the huge windows of which permitted curious onlookers to see right into them when the heavy curtains were not drawn. Here was the frozen anonymity of the most famous lodgings in history, decorated in a haphazard way to the taste of the superintendents of the national furnishings, in which no occupant had ever been able to feel at home; not a queen, not an empress, not even Josephine, had been able to cheer up these premises, which had previously crushed Louis XIII. Flowers were nowhere to be seen; the harpsichords were falling into decay—besides, who would have thought of playing them at the Tuileries?

The present tenant, of course, was called Louis, the eighteenth of that name. He had been living 'in private' since the very violent attack of gout that had confined him to his chair at the beginning of the month, giving rise to serious concern about his general condition. He was pushed in his wheel-chair from his room to the audience-chamber and to the great study, where a good many of those whom he received had seen Louis XVI hesitate and Napoleon at work at that same table. Apart from the audiences to delegations up from the provinces, for a stereo-typed exchange of words completely fixed in advance, there had been hardly more than ten to fifteen people to approach him since the arrival of the famous dispatch by telegraph, on March 5th, announcing Napoleon: the same ones who were placing a thick wad of cotton-wool between him and the outside world, simply because that was the only chance of gaining his favour. On this afternoon we find almost all of them gathered in the council chamber, where for six days they had held their low masses in little groups, whispering, discussing, arguing and waiting—for what they were none too sure, the improbable: a decision from the King, perhaps?

Here, then, was the little club that managed France, in so far as the poor country could be guided by that regime of 'paternal anarchy'. In the absence of the one man capable of inspiration, Talleyrand, there was Beugnot, with his 'full-bottomed figure', a very clerical minister . . . of the Marine; the Chancellor, Dambray, an ancient nonentity; Jaucourt, deputy-minister for Foreign Affairs; Dandré, 'director' of the police, who directed nothing; and Clarke, Duke de Feltre, who had betrayed the Directory for Napoleon, and then Napoleon for the Bourbons:

he had just been appointed to the war ministry in place of Soult, because it had actually come to be believed, by dint of slanders and libels, that Napoleon could not have conceived his campaigns himself, the success of which was attributed to his minister. For the moment, Clarke was making a show of royalist zeal so vehement that even his colleagues were embarrassed by it.

General Dessolles, in command of the National Guard, Marshals Berthier and Marmont, alternating in command of the lifeguards, Count de Beurnonville and the Duke de Duras, first gentleman of the bedchamber, made fugitive appearances without mixing overmuch with the ministers. Now and then, Count d'Artois, 'Monsieur', showed his long and haggard face, or else the Duke de Berry, small, narrow-shouldered and harsh looking, shot through the anterooms like a cannonball.

Three men, above all, were active that day, watching each other and not missing an opportunity of tearing each other to pieces: first, M. de Vitrolles, tool of Count d'Artois, a trouble-maker not without finesse or courage, always under pressure, who had rushed to the Czar's headquarters the year before, in the middle of the invasion, to let the Allies know that the way to Paris was open to them. His intervention had brought him an equivocal post as 'Secretary to the Council', which he dreamed of investing with the former prerogatives of the Secretary of State's office. In fact, Vitrolles was only waiting for one thing: the reign of Charles X, whose Grey Eminence he hoped to be, if not his Richelieu. He has left some amusing *Mémoires*, and it is he who has given a pitiless description of the other two, naturally imputing to them all the sins of the first Restoration: the Abbé Montesquiou, first, Minister of the Interior. 'He was paler, yellower and thinner than usual; he kept his eyes fixed on the table. His voice, distorted by anger, was feebler, more tremulous, than ever.' Montesquiou drew Vitrolles' shafts all the more since the Abbé was proving to be well-disposed towards those minions of hell, the 'constitutionalists', and dreamed of heading a liberal ministry. Which did not prevent him from asserting that 'the French need to be governed by neglect'.

But Vitrolles reserved a good part of his spleen for Count de Blacas d'Aulps, acknowledged favourite of Louis XVIII, for no other valid reason but his unsurpassable nullity. Bearing the sibylline title of 'Grandmaster of the Wardrobe',[1] he watched over the King so well that it was becoming very difficult to speak to the sovereign out of his presence. 'His great reserve, which manifested itself in an insufferable arrogance, his tall silhouette, long in the body and short in the leg, the classic features, gaunt and cold, of his pale face, which never lightened, his head, completely bare and covered with an over-blond wig', all this had become inseparable from the scene in which the King was seeking, more than anything, rest after a wandering life.

Blacas was furious above all because Vitrolles, whose devotion to the royalist cause was unquestionable and whose exquisite manners would have charmed marble, obtained *'les entrées'* to the King almost as easily as himself. On this March 15th, towards five o'clock exactly, Vitrolles was about to avail himself of this privilege in order to find out whether Louis XVIII was at last beginning to realize how serious matters were. Tired of listening to the other ministers 'jabbering away like old women', he entered the study, and found there an unexpected ally: Marshal Macdonald, Duke of Taranto, who was already in conversation with the King. He was a stranger to the palace coterie; previously, under the Empire, he had been one of those angular men, difficult of contact, whose worth is revealed only at moments of great danger. Macdonald was back from Lyons, where he had vainly tried, together with Monsieur, to defend France's second city against Napoleon. He had no more love for the princes than he had had for the Emperor; his Scottish character made him a regular bundle of prickles. But he had taken an oath to the Bourbons and would not abandon it.

In the presence of the King, therefore, who had not carried graciousness so far as to invite him to sit down (etiquette before all!), was this stocky, slightly corpulent man, whose civilian clothes, worn to avoid recognition, made him look like a city solicitor. Long dress-coat in nigger-brown over olive-coloured breeches, supple boots, high black hat and cane umbrella; who would have been able to recognize in this the hero of Wagram,

---

[1] Blacas had also become 'Minister of the Royal Household', reluctantly, for he considered this to be as derogatory as the acceptance of government office.

the vanquished of the Katzbach? But the fiery eye still betrayed the man who had no fear of words, when he turned to the King his large and bony face, with its noble nose:

'All this is very fine, Sire, and I am highly honoured by the confidence which Your Majesty is showing me in appointing me first lieutenant to His Highness the Duke de Berry, in the command of the army which is being mustered below Paris. But will Your Majesty permit me to ask him a question?'

Louis XVIII inclined his head, with that movement, gracious and full of meaning, which promised all without giving anything, and so frequently saved him from speech. The King was dressed as usual in a completely plain blue coat, with gold fleur-de-lys buttons, and no other distinction except those famous gilded epaulettes, embroidered with two enormous crowns, which made him look vaguely like an admiral. All this overlaid a mountain of shapeless flesh. 'His attitude and whole appearance bore the stamp of the highest rank; his head retained a youthful air, his full cheeks diminished the prominence which his aquiline nose would otherwise have had; his broad forehead sloped a little too much to the rear. He had a lively and penetrating eye which seemed to light up his face; his coiffure was that of his youth: the hair, raised over the brow, was cut in bands, powdered and fastened at the back with a queue-ribbon.'

'To where does Your Majesty think of withdrawing, in the event of his being forced to abandon his capital?'

Vitrolles was delighted to find at last a sensible man as pessimistic as himself. The event was so rare at the Tuileries that the King was unable to hide a start:

'But we have not come to that, *monsieur le Maréchal?*'

'No, but we shall have in five or six days, Sire. Your Majesty must be aware of Napoleon's activity. He doesn't need longer to get to Paris. If his march is not stopped, he will continue it rapidly, and there is no reason to believe, after what has happened since his landing and all the way to Lyons, that any unit will offer resistance . . .'

'I am expecting a great deal of Marshal Ney. He promised to seize him and bring him to me in an iron cage.'

'Sire, I *believe* he will make every effort to fulfil his promise. He is a man of honour. But his troops could escape him;

the example is catching and unfortunately the contagion is spreading.'

This worrying interlude had exhausted the King.

'Well! I will consider, monsieur le Duc! My ministers are coming. I will talk it over with them.'

Which meant, more precisely, that he would let them talk themselves hoarse giving him contradictory advice, without breathing a word himself.

'In any case, I have decided, you know, to appear before the Chambers tomorrow, for a royal sitting. I shall make an appeal that must rally every opinion.'

Macdonald and Vitrolles left arm-in-arm by a secret stairway, which enabled the Marshal to leave the palace discreetly. They knew each other only slightly, but they esteemed and understood one another.

'Do you really believe in Marshal Ney's resolve, monsieur le Duc?'

Macdonald raised a shoulder and was silent. But a moment later, he in turn asked a question:

'And do you really believe, monsieur de Vitrolles, in the utility of this scoundrel de Bourrienne?'

'Wasn't it necessary to call on the one who knew all the old Bonapartist people best? I don't think any more of him than you do, but when it is a matter of the police, one does not look too closely . . .'

'In that case, there's someone else whom you should have thought of . . .'

Vitrolles stopped, threw a circular glance about him, to elude any indiscreet ears, and said with an air of triumph:

'You don't know how truly you've spoken. I will let you into a State secret: this evening, Monsieur is going to meet Fouché!'

'Monsieur is going to meet Fouché?'

'In the most absolute secrecy, this evening at ten o'clock, at Mme de Vaudémont's. Doesn't that show realism and audacity? Through Fouché, it is the liberals and the conspirators of all sides that we shall be able to win over!'

'Ney . . . Fouché . . .' murmured Macdonald quietly; he raised a shoulder again and was silent.

18

We are only stopping for refreshment

'The priests and the nobles? I'll treat them as they deserve. I'll string them up!'

Autun, the Hôtel de la Poste, March 15th, five o'clock in the evening: Napoleon's anger was exploding in all its violence. Since setting out from Lyons, he had been more or less holding it back. After leaving that city, where he had been supreme, here he was these three days forced to sleep at inns like a common traveller, and continually thwarted by the coolness of the authorities. He was letting fly as he marched up and down in the little salon, where the Mayor and his councillors had been thrust before him. Each time he swooped down on them, almost running, these worthies retreated comically: was he not about to spit in their faces? 'They tried to put in a few remarks to vindicate themselves, but their words were as good as lost among the vehement expressions that poured like a torrent from the Emperor's mouth, and allowed them no reply.' One imprudent phrase, moreover, had touched off the powder-barrel:

'Sire . . . your abdication . . .'

'What has my abdication to do with you? That's a large question of no concern to you. What is far more certain is the need the French have of me, to secure the benefits of the Revolution for them, and to pull them out of the slavery and misery into which the priests and the nobles would plunge them by re-establishing the tithe and the feudal dues.'

When Napoleon stood still, he frightened them even more. His pallor was accentuated. His mouth had a downward twist. His voice became shrill. And all eyes were drawn by the convulsive trembling of his left calf, clinical sign of paranoia, remarked in him after 1808 each time he lost his self-control. He repeated:

'You've let yourselves be run by them. I'll string them up!'

Appalling words, and completely unprecedented in his mouth. In his whole life he had never uttered them. All these people had lived through '93, when there had swung from the lamp-

posts in the streets the stewards, the extortioners, the Swiss
Guards, and in the Place de Grève in Paris, Foullon the Starver,
his mouth stuffed with a huge fistful of hay . . .

'I landed with six hundred men and have got here without
hindrance and without any dealings with the enemy.[1] My power
is more lawful than that of the Bourbons; I hold it from the
good people whose patriotic singing and shouting you can hear.'

The Emperor took the Mayor by the arm. He shook him
violently, a man who could have been his father.

'Who are you, Monsieur, to let yourself be ruled like this by a
few privileged people? You are plebeian, after all! And yet you
abandon those in your jurisdiction to the ill-will of the nobles!
All because they invited you to their table! I'll break you, do
you hear? I'll break you!'

And he gave the impression of wanting to use the expression
not only figuratively, but literally. Then he let the old man go,
his pretext. Already calm again, he went back to the end of the
room and addressed himself to his friends. It was for their benefit
that he continued. For history.

'The Bourbons no longer suit France, where they only have on
their side a few old periwigs without influence. Louis XVIII
should have taken France as she was given to him, with national
institutions and practices, and not tried to rig her out in old
clothes that no longer fit anybody. He did otherwise? Well
then! let him go back to his friends the enemies!'

His anger had subsided. It would have lasted only an hour,
and that was already long for him. The more violent his outbursts were, the more quickly he regained his Olympian calm.

Already, great bonfires had been lit by the peasants on the
two little hills that dominated Autun, Monjeu (Mount Jove) and
Mont Dru (mount of the Druids). They were setting fire there to
busts of the King and the princes, posters and lampoons of the
Mayor, and fleur-de-lys standards. And as if these pyres
announced the end of uncertainty, Napoleon received at supper
the news that opened to him, in fact, the gates of Paris: Baron

---

[1] As far as Grenoble he had not hesitated to let it be understood, falsely,
that he had the agreement of Austria, indeed, the tacit complicity of the
British, in order to convince the reticent mayors and prefects. Here truth was
resuming its rights: he was relying only on France.

Passinges, aide-de-camp to Ney, brought the Marshal's adherence. Hardly out of the Imperial chamber, the messenger was nearly smothered by embraces from officers of the suite.

'Ney has rallied! Ney is with us!'

They ordered from the landlord his best bottles of *vin d'Aï* to drink with Passinges, but the latter contented himself with draining a few glasses and asking for a fresh horse: the Emperor was sending him back to Ney immediately, with an autograph letter which he had just drafted:

'My friend,[1] keep your command. Set all your troops on the march right away and come and join me at Auxerre. I shall receive you as on the morrow of Elchingen and of the Moskwa.'

In fact, he had despised and detested Ney for a year, and the manner in which the latter dropped the King, without great merit, under pressure from his troops, was hardly calculated to make him change his opinion. He was irritated by the terms of

---

[1] On Ney's evidence, at his trial, where his counsel had him say everything that might save his head by relieving him of the initiative for his rallying, it has been believed for a hundred years that this letter was written at Lyons and that he received it at Lons-le-Saunier. And the editors of Napoleon's *Correspondance*, relying on the *reconstituted* text which he repeated before his judges, were to publish it as official and as dated March 12th. The works of Frédéric Masson and Henri Chouet have restored things to their order: there had been a letter, from Lyons, from Bertrand to Ney, written under Napoleon's inspiration, but not signed by him. It was probably in this that the phrase occurred: 'I have no doubt that when you heard of our arrival in Lyons, you had your troops resume the tricolour cockade.' But, psychologically, it was impossible for the Emperor to make the first move towards a senior officer appointed by the King to bar his way—above all where Ney was concerned, who the previous year had shown himself obnoxious with respect to him. During the return from Elba, Napoleon from beginning to end maintained the attitude of a sovereign who was re-entering his dominions and accepting all the rallyings without having to solicit them. He had not been the first to write, therefore, to *any* of the civil or military leaders placed before him, freed from this by having them written to on many occasions by Bertrand, under the fiction of the latter's personal initiative. On the contrary, in the present case it was Ney who, on the evening of March 14th, wrote him a letter, informing him of his rallying and sending him his proclamation, in which *he offered his resignation* and begged to retire to his estate of *les Coudreaux*, fearing or pretending to fear that Napoleon still bore him a grudge for his attitude at Fontainebleau.

'On receiving this letter at Autun,' Napoleon later confided to Gourgaud, 'I dissembled my feelings. To Ney's aide-de-camp, I laid on every possible flattery of his Marshal, whom I did not fail to call "the Brave of the Brave".'

his proclamation ('is it up to Ney to give the French a sovereign?'), which he would correct, polish and refine, before having it printed the following morning. And if he declined the resignation, he declined to accord him any kind of promotion: 'Keep your command.' In other words: stay in Besançon while I go to Paris. It was not much, compared, for instance, with the advance guard entrusted to General Brayer at Lyons.

Still gloomy, Napoleon would thus be one of the least expansive people amid the febrile joy that prevailed in Autun that evening. Arriving there by every road until after midnight were peasants, half-pay soldiers, delegates from the neighbouring towns, and always the inexhaustible ant-hill of individual officers, who had got away from their regular establishments. The windows were decorated with little lights. Every house was festive, and never perhaps since the days of the Roman garrisons had ancient Bibracte harboured so many drunken men on its streets . . . at the foot of the episcopal chateau where Mgr de Talleyrand-Périgord, the youngest bishop of France, had come thirty years earlier to spend as few days as possible each year, to justify his title and to reap his benefices.

Sheltered after a fashion by the four bare walls that remained of the Saint-Andoche tower, at the gates of the town, a company of old sweats were warming themselves round a fire fit to roast the very stones. They had received triple rations of a brandy rougher than gunpowder. One of them, Alexandre Gauvilier, who knew how to write almost as well as a gentleman, was at a drum laid on the ground, composing a letter which would never reach his native 'country', his comrade in La Haye-du-Blaisis: seized the following day by the last of the King's soldiers, it would be preserved in the war archives, where it still brings back to us today the boisterous joy of the men at Autun that evening:

'In the name of the Emperor, Alexandre Gauvilier sends you his greetings. We are only stopping for refreshment and we are advancing by forced marches on Paris, where the eagle and the tricolour flag will soon be floating over the tower of Notre-Dame. I send greetings to everyone. Embrace for me all who cry from the bottom of their hearts "*Vive Napoléon*".'

During the evening—who would have believed it?—Napoleon behaved as Louis XV might have done. Three women, 'one of whom was very pretty', appeared at the window of a house situated 'opposite the Hôtel de la Poste'. The Emperor noticed them (they had done everything to ensure this) and asked:

'Who is that pretty woman between the two ugly ones?'

'Mme Véru, Sire, the wife of that reputable property-owner who has always supported your cause in Autun, and who paid his respects to you just now.'

'Have the man called for me.'

An hour later, M. Véru, dumbfounded, took cognizance of a brief decree which Napoleon had just dictated: 'Mr Véru has been appointed Mayor of the city of Autun, in place of Mr Pignot.'

19

Monseigneur, save the King! I'll take care of the Monarchy

March 15th, ten o'clock in the evening. The moon was still too young to show up whatever there might be in the Faubourg Saint-Germain, the worst lighted district in Paris. Hardly any more lamps had been erected there than under Louis XV; what was the point of lighting this quarter, where no pedestrian was abroad after nightfall? Round here, the streets belonged to the fine carriages, escorted by torch-bearers. However, a barouche without arms sneaked in discreetly this evening, by the unaided gleam of its two bright lanterns, between the high walls broken by magnificent porticos. Here was the region of great town houses and beautiful trees: the quiet of a sly bit of country in the heart of Paris. One of the porticos, already wide open, promptly closed again behind the little carriage belonging to M. de Malartic, first equerry to Monsieur. He was conducting the King's brother this evening to the house of Princess de Vaudémont. To an amorous rendezvous, it might have been thought: actually, it concerned a historic event. The leader and hope of the 'ultras', the man above all of the *ancien régime*, was

meeting on neutral territory, as equals, one of the most bloody
of the terrorists of '93 : Count d'Artois was coming to canvass
Fouché.

A little salon with a touch of the boudoir, as few servants as
possible, and a fine lady with beautiful powdered hair, who was
about to disappear with good grace and invite M. de Malartic
to a game of trick-track . . . Next to her a man stood up and
bowed deeply before this prince for whom he had been waiting
for an hour . . . for a year, rather, and who was holding out his
hand, saying:

'*Monsieur le duc d'Otrante*, I am delighted to see you . . . '

They were of a similar age, and life had left them both well
preserved : the first gentleman of France was fifty-eight and the
first policeman fifty-six. If his bearing had grown a little heavy,
Fouché's figure remained spare and upright, and his face manifestly had the same expression as in 1785, when he had been
deacon at the Oratoire; as in 1793, when he had made donkeys
parade through Nevers caparisoned with stoles; or in 1800, when
he used to enter the office of the First Consul every morning to
supply him with his daily ration of underhand information on
the whole of France. Fouché of Nantes, Fouché of Lyons, Fouché
of Thermidor had not changed his mask in becoming a high
dignitary of the Empire : it was still the same death's-head, with
its muddy complexion, its eyebrows missing under the vile
crown of tow, and its lipless mouth like a sabre-cut, whose smile
sent shivers down the spine. But the eyes 'like soap-suds',
amazingly light, gave out a curious effulgence, as of a glacier
under the sun. There had undoubtedly never been a man of an
ugliness more fascinating than his. Above all, he imposed, by a
force of character at once firm and supple, and by an unshakable
certainty of being under all circumstances the indispensable
man.

Fallen out of favour with the Emperor in 1811, he could claim
not to have had any part in the great misfortunes of the last
years. Since the return of the Bourbons, he had tried to work
with them, bombarding them with memoranda that were
prodigal of advice, often excellent, without hiding his claims to
a ministry. But all the same, he had voted death to Louis XVI.
The Court had gladly forgiven him the two thousand shot on

the plain of *les Brotteaux,* but that vote still weighed too heavily in the balance. They had kept him at a distance, but without discouraging him, for he was one of those men whom every absolutist regime likes to have in reserve, and they left him the leisure to speculate in order to enlarge his hoard, the most considerable landed fortune in France.

So he had stayed in his corner on March 1st, like a spider ready to seize the opportunity, wherever it might come from. Through failing to impose his influence on the King, he had extricated himself in time from the catastrophic gamble of the Restoration. Like almost everyone else in Paris that winter, he had conspired. For Napoleon? Certainly not: he detested him and regarded that card as played out. For the Duke d'Orleans? For a Regency under Marie-Louise? For a Republic of oligarchs and financiers presided over by La Fayette or Carnot? Perhaps, and, more probably, for all three solutions at once, free to choose at the right moment. In each case, he had conspired for it without overmuch concealment, but without laying himself open to the least precise accusation, and this mastery of the triple game, this prudent temerity, literally fascinated the royalists.

Since March 5th he had been playing for high stakes: one of the first to hear of Napoleon's landing, thanks to his network of private informants, he had immediately launched the military conspiracy in the north, the strings of which he had held through his friendship with the Lallemands and Drouet d'Erlon. It seems that for a couple of days he had dreamed of getting the Bourbons overthrown by the praetorians, and of proclaiming a provisional government in Paris, which would then have turned to the Emperor, either to crush him, or to negotiate with him. Supreme dexterity: at one and the same time he was sending information to the Bonapartists to encourage them, and to the princes to denounce the Bonapartist schemes. Once aware of the check to the conspirators in the north, he had stigmatized their attempt, and through the agency of Mmes de Vaudémont, de Custine, and some other noble ladies, attracted to him by a somewhat morbid interest,[1] had convinced Count d'Artois' coterie

---

[1] Fouché, a widower for three years, was on the point of buying from her parents (there is no other possible expression) the charming Gabrielle de Castellane-Majastres, younger than he by thirty-two years, whom he was to marry within a few weeks.

that he alone could retrieve the desperate situation. At the same time, to Queen Hortense and Maret he had let it be known that he would be glad to accept a ministry in Napoleon's government. 'For twenty-five years, I have not been lacking in loyalty to anyone,' he had written to Mme de Custine on March 12th. 'If the political situation has not allowed me to serve the King up to now, I am ready to be of use to him in misfortune.'

In the royalist camp, the manoeuvre had now apparently succeeded. As early as the 12th, Blacas had consulted him; on the 13th the Chancellor, Dambray, had come to offer him the Police portfolio; and on the 14th he had come back, to propose that he head the government. Too late: Fouché, well informed about Napoleon's progress, was no longer thinking of compromising himself with the Bourbons in the immediate future. On the contrary, convinced that the new Empire would not last, he was trying to secure himself the King for the day after tomorrow. This incredible labyrinth, in which everyone else but he would be lost, ended this evening in a move that must have filled him with peculiar pride: Monsieur had come in person to appeal to one of his brother's three hundred assassins.

Of the details of this interview nobody has ever learned anything, except that it lasted two hours. The next day, Count d'Artois did not conceal 'his favourable impression', but he used the same formula after the least important agricultural show. For his part, Fouché confided to Vitrolles that he had been happy 'to place himself between the shafts in order to avoid being crushed by the wheels of the chariot'. This sibylline formula hardly tells us much, but the attitude of Fouché and the Prince during the Hundred Days, and then their agreement, indeed their complicity, after Waterloo, allows the spirit of the interview to be reconstructed if not the dialogue.

Monsieur renewed the Court's offers to Fouché: that he should form a liberal ministry, made up of men of his choice; he would be given complete power in order to stop Bonaparte, and his advice would be followed afterwards. In reply, Fouché made a play of frankness: he repeated that in his opinion it was too late to resist a tidal wave; he declared that the whole of the army was about to pass to the one he still called the 'enemy', and made no secret of his intention to remain in Paris and accept a post from the Emperor. But here (and what risk was he running in making the claim, free not to keep his word?) he told Count d'Artois that in pretending to serve Bonaparte he would be working for the King, that he would protect the royalists, and that when the moment of inevitable defeat should come, he would act behind the scenes, and then openly, to set aside the Emperor and restore the Tuileries to Louis XVIII. For the present, he strongly advised the only sensible solution : departure, a dignified departure that would not expose the royal family to capture and would preserve every chance for the future. By the same stroke, he would be able to pride himself with Napoleon on having pushed the Bourbons into going by avoiding a fight.

At midnight, the two men parted, apparently delighted with each other. Fouché had managed not to commit himself, but here he was now 'introduced' to the heir to the throne. Had Monsieur, for his part, made him any promises? One observation has to be made : throughout the whole of his exile in Ghent he was to allow no word against Fouché, although the latter was to become the Usurper's Minister of Police, and he was to repeat on many occasions that 'Monsieur Fouché has no evil intentions'. For a historian who has sifted the chronicle of those days for twenty years, the evidence seems to establish that on March 15th Fouché sold himself to the Bourbons, but on credit.

One phrase has been attributed to him, which in fact sums up the interview : 'Monseigneur, save the King; I'll take care of saving the Monarchy.'

It is a matter here of one of those historic remarks of a truth so profound that they need never have been made.

* *March 16th* *

20

A surprise for the surpriser

High drama in Paris! Fouché, for the only time in his life, was about to be surprised, though not as much as he would appear, however. At eleven o'clock on March 16th he left his establishment on the Rue Cérutti in his magnificent town-carriage, almost a state-coach, with the arms of the Duchy of Otranto in yellow, red and gold on the side and two footmen in livery standing up behind the boot. In this great pomp he was about to show himself on the boulevard, and then parade his triumph in a few select salons. Why should he let himself be alarmed by that speedy little coupé that was following him at the trot? He was the man from whom the King's brother had sought advice at midnight . . .

'Stop! Pull up there! Halt!'

At the corner of the boulevard the coupé overtook the carriage and pulled in; two men in glossy top hats brought the Duke of Otranto's coachman to a standstill. An attempt on his life? They would have fired by now. Besides, Fouché was not frightened. But he had already understood: not for nothing had he been the master of these men for ten years . . . How many similar scenes had taken place on his orders throughout the whole of the Empire?

'Monsieur le Duc, we have orders to secure your person . . . '

Brazen it out, pretend, contend . . .

'You have a warrant?'

They produced it, in due and proper order, signed 'Bourrienne, Prefect of Police'. The blow was a harsh one. Why! It was less than twelve hours since he had kissed Monsieur's hand; was the 'flower of French chivalry' capable of quite such duplicity? Fouché, just sounded for power, and now under lock and key? All his life he had felt the proximity of that prison door through which he had thrust so many others. But the man who had fooled Bonaparte so often was not going to let himself be hoaxed by these puppets. They had made the mistake of entrusting this delicate mission to police officer Foudras, an old-timer who would rather have been a hundred miles away. To arrest Fouché, for a policeman, was like asking a cuirassier to sabre Ney or Murat. Foudras, hat in hand, seemed to be soliciting orders from his former chief rather than thinking of laying hands on him. Fouché profited by this to treat him loftily:

'One doesn't arrest a former minister like this, a senator of the Empire, in the middle of the street! Coachman, drive home!'

The two agents were very lucky just to be able to hurl themselves on the tracks of his carriage and get into the house behind him. In the salon Fouché sat down, left them standing, and admonished them as though he were still at the ministry.

'There is an absurd misunderstanding here. First, since when has M. de Bourrienne been Prefect? Has he even the powers? And besides, your warrant is irregular. Have them fetch the National Guard!'

The policemen were already exposed to the hostility of the servants: a crowd of footmen, ostlers and scullions were preparing to give them a rough time. On top of that, a little army of twenty-five civil guards came running up: the whole of the post from the Rue Lepelletier, led by Majors Gilbert des Voisins and Tourton-Havel.

'Is someone trying to harm you, Excellency?'

Fouché had always carried on a flirtation with the National Guard, with whom he was very popular. Foudras, become the accused, had to show his warrant of arrest again.

'It's not genuine . . . ' asserted the Duke of Otranto calmly.

But the policeman, who no longer knew which way to turn, regained some of his vigour and called upon the officers of the Guard to lend him a hand. Fouché then loosed his secret shaft:

'Do you really intend to lock up a man who conferred last night with the King's brother?'

There they all were, these worthy fellows, at the height of embarrassment, and quite sure in any case of getting themselves crushed in this family quarrel. Major Tourton-Havel found a solution:

'We'll suspend your arrest, monsieur le Duc, while I send two men to the Tuileries in order to have it confirmed: one to Monsieur's, the other to the King's cabinet. No doubt this misunderstanding will be cleared up . . . '

Fouché did not delude himself. He was well aware that the warrant was in order, and he knew Bourrienne, his mortal enemy, too well to suppose that he would have him arrested lightly. But he had got what he wanted : he had gained time in order to . . .

'While awaiting the return of your messengers, Major, do come with me : I see you are interested in beautiful things. I'll show you my Venetian glass . . . '

While Foudras, his acolyte and the Guards remained penned in the vestibule, where they were served with refreshments, Major Tourton-Havel, hat in hand, was conducted as in a museum through the luxuriously furnished mansion by the master of the house turned cicerone. He's really not a bit stuck-up, this Duke of Otranto, and what urbanity ! Under the threat of prison, to think of doing the honours of his house ! . . . The English salon, the 'Chinese' salon, the work-room, almost maniacal in its order . . .

'Please excuse me for a moment, Major. . . . '

Tourton-Havel rubbed his eyes and remained all on his own for some time, hopping from one foot to the other. With a completely natural movement, the prisoner in his charge had leant against the wall, which had given way under his weight, opening, as in a cloak and dagger romance, a secret door that had at once clicked to under the poor man's nose. He waited for some time : M. le duc d'Otrante, after all, was no doubt in the process of satisfying a natural need? . . . It was not until a good quarter of an hour later that he decided to drum on the wall, and after that call his comrades to break in the panel. The spiral staircase they then found led them straight into the garden . . . from which Fouché had long since flown.

The word is exact : for several days previously, a high ladder had been placed as if by chance against the wall of that garden, which adjoined the park of Queen Hortense's mansion, next door to Fouché, where the punch during those days flowed freely for Bonapartists. There, everything was prepared for this escape, arranged a long time since. A carriage kept in permanent readiness by the Queen's stables—one spoke now of 'the Duchess de Saint-leu'—bore the fugitive away in five minutes and took him to the house of one of his creatures, Lombard, ex-secretary-general of the police, who was to hide him, in his apartment on the boulevard, until Napoleon arrived.

It was a real bit of vaudeville, in which all Paris delighted. The thirty or so worthies hoaxed by this arch-hoaxer, after so many others, dared neither complain too much nor even probe too deeply, still less since the two men sent for news brought back contradictory stories: Monsieur was indignant and swore by all the gods that he was not kept informed about anything, but Louis XVIII had confined himself to saying: 'I am aware of the warrant; let it be carried out.' It was necessary, therefore, to obey the King of today, but not to vex the King of tomorrow.

Who was behind this rude reversal? M. de Blacas. For two days he had had in his hand a first list of names provided by Bourrienne, and had only been waiting for an opportunity to act at last by a brilliant coup that would make him, he had no doubt of it, the saviour of the Monarchy. This opportunity was presented to him during the night of the 15th to 16th, when he learned from Malartic of the refusal with which Fouché had opposed Count d'Artois. At the King's awakening, he had had no difficulty at all in persuading him that Fouché's attitude confirmed his suspicions: he jibbed at an honourable and magnanimous offer, therefore he was conspiring. The moment was no longer one for clemency. The King, for his part, saw in this arrest an excellent means above all of annoying his brother, whom he had left to involve himself in this flirtation with a regicide without saying a word, free to repudiate him afterwards. The little war between the two wings of the Tuileries, the Pavillon de Flore against the Pavillon de Marsan, explains quite a number of royalist aberrations during those days. Louis XVIII had agreed, therefore, and was to be in a good mood all morning at the thought of Count d'Artois' suppressed gall, since he would be unable to complain with decency in public: this would be to acknowledge his attempt at a collusion against nature!

So that very morning Blacas had written the order to Bourrienne to proceed with the arrest of Messrs Fouché, Davout, Savary, Réal, Maret, Lavallette, Flahaut, Exelmans, Sieyès, Arnault, Thurot, Gaillard, Hinguerlot, Monnier, Norvins, Gérard (the painter), Méjean, Étienne, Lecomte, Lemaire,

Legrand, Bouvier-Dumollard, Duviquet, Patris and Pierre-Pierre.[1]
Not one of them, however, would be forced into martyrdom,
even a symbolic one. Bourrienne was far from being a fool. On
March 14th, when he drew up the list, the service of the King
had still presented an acceptable risk for an adventurer; to persist in it on March 16th would have required a certain dash of
heroism (or stupidity), of which he was destitute. So on
receiving for execution the list of arrests that he had proposed
two days earlier, he decided not to press matters, and had the
residences of those suspected watched so indiscreetly that they
all went into hiding shortly after Fouché, the news of whose
arrest had in some cases been obligingly communicated to their
servants by the policemen on duty. Davout left for the country.
Lavallette hid himself in the domestic quarters of that same
mansion occupied by Queen Hortense that had served for
Fouche's escape. Hortense herself had preferred to seek asylum
with one of her old creole nurses. Carnot, though not down on
the list, also left his residence. So the morning of March 16th
saw the disappearance of all those whom M. de Blacas had hoped
to imprison.[2]

[1] The list, carefully kept by Bourrienne, and published in his *Mémoires* with
Blacas' capricious spelling, deserves to be given in full, for at the behest of
history it cites the very small number of men whom the Court was able to
suspect of militant Bonapartism, and yet we have seen that it made the
mistake of claiming to catalogue Fouché so precisely. However, we are at
March 16th. Everybody knew that the Emperor had got beyond Lyons. But
Napoleon had so few faithful friends among the people of 'good society' that
even Bourrienne could do no more informing on them. Yet he did not consider it expedient to worry Cambacérès or Lebrun, the ex-consuls, who had
just sent the King declarations of loyalty, or Caulaincourt, covered by the
protection of his friend the Czar.

[2] Then why Fouché? Why the actual attempt to place under lock and key
the least Bonapartist of the opposition, the possible saviour of the regime, the
man they had envisaged taking into the government the night before? There
are three possible explanations, which for want of certainty can no longer be
disentangled:
a. A caprice, purely and simply, of the King and his entourage in order to
strike a mean blow at Count d'Artois' 'gang'.
b. Personal vengeance by Bourrienne, who failed to resist the joy of having
his worst enemy imprisoned and of placing him beyond reach of both the
King and the Emperor at the decisive moment.
c. A huge comedy, staged with Fouché's agreement, in order to restore his
political virginity with Napoleon, thanks to the halo of persecution. He would
be able to present himself to the Emperor, whom he disserved however to the
very end, bringing him a proof of his devotion: this abortive arrest. How

The provinces loyal to the King

The average royalist, whose only source of information was the newspapers, would naturally have known nothing of the Fouché episode for a long time; how, for him, did matters look on March 16th?

Excellent. The morning papers—never distributed, moreover, before eleven o'clock—brought him good news by the armful.

First, for whoever opened the pages of the *Moniteur*:

'The most recent news suggests that Buonaparte left Lyons on the 13th, heading in the direction of Mâcon and Chalon. The combined dispositions which we revealed made it fairly evident that this movement was foreseen. Marshal Ney, who has been watching it, is marching in strength to follow it.'

The last phrase was particularly piquant for anyone aware of the events of the 14th at Lons-le-Saunier. For those who might have had the bad taste to be alarmed still, the *Journal des Débats* added:

'Within a fifty-mile radius of Paris, there is an army of 35,000 men filled with the finest spirit. Buonaparte is dismayed to learn of loyal troops everywhere and Paris undisturbed.'

The same paper informed the brave men that the sinews of war would not be lacking to them; some noblewomen had scaled the heights of heroism:

---

would Napoleon then be able to refuse him an important post? It is not altogether impossible that the matter had been agreed in hints, and without forcing Monsieur to 'stoop to details', on the night of the 15th. In that case, the Prince, delighted to play at high politics, would have pretended surprise, indeed anger, on the morning of the 16th, on hearing of the attempt at arrest, while the King would have sincerely believed he was playing a good trick on him. Vitrolles would have been the secret intermediary in this farce, between the Prince and Bourrienne. It is in fact rather strange that this very prolix memorialist breathed not a word of the incident. The second solution, however, seems the most probable.

'Several ladies have just deposited a considerable sum with M. Delacour, Rue Neuve-des-Petits-Champs, No. 77, to be distributed to the brave volunteers who are leaving to go and fight the enemy of France, as also to the wounded soldiers; they invite all the ladies of Paris to add their patriotic donations to it.'

In certain salons it had come to be wished that Napoleon would speed his advance, in order to arrive the more quickly at his doom. He was about to be crushed in a pincer-movement: not only was Ney driving him back on to the bayonets of the army of Paris, but in addition Masséna, from Marseilles, was organizing a pitiless pursuit 'against his rear', according to the expression of the time. It is true that the white flag still floated firmly over Marseilles and that if Napoleon, against all probability, had sought to re-embark, not a single port would now have been available any more, either on the Mediterranean coast, or elsewhere.

As in 1814, it was Bordeaux that from this point of view set the tone. By tradition, the bourgeoisie of the Gironde was opposed to anything that resembled the Revolution, closely or remotely, and would prevent them from trading with England. The news of Napoleon's return had fallen like a thunderbolt into the midst of the anniversary festivities of March 12th. They had been celebrating the day on which Count Lynch, Mayor of Bordeaux, had acquired the imperishable merit of being the first notable of France to be able to open the gates of his city to the invader. The Duke of Angoulême, on that occasion, had been the first prince to come back 'in the foreigner's train', that of the Duke of Wellington in the circumstances. He had certainly owed it to himself to return to Bordeaux for the first commemoration of such a glorious day. This time, the Duchess of Angoulême had accompanied him, and everyone was wallowing in thanksgiving when a messenger from Vitrolles had been allowed to disturb the Prince in the middle of a grand ball, at which the august couple had been spreading, as everywhere else, a discreet dismay, he by his wild eyes, his twitchings and brusque manners (he kept asking the Prefect abruptly: 'Who's this?— What's that man's name?'), she by her mannish bearing, her grenadier's voice and look of a living relic.

Delighted at the opportunity to be rid of boredom, the Duke had left at dawn the next day for Montpellier, and then Nîmes, where he proceeded to establish the headquarters of the royalist reconquest of the south-east. But Bordeaux had remained the scene of great indignation. There, it had been proclaimed that:

'This city will be as loyal as its inhabitants are brave and devoted. The news of danger to the motherland has sufficed to electrify all the inhabitants, to increase, if that were possible, their attachment to the best of Kings. We still have within our walls this Princess, worthy object of our respect and love. Every day Madame receives fresh evidence of the sentiments that inspire us, the strength of which grows and develops with every advance. Volunteers have flocked to offer themselves, corps are rapidly forming; the royal horseguards are setting out; the National Guard is providing numerous detachments; the same spirit has seized all the departments of the Midi, especially Toulouse.'

In fact, for March 16th, this little review of the regional press gives the palm to Toulouse:

'The theatre advertisement had announced *Games of Love and Chance*. The news that arrived during the day caused Monsieur the Mayor to give orders for *The Michaud Heirs*[1] to be substituted for the piece by Marivaux. Long before the rise of the curtain the hall was filled with an extraordinary number of spectators, who showed by their signs of impatience the enthusiasm to which they longed to give vent. They demanded the beloved air *Vive Henri IV!* and the orchestra played it: instantly cries of *Vive le Roi! Vive la famille royale!* repeated a thousand times, came from all quarters of the hall. Monsieur the Lieutenant-general, Baron de Cassagne,[2] appeared, standing up in his box; he held out his hand to the spectators; they were silent: the general staff, the officers of the garrison and the

[1] A gloomy musical melodrama in which an abracadabra of intrigue had no other purpose but to give expression to extreme royalism. Into it had been slipped, amongst others, the well-known tune *Vive Henri IV!* 'the Marseillaise of respectable people'.
[2] Military commander of the area.

public remained standing and uncovered. In a resolute and spirited voice Monsieur the Lieutenant-general uttered these words: *"Vive le Roi! Vive la famille royale! War to the rebels who would seek to disturb the peace of the State. This is the vow, this is the cry of the army!"* The words were received and repeated with an enthusiasm bordering on delirium. Throughout the rest of the performance outbursts of much the same kind were renewed time and again: all the couplets of *The Michaud Heirs* had to be repeated; all the words that contained any kind of allusion were seized upon with unparalleled rapture. The tune of *Vive Henri IV!* was demanded again and repeated several times.'

The people of the west had also received a Prince to fire their zeal. The King had sent them the Duke de Bourbon, last descendant of the illustrious Condés. He was the only one of this branch available, his son, the Duke d'Enghien, having been shot by Napoleon, and his father, the titular Prince de Condé, being hopelessly senile. On March 16th, Bourbon was in Angers, where he was displaying his myopia, 'his highwayman's face, wreathed in wrinkles and a sordid air', and from the very first evening had been anxious for addresses where his servants would be able to find him 'some discreet and understanding young ladies'. He had the family's sexual obsession, passed from father to son, and he had been vainly empowered by the King to prepare the raising of a new Catholic and royal army; he was no less a man for that.

For want of princes, Normandy was kept in hand as well as possible by a man who had no choice: Marshal Augereau, military governor of the area, who knew that he could expect nothing from Napoleon. The proclamation to the army, dated from Golfe-Juan, had denounced him along with Marmont as one of the two great traitors whose attitude had brought about the catastrophe of 1814. And he remembered the painful scene, less than a year before near Valence, when he had insulted Napoleon, defeated and on the way to exile, and had refused to raise his hat to him. A dispatch from Caen informed Parisians that:

'Yesterday, all our brave young men who had enrolled to

107

march against Buonaparte were assembled in the Rue Neuve-des-Carmélites, and went into quarters at the chateau. In all the streets through which this bright company passed, it was received with cries of *"Vive le Roi!".*

'Monseigneur le duc de Castiglione (Augereau) arrived today at four o'clock. He was received with all the honours due to his rank. His Excellency will be able to give the King a very good account of the spirit that animates us.'

Thus, to the four corners of France the little royalist ballet went its superficial way, like the flight of dragon-flies over troubled waters. The great mass of the people remained apathetic, save in certain regions of the west and south-west, where it was at one with the notables. But it is a fact that Napoleon had to hurry, under pain of seeing the latter re-awaken the feeling of compassion and sentimental attachment for the King which slumbered in the depths of the people. This skimming of the press of March 16th shows that the royalist reaction was stiffening and becoming organized in the provinces, after a few days of wavering.

In Paris a great hope was rising: leaving his seclusion, the King himself was about to perform that day the only action left to him: to make an appearance.

The 'royal sitting' of the Assemblies was announced for three o'clock that afternoon.

22

The arrest of General Ameil

March 16th, eleven o'clock in the morning. Auxerre. Two generals confronted each other in the office of the military commander for the King of the department of the Yonne. The rays of a weak sun played with the files and papers piled on the desk, and gleamed outside on the dark mirror of wet tiles on the roofs of the old town.

Behind the desk, a noble: General Boudin de Roville, who only needed lace at his sleeves and powdered hair to recall the officers of the old monarchy. Standing before him, a plebeian in impeccable uniform, though dusty, covered with a long blue coat, raised by the tip of a light-cavalry sabre: General Ameil. They knew each other vaguely; they detested each other greatly. Ameil, without being announced, had just made his appearance in his colleague's office, like a bomb; alighting from a post-chaise he had, on the strength of his uniform, thrown the orderlies and doorkeepers into confusion.

'General Boudin, I command the light cavalry of the advance guard of His Majesty the Emperor. All is lost for the Bourbons. Marshal Ney has just declared for Napoleon with all his troops. The Emperor will be in Auxerre tomorrow. Kindly have the national colours hoisted and announce the rallying of the garrison.'

'General Ameil, we are men of honour here. We have taken an oath to the King and we cannot break it. So what is it you are coming here to do? Disturb us, subvert us afresh? . . . We are happy and at peace, and we don't want Bonaparte. And right now, what is your purpose?'

'I am going to collect the lancers of Joigny.'

'Do not imagine, General, that I shall allow you to carry out your plans.'

A sign from General Boudin; his two aides-de-camp, silent supernumeraries, horribly embarrassed, placed themselves on either side of Ameil. The latter paled and suddenly realized that he had thrown himself into the lion's mouth. Rash! What had got into him to make him go beyond the Emperor's orders and try to take the town of Auxerre all on his own?

Ten days earlier, he had been ruminating in rancour and boredom in Paris among his boisterous companions. The royal government had discharged him on February 13th, for the misdemeanour of insolent opinions. These had in fact been made so clear that Ameil had been one of the very few of the Emperor's friends in Paris to be informed (by whom is not known) of the landing at Golfe-Juan, at the same time as the ministers. On returning from the theatre in the evening of March 5th, he had found an anonymous note: 'The Emperor has landed on the coast of Provence. See what your devotion will prompt you to, for the sake of his person and the glory of the Motherland.'

His devotion had prompted him to rush to Marshal Soult, Minister of War, who was busying himself in all directions in order to give evidence of a royalist zeal the sincerity of which had begun to be seriously doubted by the princes. The latter were mistaken: it was Soult's common sense that they should have mistrusted. He gave nice proof of this by attaching Ameil to Count d'Artois; he was to go by way of Lyons to 'fall upon' Bonaparte. Once in that city, Ameil had imitated Brayer and placed himself, overjoyed, under the orders of Napoleon, who had known and esteemed him. The Emperor had just received a deputation of officers from the 6th regiment of lancers, named during the Restoration the 'de Berry regiment' because the Duke de Berry bore the title of Colonel-in-Chief of the lancers and light cavalry. In garrison at Joigny, they had asked for orders.

'General Ameil, go by post to Joigny. Take command of the 6th lancers there, and march from Joigny towards Montereau in order to open up for me the route to Paris.'

He had enjoined him to do nothing else, and above all not to unmask himself foolishly on his way through a town still dominated by royalists. A brave soldier but a bad conspirator, poor Ameil went and risked all to win all: he lowered his head, after blasting Boudin with a look.

'*Eh bien! monsieur,* I am your prisoner then! . . . '

He made a half-turn, walked to the door, and there suddenly slipped away from the two aides-de-camp, who, moreover, had carefully avoided pressing him too closely, and then dashed into the anteroom shouting:

'*Vive l'Empereur!*'

Alas! The four gendarmes on duty jumped on him together: the cry was still officially listed as subversive in the latest circulars.

'Grab him,' cried Boudin. 'Search him! Take away his weapons!'

All Ameil's pockets and even his belt proved to be stuffed with dangerous explosives: the Emperor's proclamations. Two high royalist officials were on the point of leaving Auxerre, where the position appeared to be growing unhealthy for them: de Bongard, Inspector-general of Posts, and Augustin, an officer in the light cavalry of the Royal Household. Boudin entrusted the prisoner to them. The berlin containing the three men moved off towards midday, with orders to the postilions to whip along as fast as possible: some of Buonaparte's light troops were reported to be five miles from the town. The capture of General Ameil was to be the only serious check to Napoleon along the route of his return, with the resistance of the garrison at Antibes. It allowed the royalists of Auxerre a flash in the pan. If events were about to take a turn, was not one man of mettle enough? For an hour—only for an hour!—Boudin de Roville was all set to become the Charrette of Burgundy.

23

Nothing nobler has come from the pen of a king

March 16th, midday. The centre of Paris was in a stir, still under the same lid of grey sky. The weather was not to co-operate, but the onlookers cared nothing for the elements. They were about to be offered one of those great spectacles so well arranged as to suffice in most cases to dictate their political opinions: the King was about to leave the Tuileries in great pomp, cross the Seine, and proceed to the Palais-Bourbon, which had become the Palais du Corps Législatif, in order to hold a royal sitting before the two combined Assemblies.

On this occasion, the new Prefect of Police had published an order forbidding all traffic along the route of the procession:

'We, Councillor of State, Prefect of Police for the department of the Seine and for the communes of Saint-Cloud, Sèvres and Meudon, of the department of Seine-et-Oise:

'Having regard to the letter of Monsieur le Marquis de Dreux-Brézé, Grand Master of Ceremonies of France, in which his Excellency gives notice that His Majesty will proceed to the Corps Législatif tomorrow at three o'clock,

'Order as follows:

'*Article 1.*—On Thursday, March 16th, the day on which the

King will proceed to the Palais du Corps Législatif, traffic and the stationing of vehicles other than those of the authorities or invited persons will be forbidden, as from one o'clock until after the return of His Majesty to the Palace of the Tuileries:

'On the embankments of the right bank of the Seine, from the Rue du Petit-Bourbon as far as and including the Quai de la Conférence. On the embankments of the left bank, from the Pont Neuf as far as the Esplanade des Invalides.

'In the Rue de Bourgogne.

'In the Rue de l'Université, from the Avenue de la Bourdonnais to the Rue du Bac.

'In the Rue du Bac from the Rue de l'Université to the Pont Royal.

'On the Pont Royal.

'In the Place Louis XV.

'And in the Place du Carrousel.'

In the Place Vendôme, at the end of the morning, the monarchy was already offering the bystander a substantial hors-d'oeuvres: Count d'Artois was holding a general inspection of the National Guard, the only military body on which it could found any hopes, in view of the 'rottenness' of the army. It was relying on the commanding presence and allure of the Prince, who still had a firm seat on a horse, to prompt a large number of royal volunteers to enrol. General Dessoles, in an order of the day, had warned his troops that at the end of the inspection an invitation would be issued to 'all citizens whose age and situation allowed it, to yield to the impulse of their patriotism' for the purpose of forming a special legion, placed under the direct orders of Monsieur.

According to the official accounts, it was a triumph:

'Today, the twelve legions of the National Guard of Paris, and the 13th legion, consisting of the National Guard on horse, were assembled for inspection by the Prince Colonel-in-Chief. On appearing before his legions, Monsieur was greeted with the unanimous cry of *"Vive le Roi! Vive Monsieur!"* His Royal Highness, accompanied by a numerous general staff, passed along all the lines, receiving the most striking tokens of zeal, devotion and loyalty. After the departure of the Prince, the commanders and senior officers of each legion gathered together to receive the enrolments of all those whose enthusiasm had caused them to leave their ranks in order to make up the Legion of the Colonel-in-Chief, and march with the Prince against the enemy of France and Europe. The lists of voluntary enrolments were opened at once in all the companies.'

Though indeed *open* on all the tables, the lists were very far from being *covered* with signatures. Cheers, certainly, there were, vigorous and well-sustained, above all as the Prince passed along the front of the first legions, those that upheld the solid royalist tradition of the central arrondissements. The people there had not entertained Napoleon in their hearts since he riddled them with grape-shot on the steps of Saint-Roch on the 13th Vendémiaire. At that time they had already been pinning their hopes on this Count d'Artois, still attractive under his grey hair, and so affable, so benevolent, when he leaned towards a man from the height of his white horse, with a thousand years of condescension in the inclination . . . The inspection, more-over, had taken on the look of a remembrance meeting: the average age of the National Guard was about forty. Many were growing stout. This created an atmosphere of compassion, but not of heroism. Misled by the cheers of the 1st Legion, Monsieur went so far as to fear a rush at the moment of enrolment, and called out:

'No disorder, lads! Only leave your ranks one at a time!'

Ten stepped forward, no more. Among them, an old man with an angelic smile, Dupont de Nemours, a veteran in the struggle for liberty, who had offered himself for dangerous missions before, when the Commander-in-Chief of the National Guard, his friend La Fayette, on a white horse just like that of today, had called upon them to fight this same Artois, then the soul of the counter-revolution. Dupont's religion was still liberty—one could only think that he had changed devils.

Further on, it was less pitiful: eighty volunteers, for instance, from the 2nd Legion. But when the final balance-sheet was drawn up, once the Prince had returned to the Tuileries, the effective painfully reached was four companies, which would not even be directed against the army. Here ends the tale of the Legion of the Colonel-in-Chief.

During this time, at the Tuileries, Vitrolles had arrived to inquire into the King's 'form':

'His Majesty, holding a small square of paper in his hand, read me the address that He was to give. I had no need to call flattery to my aid to find the sentiments and the expression admirable; nothing nobler has come from the pen of a King. I said it, as I thought it. His Majesty directed me to assemble all the ministers at eleven o'clock, in order to make his words known to them.

'We were all standing round the King's table. At the moment when I heard it being read for the second time, I was struck by this phrase: "He who comes to light among us the horrors of civil war . . . "

' "I don't think," I said very quietly to Blacas, "the horrors of war can burn."

' "What did you say? . . . " asked the King, breaking off.

'A little embarrassed by my criticism, I did not reply. Blacas passed on my remark.

' "He is right," the King went on.

'And he wrote: "the torches of civil war". He was so sure of his memory that after this reading he handed me his paper, in order to have his address printed and published during the meeting itself.'

Meanwhile, an enormous crowd had invaded the two embankments of the Seine. The King got into his carriage very late, towards three o'clock, accompanied by Count d'Artois, the Duke de Berry and the Duke d'Orleans. He showed the son of Philippe-Égalité the badge of the Légion d'Honneur which he was wearing on his blue coat.

'Do you see this, monsieur?'

'Yes, Sire,' replied Louis-Philippe—or at least, so he boasts in his Journal—'but I should have preferred to see it sooner.'

The procession was magnificent. It included the principal officers of the Royal Household, the deputations of the Marshals of France, of the Grand Cross of the Order of Saint-Louis, of the Grand Cross and Grand Officers of the Légion d'Honneur, and of the Lieutenants-General, Vice-Admirals and Marshals of the Army. The carriages were preceded and followed by detachments of the National Guard—smiling—and units of the line—sullen—as also by red musketeers, black musketeers and some of Monsieur's Guards in green uniforms. A serried double line of National Guards and soldiers formed a barrier to contain the crowd. The soldiers, in spite of a distribution of money and brandy received that morning, in no way echoed the lively outbursts that rose from the crowd and gratified the officials. For a moment, one might have thought that Paris was holding a plebiscite on the Monarchy that was filing by in its incomparable bright pageantry, fashioned by centuries of display. But . . . 'Ah, how well the Bourbons can dig their own grave,' whispered mischievous tongues. At the corner of the Pont Royal an officer managed to grub up a few 'Vive le Rois!' from his men. These were enough to delight the Duke de Berry:

'Ah! how well they'll fight! A few of them look a bit sullen, but the mass will sweep them along!'

The Duke d'Orleans made no reply; he was generally silent, and still more so these days, but he thought none the less. The King, too, said nothing: fully occupied in reciting to himself several times the address which he had learnt by heart, he took no notice at all of the crowd.

For a long time now, peers and deputies had been waiting, packed into the crowded hall, where the galleries overflowed with a picked audience. The irony of fate! These were the representatives of the last days of the Empire: these barristers, magistrates, landed proprietors and merchants, who had been nominated by Napoleon's prefects to the docile grand electors, and who had hastened to grovel at the feet of the Bourbons in the name of a France who had never deputed them to anything of the sort. As for the Chamber of Peers! . . . It was the senate of fawning dogs that had voted the deposition of the Emperor the previous April after ratifying all his abuses of power for ten years under the form of *sénatus-consultes*. Amputated of the former members of the Convention and augmented by a strong contingent of commissioned dukes, the august assembly filled the benches with quite a picturesque assortment of well-worn men. The King, in order to speak to the country, was going to have to pass through the most contemptible symbolic assemblage that could be produced.

In the galleries was Count de Lamothe-Langon, a minor aristocrat, pretentious and boastful, who would leave under the name of *Mémoires* an improbable farrago of intimate tittle-tattle. But occasionally, when he took part in the event himself, he knew how to describe it:

'On going to the Palais-Bourbon, I saw the troops complaining at forming the barrier; it was raining in torrents, they were wet, and to pass the time they were shouting: "Long live the King! Long live the King!" at the tops of their voices; and then more quietly: "of Rome! of Rome!" This then was the spirit of the regiments in garrison in Paris; what must the others be like?

'If dispositions outside had appeared to me disquieting, inside the hall I perceived a different manifestation. Although I had arrived in good time, I obtained possibly the last place, so great was the crowd of spectators which the danger to the motherland had gathered, and which filled not only the galleries, but also the first four rows of benches. They had left the Peers, seated on the right, and the Deputies, ranged on the left, the places that were strictly necessary for them. The magnificence of the costumes, the richness of the adornments, and still more, an almost universal feeling of love, interest and concern, gave this solemn occasion a character all of its own.

'This time, the King, whether from pressure of business or from indisposition, perhaps from both, forgot his charming motto: "Punctuality is the politeness of Kings". The sitting had been announced for three o'clock; it did not begin until nearly four. There are moments of crisis when confusion finds its way everywhere.

'The prolonged booming of the cannon of the Invalides, the sounds of cheering from the multitude, which carried to the vicinity of the Palais du Corps Législatif, the drum that beat a salute, the symphonies of a military band, and then the electric thrill that travelled nearer and nearer, told us of the King's procession.

'Then we saw a deputation, composed according to rule of

twenty Peers and twenty Deputies, leave to go and receive His Majesty at the outer doors of the Palace; then the two leaves of the inner door were opened with an unaccustomed crash, while the troops drawn up in line presented arms. Finally a powerful voice cried: "The King, Gentlemen, the King! . . . " Silence suddenly reigned in the hall, and with eyes fixed, mouths half-open, necks stretched and bodies bent, we all awaited this King who was about to appear to us in such solemn circumstances. First to file by were the ushers of the Chamber of Deputies, the State messengers, the ushers and lesser officers of the King's Bedchamber, his heralds of arms, his pages, equerries and gentlemen; then, after a space, Monseigneur the Prince de Condé, hero of misfortune, more overwhelmed by sorrows than by age; alas! his reason occasionally left him; at that moment, he enquired the purpose of the ceremony, and no one dared tell him that the head of his house was coming to request help from his subjects against the man who had sent the Duke d'Enghien to his suffering.

'Monsieur the Duke d'Orleans followed; his bearing proclaimed that he expected a catastrophe; then came H.R.H. Monseigneur the Duke de Berri and H.R.H. Monsieur, *sans peur et sans reproche.*

'The Duke de Duras and Count de Blacas supported the King. The monarch walked slowly; suffering marred his features; but his eye was calm and his brow radiated that majesty which never left him. The usual cries and cheers accompanied him right to his throne. Was it an illusion? it seemed to me that the throne tottered.

'Fanfares filled the air with harmonious sound; the ladies waved bunches of lilies and white handkerchieves; the Peers and Deputies bestirred the elegant plumes of their Henri IV hats; it was like a thick fall of snow, the effect was singularly graceful.

'Meanwhile, the King bade the Peers be seated; Monsieur the Chevalier d'Ambray, Chancellor of France, conveyed the same invitation, in the name of His Majesty, to the Deputies.[1] The

[1] This procedure is to be noted: it recalled France to the glorious days of May 1789, when the insulting difference in treatment between the Nobility and the Third Estate brought on the revolt of the latter in the States General.

King took his seat on the throne; to his right and to his left, on folding-chairs, H.R.H. Monsieur, H.R.H. Monseigneur the Duke de Berri, H.R.H. Monseigneur the Duke d'Orleans, and H.R.H. Monseigneur the Prince de Condé.

'The King, after putting on his hat, and without losing any of his noble serenity, his love and confidence in his people, greeted the assembly, and then, in a strong and clear voice, delivered this address:

' "Gentlemen, in this moment of crisis which, having arisen in a portion of the realm, menaces the liberty of all the rest, I come into your midst to draw closer those bonds which, uniting you to me, are the strength of the State; in addressing you, I come to disclose to France the sentiments that animate me.

' "I have seen my native land again, I have reconciled it with all the foreign powers who will be faithful, have no doubt of it, to the treaties that have restored us to peace.

' "I have worked for the well-being of my people, I have received, I receive every day, the most touching tokens of their love for me. Could I, at sixty, better end my career than by dying in its defence? . . . I fear nothing for myself, but I fear for France. He who comes among us to light the torches of civil war brings with him also the scourge of foreign war.

' "He comes to place our native land under his iron yoke.

' "He comes to destroy that constitutional Charter which I have given you; that Charter, my finest title to glory in the eyes of posterity; that Charter which all Frenchmen cherish, and which I swear to uphold . . . "

'Here the four princes, all four, extended their hands to those of the King, and joining themselves to him, cried: "Yes, Sire, we also swear to uphold it." [1]

' "Let us rally, Gentlemen," the King went on, "let us rally round it; that it may be our sacred standard; the descendants of Henri IV will be the first to take their places there; they will be followed by all Frenchmen. Finally, Gentlemen, let the concurrence of the two Chambers give to authority the power that is necessary to it; and this truly national war will show, by its happy issue, what can be done by a great people united by the

---

[1] A scene laboriously arranged that morning, which electrified the audience none the less for that.

118

love of their King and by the fundamental law of the State."

'These last words called forth fresh transports; people were already beginning to move, everyone believing the sitting to be ended, for in France custom forbids subjects to speak when the King has spoken, when to our great surprise we saw Monsieur rise, leave his place and go to the King. All at once silence was re-established as if by magic, and we heard the following words come from the troubled lips of the august Prince:

' "Sire, I know I am departing from the customary rules in speaking before Your Majesty, but I beg him to pardon me and to approve when I express, in my name and in that of my family, how much we share from the bottom of our hearts the sentiments that animate Your Majesty."

'Monsieur then added, turning towards the assembly—a nod from the King having given his consent—and raising his voice so as to make himself heard clearly:

' "Let us swear, on our honour, to live and die loyal to our King, and to the constitutional Charter which ensures the well-being of the French." [1]

'On hearing these words, the whole of the assembly, in a movement of spontaneous enthusiasm, rose and repeated with the noble Prince the oath he had just called forth. The King, moved, held out his hand to Monsieur, who seized it and kissed it with rapture. The King himself, more and more carried away by his chivalrous sensibility, clasped H.R.H. in his arms with the dignity of a monarch and the fondness of a father.

'At this noble and touching sight, a sudden emotion seized those present; all eyes filled with tears. The cheering was not resumed, with fresh vigour, until the moment when the procession set off again.' [2]

Another witness, however, did not lose his lucidity: seated in the galleries, very near those Peers he was so furious not to be among, François-René de Chateaubriand 'thought he heard, in an interval of silence, the footsteps of Napoleon'.

---

[1] This was the first time since his return to France that Monsieur had mentioned the Charter, to the granting of which he had been strongly opposed.
[2] The *Mémoires* of Lamothe-Langon. I have quoted the whole text because it shows, ingenuously but with sincerity, the real emotion that seized those who witnessed this piece of theatre, well prepared and well acted.

24

The fifty miles through the Morvan

Roule ta boule
Roi cotillon
Rends la couronne à Napoléon!

On the road from Autun to Avallon, songs were improvised and people danced; they formed rings and stamped their feet vigorously to keep themselves warm. All along the fifty miles that he was to cover on March 16th, Napoleon would be acclaimed by more than ten thousand peasants, whose drawling accent and rolled *r*'s greatly amused him. They said '*Vive l'Empairreur!*', the master-cry of the day. Lively, with a quick eye for a wink and ample of bosom, the women were ever ready to pour the good wine, and hardly fought shy of kisses. 'All the young girls were there . . . ' an old campaigner would relate thirty years after, still bemused. And the pay-master of Elba, Peyrusse, noted in his Journal that 'On the way to Avallon His Majesty met with the same sentiments as in the mountains of the Dauphiné.' Which is saying a lot. The profound assent of Burgundy is witnessed further by that sudden flowering of popular songs, composed spontaneously by rural poets.

Bon, bon, bon
Voilà le grand Napoléon
l'Empereur élu des Nations

Le Père la Violette
est parti, tireli . . .
Mais le v'là de retour
Mes amours!

Les Princes ne sont pas contents
Lanturelan . . .
Voilà Napoléon-le-Grand
pour longtemps . . .

Napoleon remembered some of them himself, and hummed them later, as he passed—rapidly—through tricoloured townships, where the bells pealed, and long stretches of bare and dismal countryside, the region of gorse and heather on either side of Chissey. 'The most dismal of valleys,' according to one of the suite, 'presented itself to us when we left the Saône-et-Loire to enter the Yonne. Destitute of shade, like the rounded outcrops by which it is flanked, and covered with barren grass-land where the scythe encounters more furze than hay, this valley has a wild aspect without being picturesque.' This was the harsh Morvan. On leaving Autun at ten o'clock, the Emperor noticed the patches of snow at the sides of the road. The sun itself, which would shine at intervals, was white as yet. It was still winter.

Relays were changed at Pierre-Écrite; then came a very long descent to Saulieu, where the three thousand inhabitants were out of doors, swelled by at least two thousand of their neighbours, all those who came to the twelve annual fairs. The workers from the large barrel-works had rolled some enormous casks to the foot of the houses. Mounted on these improvised platforms, the people yelled their delight at seeing for an instant, as it went by at full speed, 'that face, very pale and plump', which they recognized in the Napoleons in the palms of their hands. A good many soldiers had passed through the day before and that same morning, but there was great surprise now at the very simple state in which the Emperor was travelling, 'light' by his own wish, in order to move faster. A posting barouche with six horses; a weak red and gold escort of Polish lancers, caracoling as best they could on an assortment of mounts, requisitioned en route—and in their midst, that sudden flash of grey which intrigued and amused the spectators; this was the famous Tauris, led by the bridle and without a rider, marvellously delicate of form and 'white Persian' in colour, that is to say, silvery white-grey, lightly dappled, with a mane of white and a tapering tail: the Emperor's horse, 'the Emperor of horses', known to all the army. Bought in Russia in 1809, thanks to the kindness of the Czar, he had quickly become Napoleon's favourite mount, which he had aptly chosen for the cavalcades in Russia, at Vitebsk, at Smolensk, at the Moskwa, and at the time of his victorious arrival in the Kremlin. After that Tauris had carried or accompanied his master during the whole of the retreat; it was with him that he had escaped capture by the Cossacks on the road to Kaluga. And then the German campaign, Lützen, Bautzen, Dresden, Leipzig, and the French campaign, Fontainebleau, Elba . . . He had cost 1,260 francs.[1] In 1815 he could no longer be priced. Napoleon was not to mount him once during the return from Elba : he would be continually on foot or in a carriage. But Tauris was kept in reserve for the great reviews tomorrow, at the Carrousel, and who could tell? for war the day after, the battle that would bend the backbone of Europe.

Sand choked the road. That to Dijon was left on the right, and also the little township of Arnay-le-Duc, which was falling into decline following the abolition of the diversion because it formed a pointless duplication with that passing through Autun, thus giving travellers a choice of two routes from Saulieu to Chalon.[2] So a strong delegation of citizens from Arnay were at the side of the road. They profited by a relay to surround the Emperor and beg him to reinstate the two routes. This took place amid the good-natured jostling that had become obligatory since his landing, quite contrary to his nature and to his conception of a sovereign. How many times had he not repeated : 'I'm not Louis XVI, to let myself put on a red cap !' Now, here he was, like a vulgar Capet, surrounded, importuned, interrupted and contradicted by country bumpkins. He was at the same time furious and touched by it : for after all, it was in fact the collective phenomenon of which he had had a presentiment at Porto-Ferraio; here he was again, and even more than ever in the whole of his life, embodying the hopes of the poor, who rushed to him as they once did to Saint Louis under his oak, and who stretched out their hands to this god whom one could touch, who was not a prisoner of the fine gentlemen and the gilded musketeers, and who would grant this bridge, that posting-stage, this mill, on which depended the happiness of the day . . . Here, as so often already on his journey, he extricated himself with 'I'll see . . . ', which is ever the expedient of the powerful in this position. And he had the pace increased, fast, faster ! between Roche-en-Brénil, 'that village where one was

[1] About £300 today.
[2] Since re-established, as we know, this branch has now become, luckily for Arnay, an integral part of Route Nationale 6.

surprised to see several shops', and Rouvray, a town or a village? —scarcely a thousand inhabitants under roofs of thatch. They went on, rising and falling endlessly over the humps in which the Morvan forest ended.

Napoleon was in a hurry to reach Avallon, where he knew fresh regiments were awaiting him. On the threshold of the depart- ment of the Yonne, his companions discovered with pleasure 'a little corner of Switzerland in the middle of France: Avallon overlooks the river Cousin from a picturesque escarpment, opposite another bank no less attractive. The windings of the river and of the narrow dale which it waters, the dark masses of granite that rise on either side, and the wild and wooded effect that prevails in every prospect reminded us of some of the country in the vicinity of Berne, or Freiburg.'

'A corner of Switzerland' suddenly covered by hundreds of tricolour flags, sprouting in a day like a thicket of furze.

25

This event which our descendants will scarcely credit

The sun would have shone on Auxerre for only a few moments on March 16th. From two o'clock, heavy clouds rolled low and fast over the town, coming from the west, as if to sweep away the last royalist spasm. This was the time when General Boudin de Roville, in grand beplumed array and accompanied by his staff, arrived at the archbishopric, that is to say, the prefecture. The Concordat had in fact abolished the Bishop of Auxerre and installed the Prefect in his place. The General had come to co-ordinate with the Prefect, M. Gamot, the measures necessary for the defence of the town against the troops of the Usurper, reported to be very near. The capture of General Ameil had filled him with pugnacity.

An hour later, under the rain that had begun to fall, General Boudin left the prefecture, distressed and furious, got on his horse, and without taking time to go home again and collect his baggage, fled post-haste to Paris in company with Captain of Gendarmerie Tourta, leaving Mme Boudin de Roville and his four children to the discretion of the invaders. A crowd was already gathering and growling round his house. So what had happened? General Boudin had become General Bladder: deflated by a single prick from the one hand that had the hierarchic power to do so, that of the Prefect. In the county-towns of the departments, the prefect and the military commander were absolutely dependent on each other, twinned for better or for worse. Here, Castor had let Pollux down. Everything became clear towards five o'clock, when the Prefect's carriage left the courtyard of the episcopal palace and galloped its six horses off along the road to Lyons, in the opposite direction to that of the fleeing General. The mobs were more and more numerous. Auxerre began to live in the street. Everyone sensed that something was brewing. And for the first time in his career, the Prefect Gamot was cheered by 'the populace'. He had the windows lowered so as to savour this brief triumph, and a glimpse was caught of his low forehead, thin lips and occupied air, as he flew like lightning to the Emperor, to present his respects . . .

Poor Boudin de Roville! He did not come back. Five days earlier, M. Gamot had written to the Abbé de Montesquiou:

'In these circumstances, the peoples of His Majesty the King cannot surround him with too much veneration, confidence, admiration and love.

'I believe I can safely say that the department of the Yonne is generally sound in spirit. Should any turbulence manifest itself, I shall give a good account of it. My horses are saddled and my measures taken to ensure that order shall not be disturbed.'

He had repeated the offence on March 11th, again to reassure the Minister of the Interior:

'I am going to maintain the most active surveillance at all points, and if the least movement should take place, I shall at once go to wherever the need may be; but I believe I can assure Your Excellency that we have nothing like that to fear in this department, where everything is most calm . . . '

Finally, only the day before, on the morning of March 15th, Gamot had passed a decree proclaiming to all in his jurisdiction that:

'1. An appeal is made to all men of good will who, for the safety of the Motherland and the defence of the Throne, will wish to be a part of the reserve army formed at Melun;

'2. For this purpose, a register of enrolment will be opened in every commune;

'3. When the men enrolled are sufficient in number to form a detachment, they will be sent to the town of Melun under the direction of an officer, who will be nominated by the sub-prefect from among those who shall have given proof of their attachment to the King . . . '

So when General Boudin, all fire and flame, had entered the Prefect's office, he had not been at all uneasy at finding him pen in hand, busy drafting a fresh proclamation to the inhabitants of the Yonne. Another appeal, no doubt, to shed their blood for Louis XVIII? But then why the long face, the shoulder-shrugging and the great gesture of disillusion? . . .

'Read this, General. I am going to have this text printed, so that it can be posted tomorrow for the arrival of His Majesty.'

'His Majesty? The King is coming to Auxerre?'

'Read it, General . . . '

'Residents of the Yonne, Napoleon's life has been a succession of prodigies. The greatest undoubtedly is that which is bringing him back into our midst. This event, which our descendants will scarcely credit, augurs a happy future.

'Let us unite again with this hero whom the national glory is recalling. He alone can assure France the independence which will enable her to enjoy every kind of prosperity and give her a constitution appropriate to the character and present customs of her inhabitants.

'Honour is the sole sentiment that guides our armies. May all Frenchmen imitate them! May all passions merge in one alone: love of Motherland and Sovereign.'

Signed: 'GAMOT'

Between morning and evening, therefore, His Excellency the Prefect of the Yonne had changed sovereigns, though without losing his style. This change had been induced so abruptly by the arrival at midday of a breathless courier, who had come from the Jura. One of Marshal Ney's first cares after his rallying had in fact been to get news of it to Gamot, who turned out to be the Marshal's brother-in-law: this former planter of Saint Domingo, ruined by the emancipation of the Negroes, had married one of the Auguié daughters shortly after his return to France, and a little later the other one had married Marshal Ney. A banker and good administrator, he had cleverly known how to thrive on the wealth gathered all over Europe by the sabres of the soldiers, while he himself pursued a quiet official career. Bound, therefore, to the fortunes of Ney, his lightning reversal was a condensed symbol of what took place in France that week: the soldier oscillated, under various impulses; the financier held him back as much as he could, and then fell into step with him and forced the pace so as to overtake him when there was no way left to do otherwise.

With the removal of the royalist lid, Auxerre suddenly expanded in freedom. It began with the children: towards evening they emerged from a long catechism session at which a certain Abbé Fortin had been indoctrinating them with Clovis, Saint Louis and the Martyr-king of the Revolution. This was in order to scatter through every alley shouting '*Vive l'Empereur*' at the tops of their voices. The same cries evoked an echo from the outskirts, on the road to Saint-Bris, where onlookers had been collecting during the afternoon. Adult cries, this time, and mingled with them came the sound of drums and the clink of arms: the 14th Regiment of the Line, veteran of the Italian and Spanish wars, which now formed the Emperor's advance guard and was coming to prepare his entry into the fine town of Auxerre. The officers called out to the crowd that *he* would be there tomorrow. The revelling redoubled. The soldiers were cheered all the more since this was a reunion: four days earlier, on their way from Orleans, they had passed through the town at breakneck speed, ostensibly to go and resist the Emperor. But certain tremors were not to be mistaken: soon, the officers had been forced to halt their advance, and their colonel (still royalist) had written to the Minister of War—this was still Soult:

'I am taking it upon me to halt my regiment at Avallon. I was afraid that if I advanced any further, the spirit of the people would corrupt that of my soldiers, which has remained very good up to now.'

One can only think that the stagnation at Avallon had enabled the spirit of the civilians so to corrupt that of the military that the contagion had not spared the Colonel: the latter was riding at the head of his men, maintained in his command by the Emperor and charged—once more—with opening up the way for him. He took possession of the town hall and ordered the Mayor to have the Emperor's coming announced by Commissioner of Police Sotiveau de Richebourg, the same who, only the day before, had read all over the town the address of the municipal officials swearing to 'defend the crown of Louis XVIII to their last breath'. Now here he was, forced to run through the streets and squares of Auxerre with torches crying '*Vive l'Empereur*', escorted by abominably drunk infantrymen. Others gave protection of a sort to General Boudin's house, which the patriots were anxious to sack.

On the steps of the town hall, the Colonel of the 14th of the Line was full of himself, twirling his sabre all over the place and haranguing to left and right; he would still be strutting about till three in the morning. Among the crowd, a little man bore witness to his times, ever the same, 'venting his spleen' at the sight of the blusterer—with whom he had had words ten years earlier, when they had served their apprenticeship of war together, at Courbevoie, in the light infantry of the Guard. Captain Coignet was no longer wearing half-pay dress: he had donned his old uniform to await the Emperor, and had placed in his boots the playing cards that raised his heels to give him an extra inch or so of height. He was filled with wild joy: his life was beginning again. This was the revenge of destiny.

'For all his exaggeration . . . ' he muttered between his teeth, as he watched the exertions of Colonel Bugeaud de la Piconnerie.[1] 'I can read, me, Coignet, and at home I've got all

[1] Future Marshal of France and Duke d'Isly, future slayer of the silkweavers and the Algerians.

the numbers of the *Moniteur*. It's not six months since they published the address of the officers of the 14th to the King, drawn up by my Bugeaud:

' "The officers and men of your 14th Regiment of Infantry of the Line renew a sentiment already graven on their hearts, that of being loyal to Your Majesty until death . . . " '

Auxerre did not sleep well that night.

26

I have sung my way here

Avallon, four o'clock, March 16th. It was the day of one of the fairs. The neat little town was overflowing with men in blouses, red faces alight, already hoarse from having shouted 'Vive l'Empairreur!' all day, when the latter suddenly arrived and made his way to the Hôtel de la Poste (again!), through the wide streets lined with well-built houses and the irregular squares surrounded by public buildings, small but 'with an air full of freshness and gaiety': a sub-prefecture, a secondary school, a civil court and a commercial court. Avallon was proud of being 'the commercial centre of the Morvan'. And since she was greedy of gain and close with money, for want of reserves—distress was ever present at the end of a bad harvest—business had not been neglected. From break of day there had been trading in wood, corn, cattle, horses and mules. The horse-dealers' purses had slowly filled with ringing crowns in the four or five 'very fine cafés, equipped and furnished almost like those of the capital'. The care of keeping watch had been left to the workmen from the paper-mill or the tanneries, who had stopped work since midday and gathered *en masse* along the charming terraced promenade overlooking the valley of the Cousin.

Napoleon arrived so suddenly, however, and in such restrained style that he surprised half the town, misled by a dozen false alarms: each of the numerous battalions or squadrons that had already gone by had been thought to be accompanying him. So his barouche had time to reach the inn without too much trouble, but there the other half of the population concentrated within ten minutes: three thousand men and women beside themselves. 'People of little account', noted a royalist, who adds: 'He was received by the lowest rabble, swelled by a large number of peasants whom the fair had attracted; it was in the midst of this retinue, and the most coarse vociferations, that Buonaparte reached the Hôtel de la Poste. The rest of the inhabitants (meaning a few hundred frightened bourgeois out of six thousand souls) were dismayed and locked up in their houses.'

Fleury de Chaboulon came along in the second carriage. He too suffered the coarse embrace of Avallon and remained struck by it:

'The demonstrations of joy verged on delirium. They squeezed, they suffocated, to get near him, to catch a glimpse of him, to speak to him. His lodgings were surrounded in an instant, besieged by a crowd so numerous, so persistent, that it was impossible for us to enter or leave without passing bodily through the whole population of the district. The men of the National Guard chose to remain on sentry-duty from morning to night.'

But . . . 'not one of the authorities had gone to meet him or dreamed of appearing before him', adds the very 'ultra' Fabry in his *Itinéraire de Buonaparte, de l'île d'Elbe à Paris*. He exaggerates slightly, very slightly: out of twelve municipal councillors, *one* had been found, after much exertion, to stammer the usual compliments at the lowering of the imperial footboard. And as at Mâcon, Chalon and Autun, even more perhaps, since he has been 'snapped' in the Mayor's account, Napoleon's behaviour when faced with the attitude of the Avallon notables indicates the fundamental lack of psychological balance which would constitute the stumbling-block to his attempt of 1815. At first, he had based everything on an appeal to the people (his speeches at Grenoble and Lyons had begun with *Citoyens!*, a mode of address forgotten since the Consulate); this appeal was more successful than he had hoped and brought him a response like a tidal wave, which put him off: he had no desire to be 'King of the Rabble'. It was a question of spheres. And social sphere, at that time above all, was what conditioned a man most deeply in his reflexes and motives.[1] Napoleon Bonaparte was a bourgeois who had a complex about wanting to appear noble. He had always reacted in that way, and this is the key to the Austrian marriage, one of his greatest mistakes. One whole side of his behaviour becomes intelligible if one realizes that Napoleon was a snob, and that it was not his fault. A snob as his father had been, that father whose imprint had marked him so strongly and whose approbation, one might even say posthumous respect, he had constantly sought to merit by his actions. Napoleon placed his absolute in conformity to the customs and opinions of that rather limited circle which had, however, taken over the real power in '89 by acquiring the national wealth: the lesser nobility turned bourgeois and the upper bourgeoisie on the way to ennoblement. Though very influential, because they held the strings of the Bank and the Exchange, they were not numerous: a hundred in each provincial city, ten thousand in Paris, not a hundred thousand in France. But to him they seemed indispensable, not merely to the structure of his regime, but also to its moral safety. It was with an eye to their approval, their admiration, that he trimmed and shaped his image from day to day in the dirty clay of events. They were his public: he would never seriously be able to conceive of any other.

Well? Well, let them go and fetch M. Raudot!

M. Raudot was the Mayor of Avallon, who had been bickering since the previous day with General Girard, charged with preparing Avallon's welcome to the Emperor. Endowed with a rosy baby-face under an ebon moustache and side-whiskers, Girard concealed an intrepid heart beneath the appearance of a choirboy. This brave man, still young, who had remained on his feet under grape-shot, one of the rear-guard by the bridge over the Elster at Leipzig, when all had been lost, reddened and became confused when it was a question of arguing with a lawyer.[2]

[1] This only serves to highlight how exceptional the career of Maximilien de Robespierre was among the other actors in the Revolution. All of them, from La Fayette—a noble—to Danton—a plebeian—behaved in terms of their equals. But this little noble lawyer from one of the most closed societies in France, that of Arras, was alone able to free himself from prejudice and act to the end in the service of the people.

[2] Girard was to be killed at Waterloo.

Having arrived in the town clandestinely as early as the 14th, he had progressively made himself known as charged—he too! —with smoothing the Emperor's path. He had succeeded in convincing Bugeaud, and sent the 14th of the Line marching back to Auxerre. But for forty-eight hours he had been battling endlessly against the same opening gambit: 'My oath to the King . . . ', repeated by the Mayor with that obstinacy of the Morvanese which can only be surpassed by that of the Bretons. Girard's reply:

'You know very well that's nothing but a pure formality, which one goes through at each change of government. I myself have in fact taken seven different oaths since I came of age. Am I a rogue?'

'It's that that would make an eighth oath cost you less to take,' Raudot answered him sharply. 'As for me, General, I have taken only two oaths in my life, one to the Emperor, who released me from it by his abdication, and the other to the King, from which I don't know who could release me.'

Sempiternal dialogue! Girard having capitulated, the Mayor had barricaded himself in his house. Napoleon in his turn could have left Raudot in peace . . . Quite the contrary, through successive officers he sent not only for the Mayor, but for the sub-prefect and the Commissioner of Police, all three united in resentment. The whole town was his? No matter. He lacked these three. And it was in front of them, at seven o'clock, that he proceeded to indulge in one of the most complete and most insistent pleas on the motives for his return that any *Mémoires* have left us: 'This conversation (this monologue, rather) lasted an hour and a half,' Raudot reports. 'Ten times, we tried to take our leave. The Emperor still kept us. In his remarks he introduced gaiety, abandon, a great lack of constraint, a familiarity carried to excess.' Who knows? He had no doubt sensed in the Mayor an honest adversary, capable of acting as 'stenographer' to his remarks. And Napoleon, at that decisive hour, was terribly lacking in literate witnesses, who would be able on the morrow to become 'reporters' for History. Not Drouot, nor Bertrand, nor Cambronne could make up for the literary poverty of the Bonapartist camp in face of the abundance of sparkling accounts, impressed with the stamp of humour and good form, which a score of people in the King's entourage were in the process of brewing, from Chateaubriand to Beugnot and from Vitrolles to Rochechouart. The historian of 1815 is handicapped by this hemiplegia in the mass of evidence : the architects of the return from Elba made history, but did not know how to write it; the royalists suffered the event, but recounted it with elegance and in minute detail. In Napoleon's immediate entourage, only one man was taking notes and preparing *Mémoires*: Fleury de Chaboulon. But he was a mythomaniacal nincompoop, whom the Emperor had already seen through by then. This was no doubt the reason why, even before a hostile witness like Raudot, he explained himself abundantly, one might even say that he dictated :

'I am coming back to France where I have my army. In all parts it is receiving my orders and obeying them. There can be, and there is, no resistance anywhere. In six or eight months, you would have had a terrible revolution, the results of which could not have been controlled in a manner favourable to France by any one of those who are at the head of affairs. The King is a good man : he has ability and quite good ideas; but he is surrounded by men who deceive him, by a feudal nobility that makes him act in a sense contrary to the Revolution, whose impulses he ought to be following. I alone could spare France the evils with which she is threatened, so I left the Island of Elba.

'My calculation was this : if the people and the army were not for me, at the first encounter thirty or forty of my men would be killed, the rest would lay down their arms, I should no longer exist, and France would be at peace. If the people and the army were for me, as I hoped, the first battalion I met would give the signal by throwing itself into my arms. All the rest would follow, and the revolution would be over as from that moment.

'The people everywhere are welcoming me as a liberator. I have sung my way here from Grenoble. More than three thousand songs have been made up in my honour. They are not wonderful in execution, but they are excellent in sentiment : this is the language of the heart.

'I shall enter Paris as I entered Grenoble and Lyons. The garrison of Paris and its commanders are for me. The National Guard is half on my side. The royal household is made up of old men and children . . . There is talk of the Vendée, but, in that district, war can no longer be what it was: it was gamekeepers and millers who controlled the insurrection. Today, they would have the peoples fight to reinstate the feudal system, under the orders of gentlemen whose wealth they possess and who would like to get it back from them! The Vendée will not disturb my enterprise at all, and I shall have finished soon enough to get to the frontier before the foreign armies.[1]

'On all sides, along my way, I heard cries of 'No more collected dues!' It may well be that this form of tax is no longer suited to the French nation. They asked me on all sides to abolish it, but I promised nothing; I don't toady to the people; I promise them nothing . . . The King and the Princes, for their part, have failed in their promises. Henri IV in reascending the throne changed his religion, and this great change presented those peoples with grounds for security and submission. The King, in returning to France, should have forgotten the old ideas and, identifying himself with that Revolution whose progress could not have been stopped, governed in a popular manner, so as to bind the people to him. But the King and the Princes never knew the Revolution, and could not know it. As a result, they were incapable of governing France in the present circumstances. This care can belong only to a dynasty born in the very heart of the Revolution.

'Down there, I read all the pamphlets that have been written against me. They amused me greatly. I got a great deal of pleasure from reading those that treated me worst . . . they did no harm to my cause.

'They called me a coward! . . . The King has put me beyond the law, declared me a traitor and rebel. The King had no right at all: I am a sovereign like him, recognized by all the Powers. I am the sovereign of the Island of Elba, who is coming with six hundred men to attack the King of France and his six hundred thousand soldiers. I am conquering his kingdom. Is this not allowed among sovereigns?

[1] A phrase to note: it is to my knowledge Napoleon's first allusion to the possibility of a war since his landing.

'Last year, when Marmont, by his treason, surrendered Paris to the enemy, I still had a formidable army around me, commanders, soldiers, who were devoted to me in life and death . . . I could have organized a civil war, the outcome of which would have been hard to foresee. I didn't want that. I wanted to spare France those evils, and I had recourse to a stratagem of war[1] which, preserving me for my peoples and preserving them for me, would save France from division and deliver her from the enemy. I was urged a hundred times by the Italians to go and land among them and place myself at their head: eighty thousand soldiers were waiting for me. I replied that I was satisfied with the Island of Elba . . . I didn't have to tell them my secret: but I had to wait for my elder sons .

'I held an inspection at Lyons. People were surprised to see me reprimanding the soldiers and commanders. "It's like old times," they said, "he's holding his inspection just as he did before he left!" Did they think I had to flatter the army? No, that is not how I bind the soldier to me. He well knows that a reproach or a punishment on my part is often a mark of favour.

'From Lyons, I settled what was to be done. I am dissolving the Chamber of Peers, because it is made up in part of people who had as title of admission only that they had borne arms against their country for twenty-five years. I am dissolving the Chamber of Deputies, because their powers have expired, and because, not having been re-elected in a legal manner, they are no longer the representatives of the nation.

'I am abolishing all the feudal nobility. I am disbanding the royal household. I am convoking all the electoral colleges in Paris, in a *Champ de Mai* assembly; I shall thus gather round me three hundred thousand men, and I have no fear at all that their wish shall be made known. The Bourbons dared not do it, and I dare.'

Stupefied, the three notables of Avallon who were the occasion for this long, dispassionate roar, fall back into the shadows for ever. Napoleon went to sleep, more serenely than on the two previous nights; the news received from Auxerre had informed

[1] This was the first and last time that Napoleon presented his abdication at Fontainebleau in this way.

him that his reception there the following day would be not merely triumphal but official. His officers, on the other hand, were to have great difficulty in closing their eyes, and for good reason! A fine slice of luck! Fleury de Chaboulon reports:

'The most distinguished women of the town spent the day and night on the staircases and corridors on the look-out for his passing. Three of them, tired from being on their feet all day for want of seats, asked us for permission to sit down by us. This was in a hall (adjoining the Emperor's room), where some mattresses had been thrown on the floor. Nothing was so pleasing as to see these three young and elegant Bonapartistes grouped shyly on their pallet in the midst of our bivouac. We tried to keep them company, but our eyes closed in spite of our efforts. "Go to sleep," they said, "we'll keep watch on the Emperor." Indeed, weariness prevailed over gallantry, and ere long we fell asleep ignominiously at their feet. On our awakening, we found one of these ladies on sentry-duty at Napoleon's door. He knew it, and thanked her for her devotion in most amiable and civil terms . . . '

27

Just like a dream

On leaving the memorable meeting of the 16th, Blacas invited all the ministers and a few senior officers to his table. One dined at six o'clock in those days, among persons of quality, that is to say, of property. Two hours earlier, quite beside themselves, these men had shouted vivats and shed tears at the King's indisputable personal success. But, their exaltation having sagged, they were now flopped in armchairs round the fire, and they felt a bitter melancholy creep into their hearts, of which Vitrolles' account supplies us with so true an echo that it must be quoted word for word.[1] That evening, the noble Baron would

[1] His inevitable clash with Montesquiou would bring out in him the black humour of a squabble at a wake. Throughout that week, Vitrolles and Montesquiou appear before the curtain from time to time, and cross the stage insulting each other in the best style of the celebrated comic duos. One would have thought it was a turn by Footit and Chocolat.

let his hatred betray him into making the most abominable pun:

'I had arrived with Blacas quite a long time before the hour for our meal, and we were so tired, we had been together so continuously for a fortnight, in a word, we had so exhausted all topics, that the two of us were stretched out in armchairs quite a long way apart, without feeling the need to exchange words, when the arrival of the Abbé de Montesquiou forced us to rise and draw near the fireplace.

' "A splendid session," said the Abbé, "a splendid session!" And the difficulty he had in pronouncing the *s*'s made these words a little ridiculous . . .

' "That depends," I replied, "on the results which it may or may not have. Is the Chamber going to mobilize or place at your disposal a hundred thousand men of the National Guard? Is it going to give you a hundred millions of special funds?"

'The Abbé, provoked—he almost always was when speaking with me—mumbled something or other between his teeth, and then ended by telling me more distinctly that I had spoken of all this like a blind man speaking of colours. To which I replied very calmly that it was a great advantage to wear a dog-collar, but that it should not be abused. Blacas came between us to interrupt this friendly dialogue, and the other ministers all arrived at the same moment. We sat down to table. Everyone was very sad, nobody spoke except to his neighbours; and all this display of a great house and power contrasted painfully with the thought that it was all near to vanishing, just like a dream.

'I had placed myself next to General Dessolles, to whom I felt most attracted. Dessolles was a cold man, a man of calculation rather than feeling. Yet during the meal he let himself go with unexpected emotion, and almost with tears in his eyes.

' "Wherever we look it's hopeless," he said to me; "one can say that there is something unjust about fate when we see these unfortunate princes overthrown by this impudent Corsican; for after all, they are the bravest men in the world; and the other, if you knew him as I do! . . . he really is the most deceitful and wicked of men."

'The meal proceeded as sadly as it had begun. It recalled those funeral banquets given in the old days at the obsequies of heads of families. At the moment when the dessert was placed on the table, the Abbé de Montesquiou, with his long face, pale and wan, rose and asked our pardon for leaving us, because of the obligation he was under to go to the Chamber, where an evening meeting had been appointed: and he stressed the necessity of "going to the Chamber". I could never resist the opportunities he gave me to attack him with jests, good or bad; and this time, I descended to the execrable.

' "But no," I said, raising my voice in the midst of the general silence, "he's not going to the Chamber; you can see very well that he's going to the *cabinet.*"

'He threw upon me his mournful gaze, which he tried to make withering, and left.'

* *March 17th* *

28

Gamot behaved like a spaniel

March 17th seems to have been for Napoleon nothing but
preparation for the solemn entry into Auxerre that evening.
There, a large town, bourgeois and respectable, was awaiting
him almost unanimously, with nobody of note missing from the
roll-call—among civilians, at least, for the priests were disappearing—after the precipitate flight of General Boudin de Roville.
There, he knew the Prefect would welcome him in his prefecture.
The whole of the rich department of the Yonne, in the form of
its county-town, was adhering to him like a seamless tunic, and
was about to provide the firm springboard needed for the Eagle's
final leap, from the steeples of Burgundy to those of the Ile-de-
France and the tower of Notre-Dame.

He would take advantage of it to pause, because he needed
physical rest, though he never admitted it. He was exhausted,
he was sleeping less and less well (his physician, Doctor Foureau
de Beauregard, had to give him 'soporific broths' every night,
which had no great effect on him), and he caught cold and
became husky with every shower of rain or gust of sharp wind
he endured during his harangues in the open air. But also
because he needed to organize the last step, the most delicate
and the most decisive. On the one hand, indeed, there seemed
every reason to fear the bloody confrontation that he wanted
above all to avoid, between the royalists and himself: in the
flood of news from Paris, which he was receiving more and more
copiously the nearer he got to it, there was no means of divining
officially that the King was about to withdraw. Quite the contrary, the Moniteur, the official journals, the letters to prefects
and mayors, and the proclamations were full of allusions to 'the
King's great army in formation below Paris' and assurances that
Louis XVIII was preparing to 'shed his blood' in defence of his
throne. On the other hand, Napoleon had advanced so fast, and
the army had rallied to his cause with such alacrity, that he was
himself no longer very sure how he stood. The arrest of Ameil,
which he heard about on the morning of the 17th, brought him
confirmation that the inordinate emotion of the brave men, who

thought everything was settled once they resumed the tricolour cockade, could end in catastrophes. He wanted to see Ney, count his effectives again, and establish a better check on his advance guard and his own safety. Since Lyons, only a few Polish lancers were still at his side out of the original little army, that of the landing. All the rest of the men of his old guard were following him twenty-four or forty-eight hours in arrears, by the 'water-coaches' or the post. Cambronne, out of a job, no longer commanded anything, and went from carriage to carriage among the chamberlains and valets. Since Lyons too, no one was quite sure any more who was in command of the advance guard, from Ameil to Girard or Brayer—and of what, moreover? Super-imposed on the regiments that had rallied in good order were the battalions formed at random from those who had rallied individually.

Above all, it was necessary to see things clearly. So Napoleon lingered all morning in the last of the 'Hôtels de la Poste' that provided him with his staging posts, that of Avallon. He had them bring him all the letters that came into the town from Paris and elsewhere, whoever their addressees might be. Assisted by his two secretaries, he calmly violated their secrets and was not to leave until about noon, on quite a short stage: it was only thirty miles from Avallon to Auxerre. He was to stop again for some time at Vermanton for lunch.

In the midst of a frugal countryside, populated with sparse vines, there was the sudden oasis of this little town at the foot of the hills, on the right bank of the Cure . . . A mile or so before reaching it, they inhaled the fine smell of wet wood that hung about the whole area: the Emperor crossed a vast timber-yard that ran through the town and gave it its character. A gigantic bundle of faggots, one would have said, thrown down, scattered throughout the river: it was here that all the floating wood of the Morvan arrived 'headlong'. That is to say, the cut trunks, roughly squared, were surrendered to the waters of the Cure and the Cousin and arrived in confusion at Vermanton, where they were made fast to one another in rafts of all shapes. The 'trains of wood' thus formed then continued downstream with the current, but each now guided by one or two lighter-men, as far as the confluence with the Yonne, in order to follow that, and then the Seine, before ending up in the grates of the Parisians at the rate of 120,000 'cords' a year.

On this day a great deal of loose wood was accumulating at the beaching-ground, or even missing it and continuing its journey at the mercy of Providence: the lighter-men, the wood-cutters and the workmen from the paper factory and the mills had made themselves dozens of little platforms and were stamping about on them, waving their caps. 'Père la Violette' passed slowly through their midst, smiled, and questioned some of them before stopping at the posting-house, where a battalion of infantry presented arms while a group of notables bowed to the ground: the Prefect of the department, having waylaid the Emperor, welcomed him with the formulae for any official journey.

In front of Gamot, Napoleon felt really at home. After so much rudeness and violence to etiquette, here was the beneficent milk of high-flown eloquence, of 'Your Majesty' at every other phrase, of balm for His August Personage, a little too thick even . . . but this did not displease him as much as he would have it believed. It is true, a little smile crossed his lips when he noticed the cross of the Légion d'Honneur on Gamot's chest, whom he had never decorated. It was Count d'Artois who had accorded him the dignity of prefect, in gratitude for his servility in April 1814, when he had proclaimed the Bourbons in the Yonne. And Napoleon was to say later to Gourgaud: 'Gamot behaved like a spaniel'. He listened none the less gravely to the compliments when the worthy man obsequiously served him up a decoction of his proclamation, with which he was going to regale the people of Auxerre. He replied with a few benevolent words, and then left the Prefect and his officers to plan the arrangement of his equipage in the form of an official procession: all spaniels have a use, when they accord with our desires.

29

The grand departure of the royal army

On the morning of March 17th the royal sitting had created a hopeful effect in the ranks of the faithful. Echoes of the emotion experienced by those who had been present, and the floods of wordy tears in the ink of the newspapers, excited the enthusiasm of five or six thousand sincere royalists and puffed them up for a few hours with an impressive energy of despair. The event of the day, for Parisians, was to be 'the grand departure of the Duke de Berry's army' to meet Bonaparte. All the troops of the Paris garrison, the National Guard, the volunteers and the royal household were being marched in the general direction of Melun, in order to establish an 'entrenched camp' there, against which the enemy would proceed to dash himself to pieces. They were relying on the most fervent, the students of the Law School especially, to fire those famous first shots that were to awaken France. The military governor of Paris, General Maison, fulminated an order of the day worthy of an eve-of-battle. One can understand that Napoleon, who on the same day at Auxerre had knowledge of a similar text, would not have considered his last stage, in advance, as a walk-over :

'The Governor decrees that as from the 18th all corps are to regard themselves as on campaign. He informs the troops that from the 17th the forward movement on the enemy will begin and will be continued toward the assembly-point, until the whole of the army is formed.

'Soldiers! You are about to advance. Behold your King, full of confidence in your loyalty and fidelity; the whole of France, and most especially the inhabitants of the capital, in whose midst you have lived for a long time, who look upon you as sons or brothers, say to you "Go forth, save us from the most hateful subjection!" Soldiers! You will preserve the national honour intact. You will save our liberty, our Charter. To obtain the glorious triumph that will immortalize you, that will make you adored of a people that already admires you, you have only to attend for an hour to a commander who loves you, who has always done everything to improve your lot, and who has come from your ranks, who has never failed in his duty, and who will die content if he sees you do yours.[1]

'Governor of the 1st military division.
Signed: 'Count MAISON'

[1] Count Maison was under no compulsion to hunt out the repetitions in his style. The last paragraph is a feast of QUI [in the original] : no less than 8.

During the morning of the 17th in Paris, therefore, there was the roll of ammunition wagons and the hammering of hooves on the damp stones of the road. But how, in the end, were these eleventh-hour soldiers to be distributed? A glance at the map of the two routes from Lyons to Paris[1] shows that travellers coming from Avallon, Auxerre and Sens, like Napoleon, had a choice at Fossard, between one fork which could take them straight to Melun and the road through Fontainebleau forest to Fontainebleau itself. There, the two routes, the Burgundy route and the Bourbonnais, join up again, and a fresh choice has to be made for reaching Paris: to pass to the right, through Melun, Villeneuve and Charenton, or to the left through Ponthierry, Fromentau and Villejuif. For want of knowing which solutions Napoleon would adopt, the King's military advisers had decided to establish the 'entrenched camp' between the two routes, on either side of the Seine, whose course they followed at a good distance. One end of the bolt was to rest on Melun—the eastern route—and the other on Essonnes—the western route. Whether the Usurper passed through Fontainebleau or not, it was at the exit from the forest that he would be awaited whatever happened.

This, then, was why the gentle and vaguely hilly countryside through which the Orge wound its way, and the forest of Sénart, all black and bare as yet, witnessed the invasion on March 17th of those little troops of red, green and gilded men, who were going on a crusade without knowing any too well where they were to position themselves. Their spirits were fairly high, since they at last had the impression of doing something, of rebelling — in their turn — against the violation of destiny; and then their uniforms were new, the brass polished, their health intact. They had suffered as yet neither fatigue nor necessity; at the city-gates just now, lots of pretty girls had waved their handkerchieves and thrown flowers. A sharp fore-taste of spring was breaking through between the squalls of rain, mild or icy according to the whim of the wind.

The Duke de Berry, who had never been a complicated person, shared this mood. To him was falling the mission of vanquishing the revolutionary hydra. A wide smile lit his face, with its high

[1] See the map, pp. 14-15.

145

colour, as he made his entry into Melun towards noon, riding at the head of a large group of senior officers. Everything was going so much better since he was suitably acclaimed by a good part of the six thousand inhabitants of the county-town of the Seine-et-Marne, one of those towns 'that seemed to us to take its place so naturally among those of which all one can say,' wrote a traveller humorously that year, 'is that we ourselves are surprised to be able to talk about it to our readers.' His description is confined to indicating that a circular market-place, crossed by the main road, was its sole adornment, that 'the two little promenades hardly merit the name,' and finally that 'it has some public baths, a glassworks, two cotton-spinning mills, a manufactory of coloured fabrics, some tanneries, a considerable corn market every Saturday, and a prominent agricultural society, founded by its first Prefect, Monsieur de la Rochefoucauld. A former convent has been converted into a barracks for the corps of Mamelukes.'

Naturally enough, it was this building that had been made ready to receive the first elements of 'the last-hope army', as it was beginning to be called. But when the Duke and his general staff turned up, here was the first disappointment: there were not even five hundred men in combat order at Melun. Cavernous and icy, the barracks sheltered disillusioned little groups who had no idea either where to install themselves or from where they might expect a meal or a battle. Clarke had proved even more incapable than Soult at the Ministry of War; all these brave men had been told: 'March to Melun; there you'll be told what to do.' They were at Melun, and no one had told them anything. No commanders, no plans, no orders. The ladies of the town brought them some mulled wine at about two o'clock. For want of anything better, the Duke de Berry drank some large bumpers of it with them, and handed out some decorations in the square.

At the same hour, the bulk of his army was kicking its heels very near Paris: some twelve thousand men were floundering at Villejuif. They had left Paris by the Faubourg Saint-Marceau and the Barrière d'Italie, formerly the Barrière des Gobelins. They had left behind them those conglomerations of miserable houses, the sight of which had struck the young Rousseau so strongly, on arriving in Paris, that all the splendours of the city had never been able to wipe out his first impression. Nothing had changed very much since Rousseau. When one turned one's back on Paris there was still the same interminable avenue of elms, a long monotony with barren fields stretching on either side. Close by, on the right, in a hollow watered by the Bièvre, one left the old market-town of Gentilly, and then, on a rise, the Bicêtre workhouse, where for five hundred years the poor and the insane of Paris, under the whips of the overseers, had spun, embroidered, forged and manufactured with might and main 'children's toys, old men's crutches and soldiers' gaiters'. At the sides of the road, the court of miracles watched the soldiers of the King go by: three thousand paupers of all ages, 'infirm old men, lunatics, curable and incurable, vagabonds, criminals condemned to the rack', who for a few hours had left their nearby 'stink-holes', those dens of thatch half buried in earth which the charity of the King assigned them as prison for life. They had been plied with thin local wine, a liquor mixed with vinegar, they had been stuffed with potatoes and dripping, and then herded on to the streets and told to shout '*Vive le Roi*'. 'It hurt us to hear them,' recounts a hussar who filed by that day under their cheers, before reaching Villejuif, there to stop, stamping his feet to keep warm, for forty-eight tedious hours.

Villejuif: a village of a thousand souls where there was not even a decent inn, since Paris was so near. On looking round at noon from the height of this little plateau by the side of the Seine, which the people dignified with the name of 'the mountain', de Berry's soldiers could see a heavy grey blotch on the horizon, sprawling under the mist, in which the sun occasionally lit up the dome of the Invalides; the greatest capital of the continent was becoming once more the decisive stake in the great contest that had engaged men for twenty-five years, the struggle 'of those that have against those that have not', to use the words of Benjamin Constant.

Certain corps went beyond Villejuif and proceeded to drop off haphazardly between Essonnes, Corbeil and Melun. Some stopped where they were; others left but were recalled by a counter-order and came back cursing and swearing. It was only in the evening of the 17th, after a day of memorable chaos, that a glimpse could be had of the idea, if not the method, that had presided over the sorting out: Villejuif had constituted a kind of sieve to hold back as many as possible of the troops belonging to the regular army, hence suspected of being touched by the contagion, and to send the 'pure' ones as far as possible towards Melun . . . But at Melun, when night fell, the Duke de Berry was observed by his gentlemen, sitting in front of the office of the Prefect of Seine-et-Marne, chin in hand, eyes blank. He had slipped suddenly into a churlish silence, at odds with his loquacity of the day. Yesterday, Paris had been full of noisy enthusiasm around him. This evening was the moment of truth —and this man of cyclic moods, all inflamed or all depressed, had come to realize that he disposed, in fact, of nothing but a disorganized band of men of indifferent resolution and no experience. Opposite him was the unknown, the wilderness blowing with the wind that was bringing Napoleon. The troops quartered at Montereau were already shouting '*Vive l'Empereur*'. 'Don't go any further, *mon Prince*!' But at Ville-juif, penned up maladroitly, Maison's troops were none too sure any more whether they were prisoners or on a mission. The soldiers lowered their eyes whenever an officer wearing fleurs-de-lys went by. Should an incident occur unexpectedly, should the regiments mutiny, Monsieur's son would be caught between two fires.

The memory came back to him of an incident that morning, when he had wanted to taste the grenadiers' soup as he was passing through Villejuif. Their silence; their insulting deference. And the remark of that old soldier from whom he had borrowed the wooden spoon:

'You will find the soup cold, Monseigneur. You have come too late.'

30

Worthy heir to Charlemagne's throne

At Auxerre, from the morning of the 17th, everything heralded the Emperor. Several couriers had arrived, coming from the south, and had at once been borne in triumph. There had been a great clearing of decks at the prefecture, where the bust of Louis XVIII, which had graced the general council hall on the ground floor, was removed to the loft, with every precaution not to break it : it had cost a great deal, one never knew . . . Brought down at the same time were the busts of Napoleon, Marie-Louise and the King of Rome, which turned out to have been prudently preserved beneath the rafters, as in almost all official buildings in France. The façade presented a tougher problem : stretched across the pediment was the royal coat of arms with the fleur de lys. It was scratched off and an eagle painted roughly over it. For their part, the people dressed the town with tricolours and a group of happy young sparks stuck a red cap on the steeple of the Abbey of Saint-Germain, one of the three magnificent Gothic churches which themselves surmounted the old city with a huge medieval crown. Under successive squalls of wind, rain and sun, Auxerre was taking on the look of an old lady suddenly rejuvenated by the carnival. Since he was arriving in broad daylight, Napoleon would have plenty of time to gaze upon it during the long half-hour descent which would bring him to the bridge over the Yonne : neither well built nor well laid out, the town was all bulging churches and cascades of slate roofs, falling in a gentle slope to the river, over against a little island freshened by clumps of trees and enlivened, like a Dutch landscape, by a large number of windmills.

Four o'clock was striking in the clock-tower, with its Gothic dial, when the people, packed along the Saint-Bris road, began to cheer in an unmistakable fashion. Five carriages appeared a long way off on the hill : first, that of Gamot and a sub-prefect called Audibert; next, that of General Drouot, whose sole virtue was to maintain a perpetual air of gravity, a little sad, a little apprehensive in the midst of the chattering aviary of young aides-de-camp; then that of the Emperor, accompanied by the Marshal Bertrand, a simple posting-carriage hired at Lyons, the cost of which, for this trip from there to Auxerre, including horses, tackle and the actual hire itself, amounted to 5,600 francs.[1]

---

[1] About 15,000 New Francs [i.e. roughly £1,100]. But in this must be included the horses of the escort. These figures show that journeys at that time were unbelievably more costly than today.

Around it caracoled the Polish lancers, bearing lances tipped
with red and white pennants and dressed in turquoise blue with
crimson revers, their horses covered in shabracks, also blue.
Admired above all were the long ostrich feathers which surmounted that strange article with the diabolical name that
adorned their heads: the czapska. At the doors of the Emperor's
carriage rode Colonels Jermanowski and du Champ and Captain
Raoul, the principal aides-de-camp. Finally, came the carriage
with the secretaries, Rathery and Fleury de Chaboulon, and the
one with the servants: the first valet de chambre, Marchand;
the second, Jaillis; a Swiss giant, Noverraz; a cheerful and very
resourceful young spark garnered on Elba, Gentilini; and a noble
youth, gentle and refined, whom the Emperor called Ali; one
rubbed one's eyes at this, for he was a Parisian to his finger-tips
and was called Louis-Étienne Saint-Denis, which did not prevent
him from being dressed on certain days (not today) as a
Mameluke.

First stop, the end of the bridge, in the Faubourg Saint-
Gervais. The Mayor, M. Robinet de Malleville, presented the
municipal officers to His Majesty, all present and correct, and as
he offered him the keys of the city, delivered an address, the text
of which would be posted the following day on all the walls:

'Sire!

'Twenty years of victories, the most glorious part of which
were due to your genius, your heroism, had raised France to the
highest degree of splendour. A godless coalition sought to destroy
the very memory of so many trophies; but the people and the
army placed their hopes in you; you are come, Sire! and the
national glory, inseparable from your own, is about to flower
again, more unalloyed than ever.

'Worthy heir to Charlemagne's throne, and like him,
assembling about you the élite of the citizens, you will, Sire, ere
long, give the country laws and institutions worthy of you and
of her.

'What can be lacking, Sire, to your good fortune? You govern
free men, and the palms of immortality await you.

'The devotion to you of the people of Auxerre is great, Sire,
from these acclamations that have burst out on all sides at your

appearance. The legal organ of its fellow-citizens, the Municipal Council, renews on their behalf respectful homage to Your Majesty.'

... And it was signed by Robinet de Malleville, Sochet, Thierrat de Millerelle, Edme-Marie Hay, Boniface Paradis, Sutil, Claude Lesseré, Deschamps de Saint-Bris, Escalier, Heuvrard, Crété de la Barcelle, Cottin, Sotiveau de Richebourg, etc., hence by all the names we found on page 68 at the foot of the address to Louis XVIII, less than a week earlier.[1]

[1] A juxtaposition of the two texts brings out the difference of tone. Both in Gamot's proclamation and in this address, enthusiasm is lacking; the style is there, but not the heart. The dogs fall to their knees before him, but they lie down at the feet of the King. When the notables address themselves to the Emperor, one senses a reserve in the homage, a sort of moderation in the offer of devotion, indeed, a tendency to advise or remonstrate, which disappears completely from the rapturous addresses to Louis XVIII. It is not a phenomenon peculiar to the town councillors of Auxerre; when one runs through the columns of the *Moniteur* before and after March 20th, when one ransacks the local papers and the prefects' correspondence, one finds that throughout France the discrepancy is the same, between the sincerity (insofar as the word has any meaning applied to these people) with which the over-whelming majority of the notables gathered round the Bourbons and the formal adhesion which the reappearance of Bonaparte wrung from their lips. More than a thousand texts dated March 1815 are dramatic witness to Napoleon's mistake when he turned his back on the people, who were acclaiming him with all their heart, and looked once more to the upper bourgeoisie, whose game was essentially—and instinctively—duplicity. And a study of the third wave of proclamations, those of July that accompanied the return of Louis XVIII in the steps of the Prussians, merely confirms this observation. Having reverted again to their real opinions the notables rediscovered an outburst of hyperbole to greet the second restoration, which underlines once more their reserve with regard to Napoleon. To be noted, too, is that their addresses when they rallied to the latter almost never contain any reproach with regard to the Bourbons. Quite otherwise are the addresses to the King in March and July, which overflow with abuse of the Usurper. As one may judge: on July 10th, MM. Robinet de Malleville, Sochet, Thierrat de Millerelle, etc., were 'functioning' once again, as they drafted a text to the King which was intended to secure their pardon, and in which one may read, among other pearls: 'In the circumstances in which the return of a *dear sovereign*, who alone can bring us back the days of peace and plenty, fulfils all the desires of *true Frenchmen*, the principal functionaries of the city of Auxerre hasten to lay at the foot of his throne an expression of the enthusiasm with which they are filled by *that happy event* (Waterloo), and the respectful homage *of their love and inviolable loyalty*. What thanksgivings must we not render to Providence, *when she has by the same stroke overturned the Throne of the Usurper* who, devouring the generations, covered France and all Europe with bereavement

Napoleon was not taken in. Or rather, he was taken in
wittingly. On entering the Faubourg Saint-Gervais d'Auxerre, the
Emperor knew perfectly well what sort of people the municipal
councillors were, of whom all he caught was a momentary
glimpse of bowed backs. That very morning in the inn at
Avallon he had taken note, with a pitying shrug of the
shoulders, of their royalist address of the previous week. But here
he was this evening, listening to them gravely, accepting the
compliments of men who were treating him with perjury, and
addressing to them a few words of thanks. In doing so he became
their accomplice and joined in their game. It was reciprocal:
they hid their convictions from him; he, for his part, resumed

---

and ruin, and restored the Monarch, who reconciled France with Europe . . .
'For our part, Sire, *attached to Your sacred Person by the bonds of love and
gratitude*, we renew the oath to defend your throne against all factions and
to devote ourselves, *to our last breath*, to the maintenance of your tutelary
authority.
'*Vive le Roi! Vive les Bourbons!*'
It was their text of March 15th, enlarged. They found themselves at ease
again; nothing restrained their pens any more. And Gamot, on the same day,
would hasten to explain to those in his jurisdiction the history of the month
on March:
'Residents of the department of the Yonne!
'Hardly were we in peace and security under the protection of the good
and wise King who held the reins of the State, *than the man who had done
us so much harm* appeared in the Midi like a sinister meteor; he advanced
with giant strides, he said the army had been disparaged . . . and a great part
of the people, won over by his deceptive promises, welcomed him, and raised
him to renown!
'Nevertheless, the great European family no longer wished him to govern
the French. She advanced her armies and, at the first encounter, *this man
who was thought so great*, from whom so many things were expected, failed,
ran away, and sought to *re-enter precipitately the obscurity from which he
should never have emerged*.
'What misfortunes must we not have expected in these circumstances, if
our August King had not come for the second time to bring France his succour
and support! He reappeared in our midst, accompanied by his clemency and
pardon for the past . . . We shall not be deaf to his voice; we shall listen to
it with confidence, this good King whose virtues we appreciated . . . '
. . . And who, six months later, would calmly have his brother-in-law,
Marshal Ney, shot. When he wrote these lines, Gamot, far too compromised
by his attitude at Auxerre at the time of Napoleon's passing, felt himself,
knew himself, to be lost and assured of disgrace. Lest this should occur: he
wallowed. This text may be compared with that on page 125, stiff and con-
strained. The sovereign by choice of Gamot, or rather of the ten thousand
Gamots who were running France in 1815, was and always had been Louis
XVIII.

his contempt. At bottom no one was sincere and it did nobody any credit. But the proprieties were observed, and he had never conceived of anything more happening. Onward! The comedy was played amid cheers and smiles. Napoleon's carriage moved off in the midst of acclamations all the more vigorous since the people of Auxerre had never had the honour of offering him shelter. A worthy local physician, Doctor Robineau Desvoidy, was to write ten years later:

'The whole population[1] rose as one man and clapped their hands. National cockade in hand, I too shouted with all the effusion of my young lungs: "Vive l'Empereur!" My eyes had already seen the hordes from the north filing past the famous column. I had wept over the bodies of the last Frenchmen killed before Paris. "Vive l'Empereur!" For me this cry from that time on washed away the affront to the Motherland and assuaged her smarting wounds.'

There was no deceit about the latter. The actors were masked, even the greatest, but the public gave itself truly; three or four thousand poor people cheered the procession along the Rue du Pont, the Rue du Grand-Renard, the Rue Maison-Fort, the Place Saint-Étienne and the Place du Département. To reach the main courtyard of the prefectorial palace, the carriage then passed beneath a brand new vaulted gateway, which clashed with the worn stones of the façade: it had been rebuilt in 1810 after a mishap to Marshal Davout, who had been imprisoned in his carriage, highly displeased, wedged for an hour between the massive old walls.

The Emperor alighted rapidly from the carriage and, guided respectfully by Gamot, crossed the outer hall, ascended the grand staircase, and arrived at some apartments in which the repairs in progress had been camouflaged in great haste by a set of Gobelin tapestries. Discernible here and there, however, were bits of worm-eaten panelling and the damask wall-covering, all split, faded and yellow. But there, on the chimney-piece of the little salon, were the busts of Marie-Louise and the King of Rome. On the look-out for his reaction, they then led Napoleon

[1] 12,047 inhabitants in 1815.

into the state bedchamber, the same one that Louis XIV had slept in several times. There he found a great mahogany bed on a dais, furnished with curtains and covered in crimson taffeta, six chairs, a sofa, and two stools covered in Utrecht velvet, also crimson. On the wall, he saw himself—it was he. It really was, just as he had wished himself and still wished himself. A copy of the famous picture by Gérard showed him full-length, dressed in coronation robes, sceptre in hand, ermine cloak on his shoulders, and crowned with golden laurels. He did not turn a hair, but his attitude and mood revealed a profound satisfaction at this surprise by Gamot, which enabled him to feel supreme at last, as he had been two years previously. His suite were ecstatic. Fleury de Chaboulon murmured: 'One would have said his reign had never ceased!' [1]

[1] In connection with this episode, nothing is more illuminating than a page from one of the most intelligent memorialists to come near Napoleon during this period, also one of the least known: Pons de l'Hérault, manager of mines on the island of Elba. This honest old man, an intractable republican, had received Napoleon with wholly Jacobin distrust. Then, through a series of rows and clashes in connection with the administration of the mines, a profound mutual esteem was born between the two men, who ended by recognizing that they were of the same breed, one would say of the same character. It had developed into a friendship solid enough for Pons to be the third in the secret of the return to France, after Bertrand and Drouot, before Cambronne, and well before the Imperial family. For his part, he had unhesitatingly risked the fruit of thirty years' peaceful work and agreed to follow the Emperor into France, linking his fortune to his own. But this did not prevent him from continuing to bring to bear on Napoleon's conduct a judgment which in its penetrating analysis removes all obscurity concerning the motives for his strange weakness with regard to the 'great', accompanied by a singular lack of appreciation of the 'small', which would be the cause finally of the failure of the Hundred Days. On March 17th, Pons was in Marseilles, with the job of hastening the adherence of his friend Masséna. But to read the following lines, one would have thought he had been in a corner of the synod hall in the prefecture at Auxerre, observing the Emperor's actions and gestures over his heavy spectacles, and shaking his fine old bulldog's head:

'The Emperor stood at the peak of human greatness, but he was not at the peak of true greatness: that which is born of love of the people! He was apart from the people.

'Everything is the people in the social state: outside of the people there is no salvation at all. The Emperor made cruel proof of this. It would be unjust to say that the Emperor did not love the people, he loved them a great deal, he did everything for their sake; only, *he did nothing through them*. There lay his mistake, for all his supremacy did not give him the right to act without the people. The people will not endure humiliation, they parted from the Emperor. Nevertheless, the people were sincerely attached to the Emperor,

31

When the house is on fire

On March 17th, early in the morning (that is to say, shortly before noon), General Dessolles and General Maison had themselves announced to M. de Blacas.

Blacas did not keep them waiting: these, after all, were the two human pillars on which there rested as yet that fragile military edifice, the defence of Paris. Through Dessolles it was hoped to hold the National Guard to the end, and through Maison the capital's garrison. What important reason could there be, indeed, to merit this visit to the King's favourite? Had he not received them only the previous evening at his table?

'I should have liked to pass over this anecdote,' Vitrolles observes in recounting the interview, 'but it gives too good a picture of our position and the morals of those who surrounded us . . . '

By way of preamble, and taking it in turns to speak, as if they had rehearsed their intervention in advance, Dessolles and Maison referred to the difficulties of the times, the unhappy events that were overtaking France . . . their unshakable resolution . . . their devotion to the King . . . Blacas was beginning to wonder if they were going to talk about the weather and the price of corn, when at last one of the two worthies, followed immediately by the other, gave the conversation a certain turn, which could not deceive the man who for six months had been accustomed to handling the monarchy's secret funds:

'We cannot be unmindful, *monsieur le duc,* that in attacking

---

they would have sacrificed themselves for him. But his good above all goods was the constant exercise of his natural and imprescriptible rights. The renegades from the people flocked to the Emperor; they called themselves free men, they were proud to become slaves. It was this fraction that constituted themselves the people of the Directory, who used to be called the gilded people: Thermidorian scum, the corrupt and corrupting basis of all liberty-destroying factions.

The first Consul used to speak of the great people; the Emperor spoke only of the great nation. No attention was paid to this change, yet it was significant.

a man as terrible as Napoleon, we are sacrificing not only our persons, but our families . . . '

'Our opposition will never be forgiven . . . '

'We shall lose our fortunes without a doubt, and we shall probably be forced into exile . . . '

'In such a situation . . . '

'And with no possibility of realizing any means of existence . . . '

'We are going to be forced to fall back on the King's bounties . . . '

This plural spoke volumes: when one referred to the King's bounty, one remained in the abstract, but the term 'bounties' took on a hard and pecuniary meaning that was wholly concrete. Blacas was not so foolish as to be unaware of this, but his eternal habit of taking refuge in solemn generalities would exasperate his visitors:

'Gentlemen, you must not doubt the King's gratitude . . . His Majesty will know well how to appreciate your services and your devotion . . . The thanks of the entire nation . . . '

'General Maison,' wrote Vitrolles, 'then resumed the dialogue with that cynicism which formed the basis of his character.'

He turned to Dessolles:

'You can see he's just pretending not to understand us. We must speak more clearly. Monsieur de Blacas, either you can no longer count on our services, or you will give each of us two hundred thousand francs.'[1]

What else could Blacas do, but bow and promise to seek instructions from the King? At four o'clock, the Crown treasurer disbursed this colossal sum to each of the two generals. 'This was called,' added Vitrolles, 'taking precautions.'

But in the afternoon of the 17th, neither Vitrolles, nor Blacas, nor the Princes, nor anyone else at the Tuileries had time or inclination to be indignant. The news of Marshal Ney's defection had reached Paris, at first through rumours from postilions and couriers, and then officially through officers remaining loyal to their oath who had got away from Lons-le-Saunier. The matter was now certain. The entire army was going over to Bonaparte; nothing further would stop him before Melun. And

[1] About 600,000 New Francs each [i.e. about £45,000].

no member of the King's Council any longer dared rely seriously on the Duke de Berry's army.

It was the hour of final spasms and wild plans.

Blacas proposed a Merovingian recipe. Since Napoleon was Attila, why should the noble duke not cast himself as Saint Geneviève?

'Let the King mount an open coach with his Captain of Guards and myself; let him set out to meet Bonaparte, surrounded by all the Peers and all the Deputies on horse, and then let him call upon the Usurper to withdraw.'

Vitrolles' pin-prick did not miss the mark:

'You have forgotten, *monsieur le Duc*, to have your procession preceded by the Holy Sacrament, carried by the Archbishop of Paris . . .'

'*Monsieur*, this is no time for jokes.'

'Very well, I shall answer you seriously; if the King went out by the Barrière d'Italie, Napoleon would go round Paris, come in by the Barrière du Trône, and calmly proceed to install himself in the Tuileries. There would be nothing left to the King, the Peers, the Deputies, and to you and me, but the expedient of sleeping in the open air in Fontainebleau forest.'

Blacas hung his head. The prospect of endangering the King's comfort was enough to make him swallow his plan: he would have lost his influence through it.

'Well, what do you propose then?'

Alas! Vitrolles also had an idea:

'Let us give all the royal Volunteers a rendezvous at Orléans, Tours, Blois, Saumur and Angers, in order to hold the Loire firmly. Let us organize resistance at once in the provinces of the West: Anjou, Poitou, Vendée, Brittany, and a large part of Normandy. Let us get away to safety the fifty or sixty millions of the royal Treasury that we still have in our hands.[1] If the King is really unable to hold out any longer in Paris, very well! let him withdraw to La Rochelle, where the ramparts are easy to restore. Let him convoke the Chambers there. To this firm bastion in the West it would be possible rapidly to link Limousin, Périgord, Gascony, Flanders, Languedoc and Provence. This plan of defence would hold all our sea-ports: Brest, Rochefort,

[1] About 170,000,000 New Francs [i.e. about £12,600,000].

157

Toulon. The Navy is loyal: at worst, it would still be able to ensure the King's dignified retreat from La Rochelle. And till then, we shall have fought, damn it, we shall have shown some dignity! Isn't that a plan the great Henri would have approved?'[1]

But Montesquiou, naturally, demolished this project in his turn:

'Your idea would only succeed in undoing the King by giving him a Vendean hue (sic). In this way you would alienate him in spirit from the whole of the rest of France. The king of Vendée would never be, and would never again become, the king of France. In a word, *monsieur*, only a Chouan minister would suggest that the King should pursue such an adventure.'

'Eh! monsieur l'Abbé, I would rather give the King a Vendean hue than a foreign one! . . . My plan certainly has something to frighten you, you who see no salvation except in concessions to the liberals and resignation from the ministry. For my part, I'm looking for positions from which to fight. But you, you come along every day with fresh concessions to make. You would voluntarily throw everything out of the window, as they do in a house that's on fire.'

They were to continue like this all afternoon, evening, and late into the night also, in the presence or absence of the King, who had withdrawn into crushed silence since he had been told the news of Ney. Their house was indeed on fire. What was new on March 17th, in the evening, was that they could no longer refuse to notice it.

32

I had only to knock on the door with my snuff-box

The people of Auxerre thought the Emperor would go and

---

[1] How naïve of Vitrolles! The whole of his political career would be full of equally preposterous ideas, and of comparisons that today one would have called fantastic. Only he indeed would have been so bold as to compare Louis XVIII with Henry IV. He loved the Bourbons to the point of getting himself detested by them. How can one wonder at their ingratitude?

rest for a while. 'That's what you think!' said Coignet, who
knew him well, 'he'll hardly take time to change . . . ' Indeed,
Napoleon wanted to take advantage of the remaining hours of
daylight, and by six o'clock in the evening on March 17th, he
had emerged again from the prefecture on foot, suitably dressed,
in order to inspect the men of the 14th of the Line in the Place
Saint-Étienne. But he stopped after a few steps, near the
cathedral tower: some enormous inky clouds were preparing to
break, and he had insufficient baggage as yet to allow him to
spoil a uniform:
'Have them fetch my old redingote and my old hat!'
The aides-de-camp flocked around and re-clothed the Emperor
on the spot in a wicked grey redingote and a still worse hat, as
he passed down the ranks of the soldiers, whose enthusiasm
turned to rapture. The regiment in question was one of the
most glorious: twenty-six of its officers had been killed in action
in fifteen years of campaigning, from Rivoli to Leipzig, taking
in Eylau, a name that remained inscribed on its flag in memory
of the terrible charge of the Russian cavalry, which had deci-
mated them without their giving an inch . . . For a year, all this
had been repudiated, forgotten, insulted by the Powers; the
Sierra Morena and the plains of Russia superseded by armed
parades by the banks of the Loire and route-lining for the passing
of processions at Orléans . . . This evening, boredom vanished
from all their lives when *le Petit Tondu* entered their ranks,
pulled ears, distributed pats and spied an old sapper decorated
with three chevrons:
'And you? How many years' service?'
'Twenty-three, Sire.'
'So we were together at Rivoli?'
'Yes, Sire.'
'I can see you are a good soldier. I shall take care of you.'
He distributed 'stars of honour' to those indicated by the
officers. Meanwhile the crowd continued to invade the square,
now too small. People streamed in like the rain, which was
falling in sheets. Civilians filtered into the ranks, the regiment
was almost broken up by the scrimmage, in which the Emperor's
officers feared for his life: there he was, elbowed and jostled,
within reach of any dagger. Napoleon, in decidedly good

humour, laughed at their efforts to rejoin him. He formed his own orderly picket by asking the officers of the 14th and those on half-pay to form a circle around him. Among them, his eye fell on a worthy fellow who was openly weeping, and whom he had always liked, because his height was as small as his own :

'Ah ! There you are, Grumbler !'

Coignet came forward. In his entire life he would never have a finer hour.

'What rank did you have on my staff?'

'Baggage-master at General Headquarters.'

'Very well ! Follow me, I appoint you quartermaster-sergeant of my palace and baggage-master general !'

Coignet went off, reeling under the cheers of his comrades, who had all drawn their swords and were preparing to form an arch of steel over the Emperor, for his return to the prefecture. He still heard the latter say to them :

'We are marching on Paris. We have nothing to fear : there's only one soldier among the Bourbons, and that's the Duchess d'Angoulême.'

Next? It was almost routine : in a corner of the huge synod hall on the ground floor all the notables of Auxerre had gathered for congratulations, including fervent royalists.

'Sire !' exclaimed the royal attorney Paradis, 'for six months we have been groaning under oppression !'

And the vice-president Camelin :

'France has regained her liberator ! . . . '

Charmed and charming, Napoleon gave himself up to half-confidences and amusing remarks :

'The Court of Louis XVIII? Come, gentlemen, it's King Dagobert's. There's nobody to be seen there but old fogeys. The women are ancient and ugly as frights. There were no pretty women there except mine,[1] but they were treated so badly that they were forced to leave. All those people there have nothing but arrogance and pride. I have been reproached with being proud; I was so only with foreigners. No one has ever seen me suffer my chancellor to put a knee to the ground to receive my orders, or obliged the prefects and mayors to wait at table on

[1] Meaning the wives of the Empire nobility, tolerated at the Tuileries by the Bourbons.

my courtesans and dowagers! I abolished all that parchment
nobility at Lyons. Nobility is a myth: men are too enlightened
to believe that among them there are those who are noble and
others who are not. They are all descended from the same stock.
The sole distinction is that of talent and services rendered.'

All this was said 'with extreme volubility', while taking very
frequent pinches from his favourite snuff-box covered in gold-
plated scales: a present from Marie-Louise, whose portrait was
on the lid. So all was going well—but then why did the Grand
Marshal, who it is true got worked up over very little, wear such
an anxious air?

'Eh!' he confided to Coignet. 'That's twice the Emperor has
asked in vain for the curé! I've just sent to have him fetched by
the gendarmes. His soutane is in for a rough handling, that's
certain . . . '

All alone in his presbytery, the arch-priest of Auxerre represented the last ditch of the opposition. This discordant note
struck by the highest religious personage of Auxerre—since
there was no longer a bishop—would supply Napoleon with the
occasion for his last great rage along the route of his return.

The Abbé Viart was a survivor of the 'non-juror' clergy of
the Revolution: he had been looking for martyrdom for twenty-
five years. For him all religion was summed up in respect for the
established order and worship of the Bourbons, visible symbols
on earth of the Holy Trinity. Since the announcement of
Napoleon's landing, he had been full of appeals from the pulpit
to the Holy Alliance and repetitions of a sermon (ending quite
simply with a heartfelt *Vade retro, Satanas!*) on the duties of
his parishioners in the struggle against the Antichrist. Abandoned by heaven, by Boudin de Roville and by Gamot, this old
ecclesiastic with the tottering master, and his own unsteady
gait, affected by strange bouts of intermittent paralysis, had quite
deliberately summoned his parishioners to the cathedral for
prayer and instruction at five o'clock, the moment anticipated
for the Emperor's entry into the city. There had been few in his
congregation, but still too many for the taste of the man of
triumph. Gamot had sent no less than three messengers to summon the Abbé Viart to the prefecture:

'Not before I have finished the rosary!'

When, the office duly fulfilled, his terror-stricken curates had finally got the irascible priest to accede to the fresh injunctions, coming this time from the Emperor, he had refused to put on a long cloak and change his stock. It was in a grey soutane that he presented himself, head high, in the little salon, accompanied by two other priests, with the enraptured expression of a Christian thrown to the lions. Napoleon at once gave the interview its tone:

'The priests are all sedition-mongers, *monsieur*! The peasants all detest you.'

'Sire, the priests nevertheless obtain some trust and esteem among the upper classes of society . . . '

'Since my departure the clergy have been preaching a return to the tithe and feudal rights. The priests! the priests! it is I who made their fortune everywhere. I restored the churches. Without me they would still be buried in the cellars or begging from strangers . . . '

Where were the days—not so remote, however—when the grateful priests had paid Napoleon the Great the customary tribute: the obedience of their flocks in exchange for the largesse of their Prince? Even in 1814 the imperial catechism was still being taught throughout France, including this categorical article:

'What must one think of those who should fail in their duty to Napoleon the First, our Emperor?

'According to the Apostle Saint Paul, those who should fail in their duty to Napoleon the First, our Emperor, would be opposing the order established by God Himself and would render themselves worthy of eternal damnation.'

They were raising their heads, now. They wanted much more:

'The favour is not forgotten, Sire,' the Abbé Viart ventured to remark. 'Nevertheless, may I be permitted to say that this fortune is insufficient . . . '

'The priests ought not to have more. The Gospel enjoins them to be indifferent to worldly goods.'

'Sire, if the common people had not taken their poverty as a pretext to honour them the less, and if the success of their ministry had not been in any way compromised by it, they would have been silent concerning it. You yourself, Sire, however, have so far recognized that this is not enough, that you allowed us to have recourse to supplements[1] . . . '

The Emperor's steely grey eyes began 'to look like molten metal'. This was too much; facing him was all the brood of vipers that raise their heads, the bemitred, mealy-mouthed tribe, terrible to the small, obsequious to the Prince, those who, more than anyone else, held back the Revolution. He knew what was at stake in the fresh fight which 'the priestly mob', as he used to say at that time, had been carrying on since the Restoration, and had not been very far from winning in February: the Church in France was trying to regain control of the registry. An immense pressure had been brought to bear on the King through the medium of Count d'Artois, the Duchess d'Angoulême, and certain ministers, such as Beugnot, in order that the registry records open in the mayors' offices should be closed, and that the curés should recover the privilege of holding the rolls. What a dream! The whole of human life in thrall again, so that birth, marriage and death should pass through the parish, compulsory baptism, and the confessional! The Court had not said no : if the priests became public officers again, this would augment the police personnel by a hundred thousand auxiliaries in soutanes, able to card-index the conscience of every subject. But now, suddenly, there was this fuss in the Midi, the *Marsellaise* and '*Down with the priests!*', at the passing of this man whom not even the anointing by the Pope would ever excuse for having institutionalized the Revolution, especially in the secularization of the registry. Between them and him there could now be only war. Since setting foot again on French soil, Napoleon had had no more implacable enemies than the priests : a curé of Ain had refused communion to children wearing tricolour cockades; the one at Haineville was about to go on strike over the sacraments and place his village under interdict, as in the Middle Ages, for the crime of Bonapartism; all the bishops, *without exception*, had caused a pastoral letter to be

[1] In those days, the ecclesiastics were receiving money from two hands : the allowance provided by the State and the fees, or supplements, already required from the faithful for each religious transaction.

read from the pulpit, between March 7th and 20th, exhorting Catholics to obey none but the King. One could multiply instances by the hundred. And here today, at Auxerre, was this arch-priest, embodying all the arrogance and bombast of the clergy in France.

'Enough! Enough, enough, that's enough!' Napoleon roared in a voice that turned shrill.

'We are not sedition-mongers, Sire. We preach order and submission to the laws.'

'You adhere to the Bourbons!'

The Abbé Viart was brave:

'That is true. We adhere to them through a root that is ineradicable.'

'Go! Withdraw!'

And the Emperor accompanied his dismissal with a highly significant movement of the foot: everyone present expected to see a boot placed well down the back of the dignified Abbé.

But this rage subsided at once and failed to demolish Napoleon's good humour. Any more than the last anxieties of his entourage on the subject of Marshal Ney, whom they had expected to find at Vermanton or at least at Auxerre. The Emperor knew the Marshal was very near. And he invited to his first 'official' supper since Lyons, besides the inevitable Gamot, the three faithfuls from Elba, Drouot, Bertrand and Cambronne, and three officers who had each brought him a town since March 7th: Labédoyère (Grenoble), Brayer (Lyons) and Allix (Clamecy). Before them he gave a grand recital of happy evenings and confided high matters for History:

'I let it be spread about that I was in agreement with the Powers; I'm nothing of the kind. I am not in agreement with anyone, not even with those accused of conspiring for my cause in Paris. From the island of Elba I saw the mistakes that were being made, and I decided to profit by them. My enterprise has every appearance of an act of extraordinary audacity, and in reality it is only an act of reason. There was no doubt that the soldiers, the peasants, the middle classes themselves, after all that had been done to harm them, would welcome me with rapture. At Grenoble, I had only to knock on the door with my

1. Napoleon carried into the Tuileries on the shoulders of his men, March 20, 1815

1a. Napoleon in 1815

1b. Louis XVIII (from a painting by Gérard in 1814)

2a. The Return from Elba: bringing back liberty (from a contemporary caricature)

2b. The Gates of Grenoble are brought to Napoleon on March 6, 1815

3a. General Druout

3b. General Bertrand

4a. Marshal Ney

4b. Murat, King of Naples

5. Marie-Louise and the King of Rome
(painting by Gérard)

6a. Mme de Staël (portrait by Isabey)

6b. Benjamin Constant

7a. Mme Récamier (portrait by Gérard)

7b. Chateaubriand

8. The King's Departure from the Tuileries, March 19, 1815

9a. Marshal Marmont

9b. Marshal Macdonald

0a. The future Charles X, Count d'Artois

10b. Charles Ferdinand, Duke de Berry

10c. Louis Antoine, Duke d'Angoulême

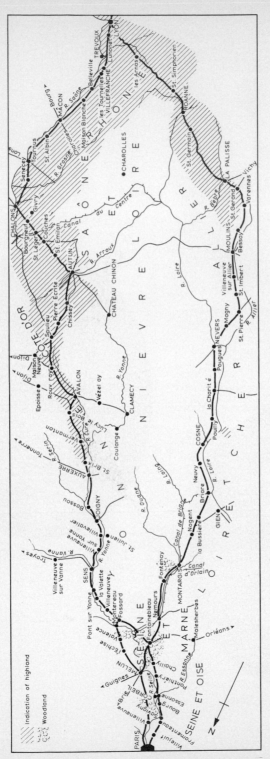

The two roads from Lyons to Paris

snuff-box and it would open. Louis XVIII is undoubtedly a wise prince, enlightened by misfortune, and had he been alone I should have had infinitely more trouble in getting France back from him.[1]

'But his family, his friends, destroy all the good that he might be capable of doing. They were persuaded that they were returning to their fathers' heritage, and that they could behave there as they pleased, and they failed to see that it was to my heritage that they were returning, and that mine could not be run like theirs. Present laws were being executed in the spirit of the past, and it was impossible for the present generation not to revolt. This is the sole cause of my success. It was maintained last year that it was I who had brought back the Bourbons. They are bringing me back this year; so we are quits.'

Having completed his unbending, he bombarded Gamot with questions:

'And the theatre in Paris? What is Talma doing? Have you been to Court? I hear they all look like green newcomers, who have no idea how to say anything or put a foot right?'

He was shown the new louis, with the King's effigy:

'Look! They've removed the reference to *Dieu protège la France* in order to put back their *Domine salvum fac regem*! That's how they've always been: everything for themselves, nothing for France.'

Drums reverberated at that moment, majestic and sedate: it was the entry into the city of the Old Guard—at least, one of the battalions from Elba that had been following him on foot since Lyons. Wrapped in their blue great-coats, sleeves heavy with chevrons, and wearing their hair in the regulation queue, the grenadiers filed by in slow time, determined by the old batteries of Rivoli and Marengo. At the head of the column fluttered the pennant of honour which the Lyonnais had handed over to them on March 13th.

At eight o'clock, when the Emperor rose from table, and as the band of the 14th was playing 'Let us look to the safety of the

[1] Napoleon, who knew the King only from hearsay, shows himself here a victim, like any bourgeois, of a 'conditioning' widely disseminated by the newspapers and salons on the wisdom and sagacity of Louis XVIII.

Empire' in the main reception-room, a carriage drew up a hundred yards from the prefecture: Ney was alighting at the Auberge de la Commanderie.

He had been hurrying towards Auxerre for two days, making his way through the flood of his own troops, whom he had set on the march and who were advancing with a speed worthy of 1792. On every hand were eagles crudely fashioned, and crowns of laurels on the pikes of the flags. By the side of the road the inhabitants supplied provisions, wine, and the requisitioning carts were full to groaning. In the evening, at the passing of the soldiers, bonfires and torches were lit by the hundred. The girls and boys danced. They drank. They made love. 'What a time of delirium!' a soldier exclaimed in recounting those hours. At every staging post Ney had been wildly acclaimed.

'Well, Levavasseur! Isn't this the national feeling? It's thanks to me that all these people are enjoying themselves.'

'Yes, *monsieur le Maréchal*, but you'll be censured for it none the less.'

Having fallen out ten times already and then reconciled at Besançon, they had not stopped quarrelling from Lons to Dole and to Dijon, so successfully in the end that when the spoilsport aide-de-camp had dared tell his chief, 'In short, you can't be sanctioned by the rabble alone!', Ney had taken him by the collar and invited him with very little ceremony to leave his company. Levavasseur, left in the ditch for his pains, had been reduced to climbing into the first carriage to have pity on him, in order to go and resume his duties that very evening, as if nothing had happened.

Now, having come to the end of his journey, Ney seemed to be seized with panic at the idea of finding himself in Napoleon's presence again. He did not want to rush along the moment he arrived, as everyone expected him to do. A last spasm, made up of shame, remorse, pride, fear and timidity, prompted him to wait. He merely sent an officer to Bertrand, and it was the latter who entered the Emperor's room, to tell him with an embarrassed air:

'The Marshal, before presenting himself to Your Majesty, wishes to collect his thoughts and justify in writing the conduct he pursued before and after the events of Fontainebleau.'

Napoleon smiled:
'What do I want with justification? Tell him I love him as
ever and that I'll embrace him tomorrow.'

33

Must Blacas be strangled?

'Baron de Vitrolles, the King is saved if you follow my plan!
He is lost if you don't listen to me!'

Poor Vitrolles would not be able to go to bed in peace during
the night of March 17th to 18th. Already exhausted by the
interminable palaver to which the King's Council had been
reduced throughout the day, he found a message on returning
home. From a woman, naturally. The Egerias of high society
were in full action: it was a matter of bringing men together,
'their men', who up to now had been shunning one another.
They became match-makers. This time the Duchess d'Escars,
whose husband held the office of principal steward to the King,
wanted Vitrolles to come and call on her—at the Tuileries—in
order to meet 'a person who wishes to make him some serious
overtures'.

At the hour indicated, Vitrolles found himself in the presence
of Marshal Marmont, who had assumed military command of
the Château des Tuileries. So the Duke of Ragusa first and fore-
most was responsible for the safety of the King's person, and
this was hardly reassuring to certain royalists. 'If he should go
and betray us as he betrayed the Other . . . ' They were wrong:
Marmont had no longer had any other resource, material or
moral, than to throw himself neck and crop into the King's
service, since that fatal day the previous April when, through
weakness and blundering rather than through Machiavellism,
he had become the archetype of traitor to the Emperor. Others,
more ignoble than he, had known how to clothe themselves in
noble pretences and choose the best moment. Marmont, for ever
after, would remain the only commander in the French army to
have surrendered his troops to the enemy while Napoleon was
still counting on him.

Always 'under pressure', this evening he exploded. Napoleon's approach, the collapse of his fortunes, the necessity of going into exile 'gave his speech an even more staccato, more severe manner than usual'. Vitrolles, stunned, was unable to get in a single word as he explained his brilliant idea :

'There is not a moment to lose in order to act vigorously. It is Blacas' privilege and incapacity that have brought matters to the wretched point they have reached. You will not contradict me there? Very well, *monsieur*, the favourite who is weighing the King down, as if his whole will were paralyzed, must be detached from him completely. Now, the King will never detach himself from Blacas voluntarily. So force must be used. And for that, I propose Blacas be kidnapped.'

Vitrolles thought he had misheard :

'What did you say?'

'I said Blacas must be kidnapped this very night. I have already taken all necessary measures. He'll be conveyed to the frontier, put on a boat for America, confined "on private authority" . . . it doesn't much matter! Once this evil genius is out of the way, we'll impress upon the King the need to centralize all powers—and we won't take no for an answer. Tomorrow, we'll have a decree published in the *Moniteur* appointing Baron de Vitrolles "Minister in chief" . . . '

'Who did you say, who? . . . '

'Why you, *monsieur*, of course, with full civil powers. At the same time this decree will confer on me the general command of the forces on land and sea. Between us, in three days, we shall save the Monarchy in spite of itself.'

Somewhat accustomed as he was to the highly unusual propositions which the times were breeding, Vitrolles had to get his breath back before reasoning with the maniac :

'Let us speak frankly : you are proposing a palace revolution. The only examples we have of this in modern times are to be found in Turkey and Russia; as yet they still govern by strangling their sovereign, which for us, you will admit, would be a remedy a little too heroic. In France, we have never managed to get rid of favourites except with the King's consent; you will recall the Duke de Guise or Marshal d'Andre. But all those who attacked Richelieu or Mazarin paid for it dearly. And tell me, what will you do with the Princes? Will you send them to the Americas too? Everyone would rise against us. I think this would be a short cut to the scaffold.'

Marmont was choking with indignation. He returned to the attack, supported by the Duchess d'Escars, who was playing Joan of Arc, eyes turned to the heavens and hands clasped, standing behind the Marshal's chair:

'We should be justified by the public welfare, surely! Is it better to let all be lost, for want of an energetic course? I wouldn't shrink from any of the dangers you point out to me in order to carry out a task in which success would be filled with glory.'

Vitrolles had to stand up, and speak sharply:

'*Monsieur de Maréchal*, the enemy is at our gates. Is this the moment when you would frame a new government, an absolute monarchy, in spite of the King, in spite of the Princes, in spite of the Chambers, in spite of public feeling, all of whom would rebel at once? The troops would not obey you for twenty-four hours. And if you should still exist in three or four days, which is doubtful, you would see Bonaparte himself enter the walls of Paris in pity at the fate of this old crowned head, the victim of such odious treachery, present himself as his avenger, and have the traitors hanged. And neither you nor I would cause him to shrink from that eventuality.'

Would he be able to get some sleep at last? 'A few further words, exchanged between the three of us, showed me that I was considered a mean spirit, a pusillanimous man with whom there was nothing great to be done, but without whom nothing could be undertaken.'

Vitrolles and Marmont parted, on bad terms for ever.

* *March 18th* *

34

But I can't count on them

At seven o'clock in the morning on March 18th Napoleon's day began with the ritual question:

'Marchand, what's the weather doing?'

The first valet de chambre, his slender silhouette impeccably braced in a suit *'à la française'* (green coat with cuffs and collar embroidered in gold, white kerseymere waistcoat, black breeches and silk stockings), opened the Persian blinds and let in a grey day that might have saved him an answer:

'No better than yesterday, Sire, alas!'

No sooner wrapped in his dressing-gown than Napoleon, sitting by the fireside, went through the newspapers from Paris and the intercepted dispatches. He then took a very hot bath and shaved himself, while Saint-Denis held the large mirror for him, taken from the dressing-case, turning it to catch the light, and Marchand proffered soap and basin, before rubbing him abundantly with eau de Cologne. The two servants noticed that their master continued to be in a gracious mood, since he hummed some airs, abominably out of tune, unceasingly between his teeth, especially the *Marseillaise*, which he had heard so endlessly the day before, and which prompted him to remark:

'Do you know who the greatest general of the Republic was? The *Marseillaise*! Its marvels were something unprecedented.'

Shortly after came the somewhat dramatic moment which everyone had been awaiting for three days:

'Show in the Prince of the Moskwa!'

They had not seen each other since the tragic days of Fontainebleau, the previous year, when a score of cowards had urged Ney to the attack on the vanquished lion: 'Speak to the Emperor, *monsieur le Maréchal*, speak to him, we'll support you!' and when he had entered the imperial cabinet crying: 'Only abdication can get us out of this!' A little later there had been worse: the indecent courtship of the Czar, denigrating Napoleon, while Ney was still claiming money from the latter, the precipitate support given to the Bourbons, and the question

the Emperor put to Macdonald and Caulaincourt, at Fontainebleau still:

'Three of you were negotiating in my name. I had deputed
Marshal Ney with you; where is he?'

'He will not be coming back, Sire.'

Napoleon had merely said 'Ah!' and talked about something else.

Now Michel Ney was entering the little salon, his face very
red under the bushy russet of his sidewhiskers, still wearing on
his chest the badge of the Légion d'Honneur with the effigy of
Henri IV. There would be only one witness to the interview:
Bertrand.

Ney bowed deeply and mumbled a few incoherent words as
he handed the Emperor the statement scribbled during the night
to justify his conduct. All they understood was his declaration:

'If I have lost Your Majesty's confidence, let him give me a
place among his grenadiers.'

Smiling, relaxed, enjoying the moment to the full, Napoleon
advanced towards him and gave him the kiss of welcome:

'Embrace me, *mon cher Maréchal*, I am very happy to see you
again.'

Ney's statement he swept with his eyes rather than read, for he
had no intention of dwelling on it; he put it down on a table and
would presently throw it in the fire, calmly telling his familiars:

'The brave Ney has gone mad.'

So the text remains lost to History, and no one will ever know
its contents.[1] Napoleon, at any rate, did not dwell on it for long:

'I have no need of explanation or justification. I have always
honoured and esteemed you as "the Brave of the brave".'

Ney then launched into some vague phrases in which the
constant repetition of the word 'motherland' remained the sole
manifestation of the right to remonstrate which he was pre-
suming to arrogate to himself:

'Your Majesty will always be able to count on me when it is

---

[1] It was probably less vehement than Ney was to maintain at his trial,
when he asserted that he had proclaimed: 'I have not come to rejoin you
through attachment or through consideration for your person. You have been
the tyrant of my Motherland, you have brought bereavement to every family;
swear to me that you will occupy yourself in the future only with making
good the evils you have caused France.' It is much more likely that the text
mixed a few innocuous shafts with protestations of devotion.

a question of the motherland. It is for the motherland that I have shed my blood, and I am ready to shed it for her to the last drop. I am devoted to you, Sire, but the motherland before all, before all! . . . '

Napoleon cut him short, for the conversation was beginning to get on his nerves:

'It is patriotism too that brings me back to France. I knew the motherland was unhappy and I have come to deliver her from the émigrés and the Bourbons; I shall render her all that she expects of me.'

Ney felt the curb and fell back on the only common ground where agreement came of its own:

'Your Majesty may be sure we shall support him: the Bourbons are lost for having wanted to go their own way and for having set the army against them.'

'Princes who never knew what it was except a naked sword . . . ' Napoleon then said, and having thus subdued his interlocutor without difficulty, applied himself to questioning him about his troops:

'What generals do you have with you?'

'Lecourbe and Bourmont.'

'Are you sure of them?'

'I would answer for Lecourbe, but I am by no means so sure of Bourmont.'

'I don't want to leave them the chance of giving us any trouble. You will give orders at once that they, and all the royalist officers, are to be secured until we enter Paris.'

Docile, Ney would countersign an order that very evening enjoining his men 'to arrest and imprison wherever they may be found those named hereafter: Lieutenant-general Bourmont, Lieutenant-general Lecourbe, Lieutenant-general Delort, Brigade-lieutenant Jarry, Major de la Genetière, Brigadier Durand, Colonel Dubalen, Baron Clouet, the town-major of Auxonne, Count de Scey, the Prefect of Doubs, and the Mayor of Dole.'[1]

[1] The majority of these officers relied so little on their Marshal's protection that they had already bolted or gone into hiding. Not one of them would be apprehended, therefore, and it would take them less than a month to be re-integrated into the French army, where at the decisive moment, along with some others, they would become the maggot in the fruit. Bourmont was to desert on the eve of Waterloo.

The conversation ended in commonplaces without ever again being warmed to true cordiality. The memory of it was to remain painful to them both, and as far as they could they avoided occasions for further meetings. The Emperor could do no other than invite Ney to lunch, but he ordered him to go back to Dijon to lead the troops of the military sub-division to Paris. So Ney was not to reach the capital until March 23rd, not without having kept a careful account of his 'posting expenses', which Napoleon would agree to reimburse him without haggling: a flat 10,000 francs.[1]

Not for a moment was the Emperor taken in: a few days later he was to say to Queen Hortense:

'Ney had the firm intention of attacking me, but when he saw the troops he commanded resisting him he was simply forced to follow the movement and sought to make a merit of what he was unable to prevent. You may be sure of this, but don't speak of it. All I have for me are the people and the whole of the army up to the captains. The rest fear me, but I can't count on them.'

35

Reveille for the Guard

On the morning of March 18th at Chaumont, where they had arrived during the night, the Guard put up the tricolour cockade and dug out their eagles. It was the end of a struggle that had been lost in advance by Marshal Oudinot, who for ten days had also tried for his part, but with more persistence than Ney, 'to hold back the waters of the sea with his hands'. Seamed by wounds and beloved of the men, 'the Bayard of the Empire' was one of the marshals who had adopted royalist ideas the most sincerely. Much influenced by a wife of monarchist background and traditions, he detested Napoleon, from whom he had received a host of pin-pricks and minor humiliations, which are more wounding than a major injustice. The King's government had entrusted him, therefore, with the thankless task of having

[1] About 30,000 New Francs [i.e. about £2,200].

to endure his exile in the east with the infantry of the Imperial Guard. (The cavalry, as we know, was at Lille under Mortier.) News of the landing had reached Oudinot on March 6th, at Metz, in his town house 'de la Princerie', where he lived in considerable style. Grasping the gravity of the matter at once, he had made no bones about exerting himself: reviews, proclamations, personal interviews with the officers . . . Wasted labour. He had rapidly felt himself surrounded with a wall of icy respect, worse than discussion. One young captain, however, had told him the truth:

'Gentlemen, with what cry will the men, and you yourselves, answer my cry of "Vive le Roi"?'

'No one here will contradict me, monsieur le Maréchal: the men, and all of us, will answer 'Vive l'Empereur!" '

Since the evening of the 10th, this cry had been resounding in all the barracks, cafés and streets of Metz, Nancy and Toul. Oudinot made a stand. He proclaimed: 'The King is relying on the honour of the soldiers of the Imperial (sic) Guard, that Old Guard to whom is reserved the glory of being the model and pattern of all armies . . . ' And he passed on to his old sweats the compliments which the Abbé de Montesquiou had suddenly heaped upon them from the rostrum of the Chamber. All they did was to laugh: 'So much flattery!' On March 13th Oudinot obeyed Clarke's order and announced that the grenadiers were about to be set on the march for Paris, in order to rally 'around His Majesty'.

'Agreed, but which?' laughed the men boisterously.

The order of march appointed by the ministry was as follows: March 14th, Pont-à-Mousson; the 15th, Toul; the 16th, Colombey-les-deux-Églises, and then Neufchâteau, Bourmont, Montigny, Langres . . . The regiments certainly moved off cheerfully. With a joy, in fact, that made Oudinot tremble. The latter, moreover, only had time to leave Metz when a sort of rising caused the three colours to be raised, from March 16th, on the towers of the cathedral. He led his troops more as hostage than as commander.

The light infantry for their part had left Nancy, but of their own accord, in order to head for the Petit Caporal. Their Colonel, the intrepid General Curial, tried to oppose this move. But what good did it do him to recall Wagram and the Moskwa if it was to lead his men to 'the fat pig'? They had not taken an oath to him, not they, and could not care less about the itchings of his conscience, that 'gentlemanly disease'. For them, all the nobility of their life was called Napoleon. General Porret de Morvan took command of the 1st and 2nd battalions of light infantry, General Michel of the 3rd and 4th, and they left without concealing their intention of going to Auxerre. They had politely discarded Curial, who followed his men gloomily at a distance, and personified those officers who were torn between two loyalties. There he was, on March 15th, making a sudden irruption into the inn, where his officers were merrily at table. Everyone rose.

'Gentlemen, do you still recognize me as your Colonel?'

'Certainly, General! Place yourself at our head in order to rejoin the Emperor, and you'll see if we don't obey you! ...'

A commander who followed his unit, subordinates who elected him 'on condition' . . . here once again was a revolutionary scene. Tens of other, similar discussions, less spectacular, took place that day throughout the army, recalling the ebullition of 1792.

At Toul, in the evening of March 15th, the grenadiers had piled arms in the Place d'Armes. Oudinot inspected on foot, impeccably saluted, tried to establish human contact, and felt such a coldness that he gave up having them shout 'Vive le Roi' the next day, on their departure. He did well: on the morning of the 16th the officers informed him that they had agreed with their men 'to go to the Emperor by the shortest route'. They were not to pass through Colombey-les-deux-Églises, therefore, but in the evening of the 16th, at Vaucouleurs, rejoined some envoys from Napoleon, who directed them to get to Sens. To do this meant doubling their marches: this was a ten-year-old habit of the Guard. 'Here's the man to get the rust off our legs, *sacré nom de Dieu!* We'd turned into radishes.'

Through a final circumspection, out of regard for Oudinot, the grenadiers put up with the white cockade for another twenty-four hours. During the night of the 17th to 18th, at Chaumont, the Marshal tried a supreme effort, and held out a glittering profusion of crosses, gratuities and promotions. He

went so far as to offer *all private soldiers* the shoulder-straps of
a second lieutenant. Beside him, as surety for this royal promise,
was a general, crippled and quite grey with dust: Mathieu
Dumas, who had just arrived at breakneck speed from Paris, in
order to keep the Guard in hand. The Court had finally grasped
that it was the keystone of the army. Mathieu Dumas knew the
road to the east . . . In 1791, he had galloped before to Varennes,
delegated by the Constituent Assembly to recover the royal
family in flight. This time, he was to take back to Paris nothing
but a sharp sense of having betrayed for nothing the best of his
youth: at nine o'clock in the morning, Oudinot and he found
themselves alone again at Chaumont, in the margin of History
and Life. The men had left, with drums and trumpets, flags
unfurled, eagles in the wind. Oudinot retired to his estate of
Jean d'Heurs. On March 18th, there were in this way half a
dozen Marshals of France who had no more on their horizon
than the prospect of a long old age in which to plant their
cabbages.

*   *   *

On the same day, at Cambrai, the Duke d'Orléans exclaimed:
'I have never seen such a fine regiment, nor hussars turned
out more smartly or in more military fashion!'
Beside the Prince, Marshal Mortier, Duke de Trévise, had
the noble bearing of a gentleman on his white horse, but General
Lion 'displayed the obsequiousness of a page-boy'. The two of
them, a few days before, had quelled the attempt at a military
revolt in the north, and the King had just sent them the son of
Philippe-Égalité as, at one and the same time, a reward, a token
of liberalism, and an aid to getting the troops in hand again.
The three of them, in the main square, were reviewing the
light cavalry of the Guard, those same whom Lefebvre-
Desnoëttes had led off on his mad circular tour. The windows
and pavements were filled with an enthusiastic crowd. At Lille,
and throughout the surrounding area, opinion was royalist:
Louis XVIII played on the Flemings' desire for tranquillity and
peaceful commerce. So they were sincere in acclaiming this
Prince, who it seemed had fought at Valmy . . . in the French
camp, for once, which was unusual. He had now assumed once
for all the air of a starchy private tutor, a little plump, a little

179

sly, amiable, affable even, continually occupied in hiding his ambition and intelligence under banalities. Throughout those days, Louis-Philippe of Orleans had also to dissemble an undeniable satisfaction. He was delighted with what was happening. A good part of the liberal middle classes, more or less led by Fouché, already dreamed of him as the tricolour sovereign who would unite in his person the Restoration and the Revolution. But the situation was not ripe, and it was impossible for him to make a gesture, or so much as wink an eye, to speed this solution. So what could be better for him than the return from Elba? Napoleon was taking the trouble to destroy the throne of the senior branch. When Europe had demolished Napoleon in his turn, the cadet branch would be able to impose itself as the remedy for all ills.

Meanwhile, of course, it would be necessary to go abroad again, but why should Orleans fear that, a gilded exile which, in ten years of speculation, had enabled him to multiply a hundredfold the annual revenues possessed by his family, since Law's bankruptcy, on the banks of London, Amsterdam and Hamburg?

This was why Louis-Philippe held his peace so much that week and stirred the men to loyalty only as a matter of form, without sparing his compliments to the soldiers who were filing past him:

'Your turn-out is all the more splendid since, as I know, you have not received either clothing or equipment from the time of the campaign of France, and since I am seeing you in your uniforms of Champaubert and Montmirail! . . .'

For these words, the light cavalry were happy to cry 'Vive Monseigneur le duc d'Orléans', but not a single 'Vive le Roi', which the Prince was very careful not to require of them. Mortier and his officers had informed him, moreover:

'We cannot answer for what will happen when our troops come into contact with those who have already resumed the tricolour cockade . . .'

The cheers of the citizens of Cambrai were answered, therefore, by the sprightly reserve of Louis-Philippe and the compact silence of the soldiers. The former was himself to observe in his *Mémoires*:

'The enthusiasm which the people displayed was unable to disturb the phlegm of the troops. The Mamelukes filed past at the head of the regiment; they wore the crescent on their turbans. I asked them if there were any among them still who had come from Egypt, but they replied that they were all French. As this regiment filed past me, I reflected on the huge mistake the King had made in not having himself surrounded, on his arrival, by troops of the Old Guard. What a difference if, instead of showing them on every occasion the antipathy which he felt for them, he had frankly applied himself to attaching them to him! Troops such as these, devoted to the King's cause, would have been far more useful to him than the Musketeers.'

In the meantime, the poor cavalry of the Guard was temporarily subdued by Mortier. The defeat of the rebellion had broken the back of the Bonapartists in the north. The Duke d'Orléans noticed that a few soldiers still had the fleur-de-lys in their buttonholes and that all the officers 'wore it correctly'.

What was to be done, then? There was no question of setting them on the march to the south, where the plague would overtake them. How comfortable one was at Lille, between the sea, Belgium and France, half-way to the Crown, with a portfolio bulging with stocks and shares in one's baggage, and surrounded by universal sympathy, if one's name was Louis-Philippe d'Orléans!

36

You can take off your boots

On March 18th in Paris, if consternation was overtaking all royalists informed of Marshal Ney's defection, official circles displayed a kind of aggressive euphoria. They diverted the public's attention to the 'grand departure' of de Berry's army. But that was not all. The *Moniteur* that morning published an extraordinary declaration by the Minister of War.

Clarke had spent all those days in drawing up dossiers. This man, loaded with military titles, who was to end up a marshal, had all the appearances—and the arrogance—of a head clerk in a prefecture. Visitors always found him calm, spick and span, well-shaven, behind a large desk 'on which reposed several bundles of papers arranged with great method, I would readily say elegance. It was borne in upon me that M. le duc de Feltre must have the bump of nomenclature to a very high degree' (Beugnot). Perhaps it was the calm of that red-tape retreat that furnished him with his victorious mentality. Perhaps, too, the conviction that as soon as he concerned himself with a matter all was well. And besides, Clarke did not set himself any problems of conscience, contrary to the majority of imperialists turned Bourbonites. He had always chosen abasement. This creature of the Directory, this lackey of Napoleon's, had astounded the Chamber of Peers that winter, however little disposed they were to rebellion, by affirming in defence of a government bill:

'Thus says the King, thus says the Law!'

Today, declared the *Moniteur*, the Minister of War, as he passed through the hall of the Lifeguards, addressed them in the following words:

'Gentlemen, for a week you have not slept. Now you can take off your boots. I shall sleep tonight as peacefully as three months ago. I had come a week too late.[1] At this moment all is made good. The general staffs, which were not organized, are now fully formed. The officers answer for their regiments. General Ameil, commanding Buonaparte's advance guard, is taken and is at this moment under safe escort in my apartments. General Marchand,[2] for his part, has seized Buonaparte's rear (*sic*) and has re-entered Grenoble. He has seized the artillery there which the latter had left behind.'

What was up with Clarke? In all that he said that day one thing alone was true: he held Ameil.[3]

---

[1] A friendly courtesy with regard to Marshal Soult, whom he replaced.

[2] Military governor of Grenoble, who had vainly tried to resist Napoleon's entry into the town.

[3] Was the latter really taken to Louis XVIII at the Tuileries? Napoleon on Saint Helena vouches for it, in attributing a neat remark to him:

'The King had him brought before him and questioned him. The General

This capture seems to have acted on Clarke like an elixir of youth, and it was on this accident that he built up his amazing harangue. As for what he went on to assert of the situation in 'Buonaparte's rear', he lied, the most coolly and calmly in the world.

In the steps of the Minister, the newspapers indulged themselves to their heart's content. The *Débats* informed their readers that, 'after having retaken Grenoble, General Marchand effected a junction with Marshal Masséna, Prince d'Essling. It is believed that they have re-entered Lyons.'

This was read in Paris on Saturday, March 18th. It is true that one can ransack the whole of the Press without finding a word about Marshal Ney. But alongside Clarke's blusterings there were sufficient anguished articles and news to be read between the lines for no one to be able to believe any longer in the lies. The *Journal de Paris* literally bawled itself hoarse in an appeal, in which the epithet of 'Corsican Robespierre' was one of the most astonishing and most significant that Napoleon had received:

'Do not believe the traitors, above all when, with sly and perfidious self-interest, they exaggerate the alarms and the danger.

'For what danger is it, after all, that threatens us? What! Because a few frantic people, deserters from honour and from glory, have passed into the tyrant's camp, should we believe ourselves in peril? What! Would a gang of five or six thousand fugitives think to achieve the conquest of France, to come and impose their laws on a nation of twenty-five million people; would they dare conceive the mad hope of placing us once more

---

admitted all he knew of the Emperor's movements and of the revolt of the provinces.

'"What," said the King, "you could violate your oath and join the Usurper?"

'"Sire," answered Ameil, "we military men are libertines: if you are our legitimate sovereign, the Emperor is our mistress" . . . ' (*Correspondance de Napoléon*.)

This audience seems very improbable. It is no doubt a bit of boasting by Ameil, later, in order to have the Emperor forgive him his folly at Auxerre. But quite as incredible—and yet true—is that the latter should have quoted a remark acknowledging the legitimacy of Louis XVIII.

under the iron yoke of the Corsican Robespierre? And who are they, these madmen who have joined the desperate cause? What do they want? What do they demand? What do they expect? That which they want, which they demand, which they expect, is ruin, desolation, the plundering of the capital; it is disasters without end, revenge without limits. Traders, it is the pillage of your rich stores that is at stake. Proprietors of all classes, it is your houses, your furniture, all that you possess of value.'

On the same day, General Augier proposed a bill to the Deputies, consisting in particular of the following articles:

'1. War is declared nationally against Buonaparte.
'2. All Frenchmen are called upon to take up arms.
'6. All citizens shall be required to stop recruiters for Buonapart.
'7. The campaign against Buonaparte shall be accounted threefold.
'8. A medal shall be struck which will be issued to all who march against the common enemy.'

This bill was 'referred to committee'.
But why should journalists and representatives not be in a panic, when the King himself was vacillating? Under the blow of Ney's desertion, he signed that day (and *no longer dated* from the twentieth year of his reign) a querulous proclamation to the army:

'Officers and men!
'I have answered for your loyalty to the whole of France. You will not belie the word of your King. Bear in mind that if the enemy should triumph, civil war would at once be kindled among us, and that in that very instant more than three hundred thousand foreigners, whose arms I should no longer be able to hold back, would fall upon our motherland from every side. To conquer or die for her: let that be our war-cry.
'And you who at this moment follow other flags than mine, I see in you only children led astray; renounce your error, therefore, and come to throw yourselves into your father's arms; and,

I pledge here my honour for it, everything shall be at once con-
signed to oblivion!
'You may all count on the rewards which your loyalty and
your services shall have merited.
                                                        LOUIS'

What was this! Threats alternating with promises? How
humble and mendicant he was, this son of Saint Louis! How the
tone had changed since the royal sitting! He was even resuming
on his own account the threat of invasion which his gazeteers
had been brandishing. Was it blackmail now? It is true that the
Count of Provence never shrank from the measure.

37

At last, everything is going splendidly

On March 18th, the sound of boots began to be heard in Europe,
a little on all sides. In Vienna, the plenipotentiaries of Austria,
Russia, England, Prussia and France held council, to decide what
course to adopt 'if Bonaparte should manage to re-establish himself in Paris'. Talleyrand, optimistic four days earlier, seemed to
have lost his illusions and no longer concealed the gravity of the
situation. No doubt he had received accurate information
emanating from Lyons. One sovereign alone was present at the
meeting: the Czar. Tortured with remorse because he had taken
credit for defending Napoleon during a part of the Congress,
Alexander was furious. Cold, abrupt, he called for immediate
measures, as if the war had already begun. That very evening,
a military commission brought the great Allied commanders
together, still in the presence of the Czar: Schwarzenberg,
Wellington, Volkonsky, Knesebeck. There it was decided to
form three front-line armies, intended, that is to say, to invade
France, and two reserve armies, which would constitute the
second wave. During the night, a revived Talleyrand wrote to
Louis XVIII: 'Prompt and extensive measures are going to be
employed.'

Already, close to the French frontier, events were being precipitated. The Congress of Vienna, without having made the least enquiry into the wishes of the Belgians, had decided to attach Belgium to the crown of William, by the grace of God King of the Netherlands, Prince of Orange-Nassau, Duke of Luxemburg, etc. . . . His actual assumption of power had been deferred to the end of the Congress, but, circumstances having changed, the Crown prince, son of William I, hurried to Brussels, where on the morning of March 18th the garrison assembled in the Royal Square took the oath of loyalty to the new king. It was a sad ceremony, ruined by thick mist, which seemed to glue the brass and drums to the ground. The crowd, with lacklustre eye, watched the Dutch High Command go by, and riding towards them, a pot-bellied individual, German to his finger-tips. These new masters were a matter of indifference to the poor people, tossed for ever between Spaniards, Austrians, French, Germans and English. So why not the Dutch! If at least they could bring them peace! . . . But the Crown prince's harangue left them little hope:

'To me is reserved the honour of leading you in battle if it should be necessary to pass, from the peace which we enjoy, to a state of war. I place complete confidence in you, gentlemen, and in these brave soldiers; the Belgians have always been famous for their courage; you will uphold that reputation.'

That very evening, Belgian and Dutch troops, preparing the way for the English, who had been announced, left Brussels and headed towards the French frontier, by the great paved highway that passed through a township called Waterloo.

*   *   *

What was that big manoeuvre, then, which echoed them in the south of Europe? The Neapolitan army was setting off for Rome and Milan. At noon, a man still young, with an athlete's body, leaned back in his armchair, and from his study threw a last glance over the most beautiful view in the world. Through the four high windows giving on to the terrace, Joachim Murat could see Vesuvius, Portici, Capri, and the whole of the bay of Naples. Under the huge frizzy mop, it was still the same face, with flat nose, thick lips, and glowing eyes, underlined by deep pockets: too much alcohol, too many women. It was still the same costume, multicoloured and beplumed, which made him look like a character out of the *Comedia dell'Arte*. But today the hour was no longer one for select parties: His Majesty Joachim I, King of Naples, was becoming Murat again, and his familiars saw him lit up with a sombre gaiety that was not unlike that of Marshal Ney, three days earlier, at Lons-le-Saunier. The war was over for Murat, that internal war which he had been conducting against himself ever since his stab in the back, the previous year, to Napoleon.

For a year, it had been hell for him: he had reigned through felony over a people who tolerated him, but he had felt the encircling pack of kings by divine right: a great part of the debates at the Congress of Vienna had turned on the means to rid the throne of Naples of the son of the innkeeper from la Bastide-Fortunière, in order to restore it to its legitimate owner, the Bourbon Ferdinand. Murat would have gladly forgiven himself for having betrayed France, but not for having betrayed her for nothing. By March 1st he had already taken defensive measures and was feeling himself cornered. And then matters had precipitated: messengers from Napoleon, news from Vienna, appeals from the Italian patriots . . . The whole of a past, the whole of a present, suddenly fused, to make this head in perpetual ferment pop like a cork . . . The prudent around him were anxious, and above all the most prudent of the lot: Caroline. The Queen had been shut up in her apartment for two days. The most intelligent of Napoleon's sisters had ended by vowing a quasi-incestuous hatred for her brother, which accorded with her sharp sense of politics and the opposing forces. Caroline! A lot she cared for the patriots and for France! It was she who had thrown her husband into the arms of Austria the previous year, it was she who obstinately held him to his alliance with Metternich, the only chance in her eyes of keeping their kingdom. Curiously enough, this artful minx was wrong, and it was the churl who was right: Austria had decided to dethrone Murat nearly a month before. But it was still necessary for the latter to provide a pretext: he was about to do so, heedlessly.

'My carriage! My horses!'

He gave a courier a last letter, which he had just written to Lucien Bonaparte, in Rome at the time, with the Pope. It was an outburst of joy, a blaze of truth, in which he recovered his soul: 'At last, everything is going splendidly. I have made up my mind. I am going to support the hopes of the Emperor and of France. I leave this minute for Ancona. Till we meet in Rome.'

He had certainly used deceit to the end, and the day before he was still declaring to Count Mier, the Austrian ambassador, that he had no other policy than an unshakable alliance with Vienna. But he had already ordered his Guard to start for Ancona, across the Italian states, followed by the three divisions of Lechi, Pignatelli and Livron. The whole of central Italy was astir, like an anthill struck by a kick. The Pope was packing his bags. The Austrian armies were preparing to defend Piedmont. Sick and tearful, Caroline barricaded herself in her room; it was the best way to avoid untender farewells, and perhaps even some trooper's language, which Murat inflicted on her during their great scenes.

An end to the hesitations, the evasions and reflections so painful to soldiers: since the great news of his brother-in-law's return had spread across Europe, Murat knew that all eyes were turned towards him, from Paris, London and Vienna. At the head of the grand marble staircase he appeared rejuvenated and liberated, borne up by a gust of pride, and at last restored to himself.

'I want to show the whole world that I was not, and am not, an enemy to Napoleon.'

At one o'clock in the afternoon, King Joachim threw himself into a travelling carriage of eight horses, in company with General d'Ambrosio, and took the road for Ancona, followed by his general staff and household in three carriages of six horses. The groups of idlers, who were for ever loitering with eager noses at the palace gates, cheered him loudly: no member of the public knew as yet that he was leaving for the war, and he was so amusing to see in his gaudy disguise, with a kind word always for the humble, an open purse for beggars . . .

The next morning, moreover, the Naples newspapers were to assert that the King was going to Ancona, on a visit of inspection, with the agreement of the Court of Austria . . . and that the latter were keeping a sharp eye on Napoleon's return!

38

Delirium was in every head

To work! The whole of March 18th was to see Napoleon organizing his final leap, the one that was to take him to Paris. Installed at Auxerre in all the pomp of sovereignty, having at his beck and call, through the medium of Bertrand, the secretaries, the aides-de-camp, the Prefect and his clerks, he was about to 'function' as on the eve of a battle and to deploy all the resources of his meticulous dynamism. Woe to those who might have wanted to rest that day, or who should fail to pretend to be informed about everything that he asked them. Roughly treated by a gust of displeasure, Fleury de Chaboulon sighed: 'His habit was to engage those who surrounded him with all that went on in his mind. He thought that we too owed it to ourselves to know everything and do everything! . . . ' And the unfortunate sub-prefect, Audibert, raised his arms to the sky at the vastness of the rations and fodder demanded for the troops. He dared to observe respectfully to the Emperor that what he was asking was impossible.

'You must know, *monsieur*, that I have razed that word from the dictionary. Go! And only come back to tell me that my orders have been carried out.'

During the morning, after the audience with Ney, Napoleon received Colonel Marin, Cavalry-major of the artillery of the Guard, who had arrived full speed from Compiègne. More fortunate than Lefebvre-Desnöettes and the brothers Lallemand, Marin had managed to escape from the royal police after taking part in the attempt at a military rising. Thus the Emperor learned at first hand the circumstances of that unhappy escapade; far from being cast down by his defeat, he was pleased, and did not conceal it. Here was proof that nothing succeeded except what he undertook himself, and that every attempt to overthrow the King's rule by making use of a lever other than his presence was doomed to disaster. Besides, through the brave officer's account, he had a good idea who was pulling the strings from Paris. He confided to Fleury:

189

'The leaders of the conspiracy would have liked to take over the business and work for themselves. They claim to have sought to open the way to Paris for me. I know now what to believe. It is the nation, the people, the soldiers and second-lieutenants who have done everything. It is to them alone that I owe everything.'

Before noon, he withdrew for a few minutes to scribble in his own hand a letter to Marie-Louise, which an officer disguised as a merchant would try to take to Vienna. It was the third since his landing; it did no more than repeat the terms of those written at Grenoble and Lyons:

'My good Louise, People are flocking to me in crowds. Entire regiments are leaving everything to rejoin me . . . I shall be in Paris when you receive this letter . . . Come and join me again with my son. I hope to embrace you before the end of the month . . . '

During the whole of the afternoon he was to concern himself with the army. He disposed, at Auxerre, of the following regiments: the 5th and 7th infantry (one still said 'of the line'), the 3rd Engineers, the 4th Artillery, with thirty field-pieces, and the 4th Hussars, all these having come from Grenoble. Further, come from Lyons, or gathered between Lyons and Mâcon, the 23rd, 36th, 39th, 72nd and 76th of the Line, and the 3rd Hussars. Plus the 14th of the Line, found there. Plus 'the phalanx from Elba', who were in process of arriving bit by bit: 600 grenadiers and light infantry of the Old Guard,[1] 118 Polish light horse, and about 400 Corsican light infantry. If one adds the battalions of half-pay and isolated men, he then had with him about 14,000 troops and would be able to forgo calling upon the 6,000 to 7,000 men whom Ney had set on the march. But the men from Elba were exhausted, after seventeen days of forced marches. The road to Paris, however, could not suffice to carry and feed the flood that Napoleon wanted to lead rapidly against the capital. So he decided to have the cavalry go through Joigny and Sens, to intensify the transport of troops by vehicle, but above

[1] In the majority of his harangues, Napoleon spoke only of these, which allowed him to play on words, and to assert that 'he had landed with 600 men', whereas his flotilla had transported 1,100 altogether.

all to embark as many foot-soldiers and artillerymen as possible on the Yonne. Those in charge of the water-coaches could guarantee the transport of only 6,000 men? Very well! Let them sort themselves out so as to send double. Let them fetch the boatmen of Sens and the other river-towns by post. Let them put into the water everything that could float: little boats, big boats, barges, lighters, and if that were not enough, let them even use timber rafts! The Emperor summoned the 'master mariners', cajoled them, bullied them, and went into such a mass of detail with them, concerning river transport, accident prevention, the draught of boats, sails and horses for towing, that they listened to him open-mouthed and 'could not conceive how an Emperor knew as much about it as a boatman'.

In the afternoon Napoleon himself went to the port to pester the officers, who no longer knew which way to turn. If those in charge had plenty of cares, among the soldiers and citizens all was still gaiety, which transformed the scene into a sort of grand nautical fair, as the river became covered with overloaded boats. Saint-Denis accompanied his master on the banks and observed:

'There was a general enthusiasm, a joy. It seemed as if the soldiers were going to a great festival, to which they had been invited. The songs, the cheering, *Vive l'Empereur! Vive Napoléon! Down with this! Down with that!* resounded on the boats and on the banks of the Yonne, along which the crowds rushed, and in their turn, did not remain silent. Delirium was in every head. The electric spark had spread to all. In times to come, it will be impossible to read the account of this wonderful voyage without experiencing the same emotions as were experienced by those who witnessed it . . .'

Why, then, in the midst of this festivity, did some men appear not to welcome it? Those who, of all, might have felt exalted? Bertrand, Drouot, du Champ and Jermanowski bore anxious brows and turned uneasy glances towards the windows. They stuck to the Emperor as closely as possible and quickly moved in on him the moment anyone suspicious jostled him too closely. Clearly, they feared an attempt on his life. Fleury de Chaboulon did not miss this opportunity to distinguish himself, and the secretary took a hand in the orderly picket. He produced a fencing-master's rapier and managed to exasperate Napoleon. It was he who was responsible for the assassination psychosis that was to haunt the Emperor's supporters for three days and seize Paris after Auxerre. The whole of the morning, in company with the other secretaries, he had sorted 'the mail' from the intercepted courier, and had been greatly amused at first, as on the other days, at the abuse, such as 'Robespierre on horseback', 'Corsican ogre', etc., gathered by the shovelful out of personal letters emanating from the most important people of Paris and the provinces—some of whom had already just been wallowing at the Emperor's feet. On orders from Napoleon, who himself derived sharp amusement from it, the secretaries contented themselves with re-sealing the letters and forwarding them to their destinations, duly marked in the corner, however, with a 'SEEN BY HIS MAJESTY', which 'like the head of Medusa, will undoubtedly have petrified more than one noble reader.'

But as the day advanced the game became more serious: a certain number of tallying bits of information, found in the newspapers and in the letters, left no doubt that some assassins had been released somewhere with the mission of killing Napoleon, since his death was the only chance that remained to the King. Some Vendeans, veterans of Cadoudal's band, had left Paris with gold and a complete arsenal. One newspaper even announced that they were disguised as women and soldiers, and that the Usurper would never escape them. The news of a subscription opened at Blois to reward the 'tyrannicide' was sprawled across the press that morning. How should these rumours have failed to alarm the Emperor's familiars, several of whom were still haunted by the memory of that terrible year 1803, when the First Consul 'lived under the dagger' of Georges Cadoudal's five hundred Chouans, who had arrived in Paris to kill him? Much closer, the dangers of the previous year were there, quite fresh, to testify that the Bourbons and their henchmen had not abandoned resorting to political assassination, used systematically by the Capetians for a thousand years in order to 'shape France' to their own profit.

In April, the mysterious wanderings of Maubreuil in Fontainebleau Forest, on orders from Talleyrand approved by Count d'Artois . . . In February 1815, hence scarcely a month before, the landing in Corsica of a man who was a criminal beneath his noble veneer; a former killer of the Vendée, the Marquis de Bruslart, officially appointed Governor by the King, unofficially charged with forming a gang of thugs destined for the Island of Elba . . . Past deeds and present threats mingled so dizzily that day that Fleury de Chaboulon burst out into alarmist remarks. 'From that moment I no longer left the Emperor during audiences and, hand on sword, I did not lose sight for a single instant of the attitude of those admitted . . . Count Bertrand, General Drouot and the rest of his suite likewise redoubled their surveillance, but it seemed that the Emperor made a point of defying his murderers' blows. This very day, in holding a review, he mixed with the people and the soldiers.' (He was thus already keeping vigil.) 'In vain we tried to surround him. We were jostled so persistently and so vehemently that it was impossible for us to remain by his person for a moment on end. The manner in which we were elbowed amused him enormously. He laughed at our efforts, and to outface us, plunged even further into the midst of the crowd.'

The assassination obsession was not to slacken its hold all evening and came near to costing two poor devils their lives, the first of whom, without a doubt, would have got his deserts, though only through his stupidity. Had he intended to pass himself off as a staff officer at the prefecture, so as to offer his services to the Emperor, but in reality to spy on headquarters, with a pair of green trousers? No more was needed to persuade everyone present that they had to do with one of Monsieur's Guards in disguise. He became confused, did not know what to say to the questions with which he was plied—and in an instant found himself covered with blows. They were getting ready to throw him out of the window when the Grand Marshal came along at the noise. Bertrand's dignity, more than his benevolence, made him revolt at a lynching a few yards from the Emperor. He had the spy referred to him, secured his confession, convinced himself that it was only a matter of an informer, not of an assassin—and let him discreetly decamp. Thus the greatest leniency continued to be the order of the day.

However, a violent quarrel was still to disturb the officers' banquet that evening. A major of hussars, with a mouth like a sabre-cut, but whom nobody knew, sat down at table without ceremony among the worthies of the rallied regiments. What was one more or less? . . . Bottles sprouted on the table all on their own, to be at once emptied. How well the wine tasted that evening! Then, there was the sponger turning into a wet blanket and taking it into his head, under the impetus of a drunken melancholy, to proclaim that the King could still count on the National Guard in Paris, indeed, on the Imperial Guard! . . . that the King was having 500 francs remitted to every loyal soldier, and 1,000 francs to every officer . . . that Napoleon had been outlawed . . . and that, in a word, if he were taken, he would be in a tight corner . . .

The wretched man was to say no more; a wild outcry rose around him. The others had drunk their wine gaily. By way of diversion, they took him by the scruff of the neck and began to beat him. This time, it was Fleury de Chaboulon who saved the life:

'Gentlemen! The Emperor wants no bloodshed! Let this spy go and tell those who sent him what he has seen. Let us all drink to the Emperor's health!'

An irresistible argument. The mysterious hussar profited by the extra toast to disappear into the unknown from which he had come, and into which he melted for all time. Perhaps it was not even a question of a spy, but of an eleventh-hour supporter whose contrariness had been somewhat provoked. Who knows?

The last to care about these threats, outwardly at any rate, was Napoleon. He was fond of repeating, during those days, his old saying of ten years before: 'When one means to have a hand in ruling, one must know how to be assassinated.' And by policy as by inclination, for nothing was further from his nature than rancour, the orders he gave General Girard, finally appointed officially to command the advance guard, were wholly benign in character:

'General Girard, I have been told that your troops, knowing the decrees from Paris, have decided by way of reprisals to lay hands on any royalists they may encounter. You will encounter none but Frenchmen. Calm your soldiers. Deny the rumours that are provoking them. Tell them that I would not wish to re-enter my capital at their head if their arms were stained with French blood.'[1]

These minor vexations did not prevent Napoleon from joking, towards the evening, with General Allix, one of the worthies to whom all things were permitted at these moments:
'My word, Sire, Marchand manoeuvred like a duffer at Grenoble. Had it been me, I should have gone about things differently to bar the way to you.'
'And what would you have done, then, in his place?'
'Instead of sending a single battalion to the Laffrey defile, I would have marched against you in a body with reliable troops, whose character I knew.'
'And then?'
'I would have killed you, *Majesté*,' was the calm reply from the man who all alone had seized Clamecy.
This was a bit much all the same. The spectators trembled. Napoleon, whose sense of humour was not his dominant trait, appeared somewhat disconcerted:
'You wouldn't have done it, Allix! . . .'
'I would, *morbleu!* I could never find a better chance to immortalize my name!'

[1] On the other hand, Napoleon later furiously denied having added: 'I forbid you to fire a single shot.' 'Thus,' he wrote in his own hand, 'if two hundred royal volunteers had held firm, would General Girard have had to surrender, since he was not to fire a shot, and Napoleon, if he had encountered resistance, would he have had to return to the Island of Elba?' . . . There is a restatement here all the more notable since it underlines the difference between the Napoleon still vowed to adventure who had actually ordered the commander of his first advance guard (Cambronne, at Golfe-Juan, on March 1st): 'I am entrusting you with my finest campaign; the French are all waiting for me with impatience; you will find none but friends everywhere. Don't fire a single shot. I don't want my crown to cost the French one drop of blood . . . ' and the Napoleon already sovereign, resolved on breaking the final resistance, rediscovering in the depths of his being the irritation that led him to have the Duke d'Enghien shot. From Golfe-Juan to Auxerre, an irreversible road had been travelled. He ordered the commander of his last advance guard, therefore, to guard *him* quite as much as to guard *itself* against brutalities. He himself would watch over what the cavalry might display at all the possible outlets from Fontainebleau Forest, which he reckoned to reach the day after the next.

Who said that men of war have no wit? Amid the general hilarity, Napoleon gave this one the supreme recompense: that light pat on the cheek, a caress of glory.

39

Load twenty-five millions into ammunition wagons

On March 18th, at midday, a military man entered one of the 'little lottery offices' that were to be found here and there selling a bit of luck cheaply. Twenty or thirty draws took place each week by districts. And everyone put what he liked on a number.

'Do you want a definite number, my lad?'

'I understand! Give me 18. He'll be leaving before long. I'll put a Napoleon on it.'

A symbolic anecdote: it was the day of rout for Paris. At an early hour great berlins with baggage left the Faubourg Saint-Germain, where the domestics were shaking the rugs, getting out the dust-sheets and closing the Persian blinds on the abandoned town-houses. Princess de Talleyrand and Countess de Blacas had set the example. The Duchess d'Orléans herself had left the Palais-Royal. The stock exchange was collapsing. The funds were fluctuating between 68 and 66 francs, whereas on March 5th they were still being quoted at 78 or 75 francs. The passport office and the staging-post were besieged. The assistant headmaster of the Lycée Henri-IV discreetly persuaded his pupils not to shout '*Vive le Roi!*' any more and saw to the cleaning of Napoleon's bust, which had been stored . . . in the latrines! However, gangs of young fanatics still roamed the Champs-Élysées and the gardens of the Tuileries in groups of ten or so, with huge white cockades in their caps; they had 'pockmarked faces, wild eyes and a conceited air — these were the eternal young swells, who were still cock of the walk.' Provoked beyond endurance, these dandies were filled with homicidal folly. That day, twenty or thirty of them—three gangs combined—rushed upon a half-pay officer who had the temerity to outface them, and slowly killed him with blows from their boots and whips. When they left him, at the corner of the Rue Saint-Honoré, one of his eyes was torn out, his skull was split open and his limbs dislocated. In that rich quarter, a crowd quickly gathered to watch the spectacle without displeasure. Two women from a fashion house clapped their hands, and a lemonade-seller gave his wares gratis to the murderers. As for the police, they took good care not to intervene. This incident frightened the Bonapartists sufficiently for them to refrain from advertising themselves, far more than on the preceding days. An atmosphere prevailed in Paris like that of a bloody Vespers. Fear gripped the city. Who would make tomorrow Saint Bartholomew's Day?

In the afternoon, Vitrolles gave proof of realism. Here it was, several days already since he had been badgering Blacas with his advice on 'measures to be taken in the event of a setback'. Financial measures, of course. A miserable emigration was enough. Let it at least be a gilded one: 'The Crown diamonds must be got to safety and a reserve of money secured.' But up to the 18th, 'his remonstrances had led to nothing'.

'And what do you want me to do about it? . . . ' replied Blacas—'with that air of surprise he had whenever one tried to get him to act.'

Today, Vitrolles grew angry, cornered Blacas in a window-recess and seized him 'by the collar of his coat':

'In short, do you want the Crown diamonds to fall into the hands of Bonaparte?'

'But what's to be done?'

'What's to be done? Why it would be enough to deliver the diamonds into the hands of M. Hue, chief valet de chambre to the King, send him off to Calais without anyone knowing the precious deposit that has been entrusted to him, and give him orders to cross over to England as soon as he hears that the King has left Paris. As for the money, load twenty-five millions into some ammunition wagons and put them on the road to one of the nearest frontiers with Belgium.'

Blacas, overcome by so much ingenuity, at last agreed to carry out this plan. There were no problems with the Crown diamonds. But with the specie, an unforeseen obstacle loomed up; the Minister of Finance conducted himself like an honest man.

It was a matter of Baron Louis, ex-deacon at the High Mass during the Feast of the Federation, who asked Vitrolles:

'Do you know the weight of a bag of a thousand francs in cash? And how many wagons would be needed to transport twenty-five millions?'

'Very well! We'll carry them away in gold!'

'In gold? Do you think it would be easy to find such a sum at once, and do you know at what rates?'[1]

'Well, then, do you want the King, a fugitive perhaps at any moment, to be forced to beg his living? For want of money, get bills of exchange on London and other places abroad.'

'But again, what is to be done?'

'Eh! *mon Dieu!* send for Laffitte or some other banker and see what they can do to supply you with bills on London.'[2]

Another fervent royalist, General Count de Rochechouart, was summoned, after midday on the 18th, by the Duke de Richelieu, whose aide-de-camp he had been for ten years at Odessa, at the time when the two of them had served the Czar. Emigration, for them, had been delightful: the whole of the Crimea to govern with the whip; absolute power over a province almost as big as France. Rochechouart had fought valiantly in the Russian army, and prided himself on having been one of the first to enter Paris the previous year, thus retaking by force, in the name of Europe, that insolent city whose inhabitants had presumed to 'live or die free'. Since then, Richelieu and Rochechouart had lived at Court, somewhat hamstrung by the strange

[1] 'For my part,' Vitrolles observed, 'it was evident that M. Louis wanted to look after himself with the returnee. Indeed, his friends who remained in France made much to Bonaparte of the fact that he had left twenty-two millions in specie in the Treasury, which he could easily have carried away.' The severe verdict of a partisan. It is not impossible that Baron Louis wanted, quite simply, to keep this sum for the people of France. After all, it was to them that it belonged. But, in matters of generosity and honesty, the historian of 1815 is reduced to hypothesis. Let us acknowledge this, however: it was not for himself that Vitrolles was working: he was to know how to risk his skin in a few days, without leaving for abroad.

[2] 'Thus it was done, and a sum of about fourteen millions was easily procured. This sum was the King's resource and comfort during his stay in Ghent, and gave him the means to provide for all the expenses made necessary by the large number of those who had followed him, as many civilians as military men. Finally, it was the balance of this sum that M. de Blacas obtained as a pure gift at the moment when he was forced to leave the King, which formed the foundation of that great fortune.' (Vitrolles.)

liberal ideas that were circulating, even in the King's cabinet. The former did nothing: he was reserving himself for the highest posts, for when he should be needed. After all, one is well able to govern France, when one has governed the Crimea. Rochechouart was an officer in the lifeguards.

'All this is going to end very badly, my dear friend,' said Richelieu to him. 'They've lost their heads at the Tuileries. So, although neither the King nor his ministers have given me the word yet, I think we are about to retreat before the flood. In the danger the King is running, I cannot decently leave him, and I shall stay by him to the end. I am sending off my secretary this very moment with my barouche, my valet de chambre and my effects. They are going to wait for me in Frankfurt. Here are ten thousand francs in gold which M. Ouvrard[1] has procured for me. If you have any money, realize it and make your preparations. You have two horses; lend me one of them; we shall be leaving together in a few hours without a doubt.'

Rochechouart went straight away to the quarters of the Black Musketeers, situated at the Célestins, near the arsenal. All the officers were there, but had received neither orders nor any communication whatsoever, 'at which he was both surprised and grieved'. He recommended all his noble subordinates not to leave, as the order to ride off might arrive at any moment. The whole of the rest of the day was to be spent by the Count in final preparations.

'I took five hundred francs in my purse and the rest was placed in a cash box, that is, a travelling case, which was put with my effects in the boot of my cabriolet, along with a little portmanteau of the Duke de Richelieu's. I left in Paris, with an old French valet de chambre, my silver, my kitchen utensils, table linen, plates and dishes, etc. . . . , plus a few hundred bottles of good wine in my cellar.'

More than a thousand were to go through the same agonies and liquidate everything in twenty-four hours. Not one thought seriously of making a stand. They had such a dread of the

---

[1] The most celebrated man of business of the time, who was beginning, however, it is true, to lose a little of his standing in favour of Laffitte.

people, before whom they had already recoiled twenty years earlier, that this March 18th was 'the day of the aristocrats' great colic', as the *Patriote de 89* was to say. The main difference, from the big flights of July 1789 and June 1791, was that this time they took their precautions. Ouvrard, Laffitte and the twenty great bankers who held in their hands all the fortunes of France were the busiest men of the day: more than twenty millions of francs[1] were to be converted by their efforts into rapidly negotiable bills on foreign banks, between March 15th and 20th: this represented more than a tenth of the total mass of specie in circulation.

*   *   *

Between Auxerre and Melun, between Napoleon and 'the royal army', there was Montereau-faut-Yonne, the pretty little white town of five thousand souls where the Yonne joins the Seine in a great bustle of boats and water-coaches, echoed by the clatter of vehicles on the highway. The whole of it lies open to the heights of Surville, from which Napoleon, aiming his guns himself, had blasted the Württembergers thirteen months earlier and saved Paris—for a few days. One could see at a glance the strategic importance of the double bridge of stone that spanned the two rivers one after the other, that same one on which the gentle Dauphin Charles had Jean sans Peur, Duke of Burgundy, butchered, in defiance of his word sworn upon the Gospels. Whoever held the bridge of Montereau covered or uncovered the capital. Now it had been held, and substantially, for several days by the 6th Lancers, whose helmets and pennons could be seen shining from afar at the two extremities. This was 'de Berry's regiment'—which was, indeed, about to receive envoys from the Prince! At the end of the morning a detachment of about fifteen lifeguards, commanded by MM. Javel and Camboulas, arrived in Montereau to 'arrange accommodation' as advance guard for the 'royal army'. They came upon a captain, who told them:

'You are perhaps unaware that we have just declared for the Emperor? You will be free to return to Paris, but after you have spoken with Colonel Galbois.'

Now Javel knew Galbois, and knew that (according to Fabry) he had been 'overwhelmed with favours by M. le duc de Berry'.

[1] About sixty million New Francs [about £5,000,000].

So he hoped a great deal from this interview . . . but understood before the first word, when he noticed the cross of the Légion d'Honneur on the Colonel's chest, with the eagle substituted for the effigy of Henri IV. Galbois was the perfect epitome of the situation of the majority of French officers: sent to Montereau by the King to defend the gateway, he had obeyed; receiving orders from Napoleon to remain there, to guard it for him, he had also obeyed. Precisely because they knew one another, the two men clashed violently: it was between friends and between parents that the quarrels of March 1815 were inexpiable.

'Arrest these two men!' roared Galbois to the lancers.

For their part, Javel and Camboulas called upon the lifeguards, in no great hurry, it is true, to be spiked on the lances of the cavalrymen who came rushing up from everywhere. After a pretence at a scuffle, the King's men fled, leaving their two commanders prisoner. Such was the memorable Battle of Montereau, the second of that name. It is impossible to pass over this feat of arms in silence: it was the only 'fight' that was to develop along the route of the flight of the Eagle.

*　　　　　*　　　　　*

At about four o'clock in the afternoon, the King, already harassed in the extreme, had to give audience to Marshal Macdonald, very much upset:

'Sire, it is with regret that I bring you my resignation.'

He had thought fit that morning to try to take his role seriously as second-in-command—hence actual head—of the last-hope army. And he had gone to the Duke de Berry to criticize most of the measures taken, but above all to assert himself. 'The Prince, already *enlacé*,[1] received the overtures that I made to him very badly. We had a sharp argument . . . ' which ended with the Marshal's decision. Great God, what a moment for it! Louis XVIII declined to accept the resignation. He knew his nephew's temperament: Count d'Artois's two sons were irascible, incapable of mastering their passions, above all when they were in the wrong. Macdonald bowed, gave his thanks . . . 'but remained none the less resolved to have no further part in anything,

[1] A picturesque application of the proper meaning of this verb, which was still used in the eighteenth century in the sense of *'pris dans les lacs'* of events, in other words: trapped.

except to follow with loyalty the path of his oath'. A loyalty, therefore, that for the Duke of Taranto did not rule out prudence. The man who could make Count d'Artois turn pale by telling him without thinking: 'As for me, I'm all for the Revolution!' . . . had not been any the less aware of how to make himself esteemed by the ultras. He was to 'follow his oath' by accompanying the King to the frontier, but had skilfully got himself out of a difficult mission in the nick of time; that of ordering fire against Napoleon. Already at Lyons, he had assumed every appearance of firmness, free to get out of the mess when he realized that the soldiers were devoted to the Emperor; and this evening, why not continue to make use of his Nestor-like character in order to avoid complications? He had come at the right moment. By dint of Vitrolles' admonitions, the King seemed quite martial, this evening:

'To what department does Your Majesty propose to withdraw?'

'To the Vendée, *monsieur.*'

Here was a pretty pickle! Macdonald shuddered at the prospect of being 'led by his oath' tomorrow into heading a Chouan rising.

'To the Vendée? All will be lost if Your Majesty goes in that direction. You will be followed there. The coasts will be seized and all retreat will become impossible.'

A remarkable courtier! He knew exactly what he had to say to the King in order to get himself esteemed for ever, while keeping up the rough appearance of military frankness. Macdonald rendered Louis XVIII the most valuable of services here: of giving the King's propensity for flight the appearance—and the warranty—of strategy.

'Go rather to Flanders, Sire. Feeling in the departments of the north and of the Pas-de-Calais is better than elsewhere; Lille or Dunkirk will afford you complete security . . . There, you will have gateways by land or sea close to the frontiers, in order to go abroad . . . '

The King thought it over, or pretended to, and then said:

'I like your observations well enough; let us await further news.'

From that moment his decision was taken, or rather he had

resolved to make it public at last. A good actor, he had only spoken of the Vendée just then in order to hear the reply 'Flanders' from a paragon of bravery. From that evening, Macdonald in his turn would be able to play a little comedy. As soon as he got back to the Tuileries, the Duke de Berry, who had left 'his army' to disentangle itself all on its own among the banks of the Seine, sent for him, gave him his hand, and embraced him.

'Let us forget what happened this morning. The King has ordered me to hand over the control of military matters to you. From this moment, you are in charge of everything.'

Macdonald pretended to be surprised. True to what he had just told the King, would he refuse this supreme command? He accepted it.

He accepted it *now*, because he knew that Louis XVIII was no longer entrusting him with responsibility for a fight, but for a retreat. Icy, he allowed himself the added pleasure of telling a 'son of France' what to do:

'In that case, *Monseigneur*, put it in the order that I shall take command at ten o'clock tomorrow and that correspondence should be addressed to me.'

That same evening an unknown hand was to hang a placard on the railings round the Vendôme column, worded thus: 'Napoleon sent a message to the King: "Don't send me any more soldiers; I've got enough." '

During the afternoon a print war was declared in the Rue du Coq, where for several days a royalist bookseller had been displaying an engraving representing 'the entry of the armies of the European Allies into Paris'. His Bonapartist neighbour decided to give tit for tat and, in order to do so, displayed quite simply new prints: 'the entry of the French into Milan, Naples, Munich, Vienna, Berlin, Warsaw, Madrid, Lisbon, and Moscow.'

40

It is Attila, it is Genghis Khan!

Another general dispersion took place in Paris on March 18th, that of the 'liberals', that is to say, of the little groups of men and women who were very active as votaries of their cult of bourgeois parliamentarianism, spurred on by the rapturous Anglomania of the salons.

'Adieu! I'm not going to go, along with all the half-pay officers of the military division, to sweep the dust from His conquering carriage by the gates of the Tuileries! . . . '

Who spoke thus, as he took leave of his friends? It was Fontanes, ex-senior-tutor at the Université, the lover of Élisa Bonaparte, for ten years the unsurpassable pattern of servile eloquence before Napoleon. A monarchist by inclination, he had only to slip a little in order to place himself under the feet of the Bourbons: he was already quite flat. This did not prevent him from parading and perorating in the centre of that little world closed about himself, the little masonic church of moderate democracy, whose prophets were called La Fayette, Benjamin Constant, Lanjuinais, Roederer, Sieyès, Laplace, Joseph Chénier, Barthélemy, Lambrechts, Boissy d'Anglas, Ducis, etc. . . . Many of them had professed the hazy notions of the Girondins in 1793; in other respects there were among them no more coherence and cohesion than among the *fédéralistes*. They used to meet a great deal in those days at Mme de Staël's, who was highly delighted to be able at last to become once again the leader of the revolutionary salon. Dumpy, petulant, with a blotchy complexion, Necker's daughter inflicted an aggressively provoking décolleté on her interlocutor and trapped him in a web of words, emphasized by 'the most beautiful hands in the world'.

'Who will call Napoleon to account for the three million Frenchmen lost between Cadiz and Moscow? And to account, above all, for that sympathy which the nations used to feel for the cause of liberty in France and which has now turned to inveterate aversion?'

No one thought fit to ask her why she had sought the tyrant's favours so doggedly throughout the whole of the Empire. Above all not Lanjuinais, the last of the great survivors of the Gironde, dressed affectedly in black, who proclaimed:

'We went looking for a master among men whom the Romans didn't want as slaves . . . '

A pleasant courtesy from a Breton to the Corsicans! Many

another was to be heard from the mouth of La Fayette, who was revenging himself vigorously after twenty years of retirement. The return from Elba (not by any means to be supported, but to be fought): this was the second chance of his life. At the beginning of March still, he had been mouldering in Auvergne, on his estate of *la Grange*, where the unfortunate Adrienne, his wife, had died eight years earlier of heroism on her part and egoism on his. After Bonaparte had ignored him, he had tried indeed to pay court afresh to the Bourbons, in 1814, but they had turned their backs on him at the Tuileries, during his one and only visit. He had had to resume the crabbed existence of a gentleman farmer, presiding over country balls and high masses —he, who had been called 'the Hero of Two Worlds'! He had been occupied in writing a memoir about his role during the 'flight to Varennes', when the news of the landing had transfigured him. Quick, the baggage, the trunk, the barouche! The ageing boy of fifty-eight had rushed to Paris, nose in the air, hair in rolls, and shrill of voice, certain that he bore within him the welfare of France.

And then! Ten days of munching petits fours with these ladies, before the collapse of everything today! It was not for want of being seen everywhere, no indeed, nor of trying to throw out lines in every direction—to the royalists, through Montesquiou, Jaucourt and the Abbé Louis; to the Bonapartists through Caulaincourt, Cambacérès, La Valette; to the 'republicans' or supposedly such, Carnot, Grégoire . . . In order to propose what, in the end? What plan, what method, what system? La Fayette had always been the apostle of the void. It was Gilles[1] again, 'the funambulist of liberty', convinced that all would be well as soon as England was imitated. The universal remedy: two chambers of notables, a feeble monarch, and, in the midst of it all, me, Gilbert Motier de La Fayette, on my white horse. Carried along by him, the liberals had thus rallied at first with one voice to Louis XVIII, in spite of his entourage of ferocious reactionaries. His scepticism and nonchalance still left them a better chance of holding the stage than the authoritarianism of Napoleon. But what was the good of offering one-

[1] A pantomime character, a sort of simple-minded, chickenhearted Pierrot, immortalized in a painting by Watteau [trs.].

self, if one was ignored? Caught between the Court, who preferred a straightforward call on Fouché, and the people, who dreamed of none but Napoleon, the liberals had been reduced to 'blowing soap bubbles'. Colourful ones, indeed, shimmering and well inflated, they would impress the historians, for these people certainly knew how to write and talk, above all about themselves. They did not advance History by an inch.

At the last minute La Fayette had found an unexpected ally: François-Auguste de Chateaubriand, who also called himself François-René when he had a mind to, and who had been frantically busy between the Tuileries and the boudoirs. Only the day before he had proposed a plan not far short of those of Vitrolles and Marmont. La Fayette and Constant topped him by a head, but he asserted himself through the magic of the word and an elevation of tone that compensated for his short stature. Then, all were silent around him. They saw no one but Chateaubriand: 'On shoulders a little too high, a disproportionate head, which had an air of being at odds with the body. A fine head, in other respects, in spite of the indelible marks of smallpox. Brown hair, thin lips and eyes of perse, that is to say, greenish-blue, which became dark blue with age, and which he knew how to use, as a technician, with women.' [1]

'Let the King keep his word! Let him stay in his capital. We have arms and money: along with money, we shall have weakness and cupidity. If the King leaves Paris, Paris will let Bonaparte come in. Bonaparte, master of Paris, is master of France . . . Let us barricade ourselves in Paris. Our old monarch, under the protection of the will of Louis XVI, the Charter in his hand, will remain in peace, seated on his throne at the Tuileries. The diplomatic corps will range themselves about him. The two Chambers will assemble in the two wings of the chateau. The Royal Household will camp out in the Carrousel and in the garden of the Tuileries. We shall line the embankments and the water terrace with cannon. Let Bonaparte attack us in that position! Let him carry our barricades one by one! Let him bombard Paris, if he so wishes, and if he has the mortars! Let him make

[1] In that remarkable work of lucid demystification by H. Guillemin, *L'Homme des 'Mémoires d'outre-tombe'* (Gallimard, Paris, 1965).

himself odious to the entire population, and we shall see the outcome of his enterprise! Let us resist for a mere three days, and victory is ours. The King, defending himself in his chateau, will give rise to universal enthusiasm. Finally, if he must die, let him die worthy of his rank! Let Napoleon's last exploit be the butchering of an old man! . . .'

Words little suited, indeed, to gain him the favour of Louis XVIII. The manner in which François de Chateaubriand confounded aesthetics and history had exasperated the Court, after wearying Napoleon. But La Fayette fed upon the same mirages.

On March 18th it had to be realized beyond doubt that all this was nothing but idle fancy. There was no worse anguish for the leaders of the 'liberals' than suddenly to become aware of the general indifference, not merely to their ideas, but to their persons. Mme de Staël barred her door, La Fayette took the road back to Auvergne, and Chateaubriand collapsed into panic. By dint of shouting for a year that it was the publication of his brochure on *Buonaparte et les Bourbons* that had restored the throne to the latter, he almost ended by being persuaded of it himself and by believing sincerely that 'Buonaparte' would have him shot within an hour of re-entering Paris. So Chateaubriand fell back desperately on the Tuileries, forced to link his fate to that of the Princes, whom he despised and served at one and the same time, all theatrically. But he had hardly any audience at the palace and that was why, towards evening, Vitrolles saw himself taken to task by François-Auguste's advocate. An advocate with a delicate velvet face, whose huge black eyes carried their fires so far as to ogle her interlocutor, over a deliciously drawn mouth. Claire de Kersaint, Duchess de Duras, was one of 'the flattering mirrors to which Chateaubriand used to go for an hour or two every day to look at himself. With these young women he found the diurnal tribute of admiration which replaced that which the public omitted to render him.'

This definition is by Vitrolles himself, interrupted in his conversation with the Director of Police by the wife of the first gentleman of the Bedchamber bursting in. Mme de Duras was at the height of hysteria: 'She began to magnify, with all the eloquence of feeling, M. de Chateaubriand's danger, the scandal it would be for us to abandon him. She demanded that the King give him a mission to Vienna at once.[1] As I was unable to tell her that her request would be granted, the poor woman ended by falling into a dead faint.' Vitrolles just had time to support her, put her into an armchair and ring. Whereupon d'André, who had vanished into a window recess, reappeared:

'Who ever is that woman?' he asked; 'with the coarse voice and stout figure.' The Director-General of the police did not know Mme de Duras, who lived on the floor above the King.[2]

*   *   *

One liberal madonna alone did not close her town house. Mme Récamier was still receiving on Saturday, March 18th. But she had few invited guests. Our Lady of Finance and of Unappeased Desire was giving her usual display that evening: that irresistible impression of candour and naïve frailty with which Juliette knew how to infatuate the great debauchees. Married by her father, the banker,[3] wooed in vain for twenty years by Joseph and Lucien Bonaparte, Murat, Fontanes, Talleyrand, Ouvrard, Wellington and the Czar, she had not made up her mind yet to surrender to Chateaubriand a virginity under perpetual siege from the élite of Europe. But that evening, among the wrecks of a quarter of a century who floated about her salon, there was this already ageless man, who was dying of love for her:

'Tall, a little stooped, shaken by tics under his straight red hair, dressed with studied negligence in a curious yellow suit': this was Benjamin Constant. How daring he felt that evening! There are not a dozen people who still know *Adolphe*, which he had just finished, and in which the love of a man for a woman was all called in question once more. Liberal? Romantic? Sublime? Idiotic? Benjamin was all these together, 'that evening, when he was at the pinnacle of his life of gambler, sinking his capital on all the gaming-tables: love, fortune and glory.'

[1] That is to say, to Talleyrand, the personification of vice, according to *Les Mémoires d'outre-tombe*. Well, well!

[2] Once, when this anecdote was recalled, Vitrolles concluded unkindly: 'It was through the efforts of Mme de Duras that M. de Chateaubriand followed the King to Ghent, and it was there that he began his political career.'

[3] With honourable intentions, so that she should be endowed with a suitable civil status.

The deceived lover of Mme de Staël lived only to become the lover of Mme Récamier. The deceived lover of liberty of the rosy years of 1789 and 1790 hoped in a confused way for revenge in 1815. Eclipsed by his large glasses, Benjamin Constant's gaze seemed feeble and false. 'A strange green glimmer seeped from between his half-closed eyelids.' But there occurred, on that evening of March 18th, in the obscure alchemy of this individual, an amalgam impossible ever to separate, of love (individual destiny) and politics (the common destiny). They had all fled or were preparing to fly: La Fayette, Chateaubriand, Vitrolles, the King. Benjamin Constant remained, only for Juliette, and because Juliette remained, no one was quite sure why:

'Juliette suddenly told me this morning that she had been reproaching herself for encouraging me and almost proposed that I should not see her alone any more. There is in her a positive decision not to abandon herself to love . . . Oh! now, let us consider and talk it over with ourselves. Juliette cannot, or to put it better, does not want, to have no part in my life. To please all and love none, there lies her necessity. Her coquetry is indestructible. I dined at Juliette's on the 14th, the 15th, when I spent an evening in a long tête-à-tête with her, and the 16th. My head is in danger and I am foolish enough to concern myself only with her. I have done an article for the *Débats*. If Napoleon should triumph and he should catch me, I am lost. No matter! Let us try to remember that life is a bore.'

Immediately after writing these lines in his diary, Benjamin Constant carried that mixture of amorous passion and ideological exaltation, which was to characterize the coming romanticism, to its limit by having that famous article[1] published in the

[1] I give the complete text in an Appendix. It is undoubtedly one of the most astonishing documents of that month of March; and why has it never been quoted except in cut form? It was not a madman writing, nor a doormat. It was a great writer of the French language, who sincerely believed in burning his boats and risking his life by uttering that cry. That voice he raised at a time when everyone else was silent, that outcry against the tide of history, was the swan song of those worshippers of a liberty which they had always confused with their own intellectual comfort. It is also one of the most inspired indictments of Napoleon, in the name of the men who were still rejecting him on the eve of March 20th.

Journal des Débats on the morning of the 19th, in which he proclaimed:

'He is reappearing, this man stained with our blood! . . . It is Attila, it is Genghis Khan, more terrible and more odious because the resources of civilization are his to use . . . I am not going to crawl, a miserable turncoat, from one power to the other, to cover infamy with sophism, and mumble desecrated words to buy back a life of shame! . . . '

It is easy to smile when one knows that, a fortnight later, Benjamin would 'crawl from one power to the other' . . . and would 'cover infamy with sophism' by drafting a Constitution for Napoleon. It is a great misfortune for men of letters that they cannot betray in silence like a soldier or a civil servant. Sainte-Beuve was to publish some extracts from Benjamin Constant's secret notebook, in which the unhappy man, sincere perhaps at last, condensed his adventures of that month into a few lines. What jury after that would have the heart to deny him extenuating circumstances?

'Mme Récamier takes it into her head to make me enamoured of her. I am forty-seven years old. "Dare," she says to me on August 31st. I leave her house madly in love. All life is upside down. The coquetry and callousness of Mme Récamier. I am the most wretched of men. Extraordinary that with my inner suffering I have been able to write a word that makes common sense. Bonaparte's landing, March 5th, 1815. I rush headlong to the side of the Bourbons. Mme Récamier urges me on. The folly of the royalists. Their refusal to do anything to regain opinion. I merely resolve more obstinately to repulse Bonaparte. My article of March 19th. The King leaves the same day . . . '

The Forty Hours of March 20th

From March 18th, midnight, to March 20th, 9.0 p.m.

'During the night of March 18th to 19th several habitués of the Château des Tuileries claimed to have heard a great commotion in the throne room and in the Peace gallery. They hurried to it and through a thick dust thought they saw some individuals of strange shape, dressed in red caps and Jacobin costumes. By means of enormous birches they were sweeping away the throne and the insignia of royalty. Their aspect was terrifying. The lifeguards were fetched: they saw nothing but raised dust, settling in eddies.'

The anecdote, naturally unverifiable, was told by Count de Lamothe-Langon. It shows us the sort of nightmares that haunted the precarious sleep that night of the gentlemen prostrate on the sofas of the Tuileries.

It was Palm Sunday. At six o'clock in the morning, Paris observatory recorded 8°, a fine rain and light mist. At midday the rain had stopped, but the weather was cloudy, and the light mist persisted. The temperature was 12·2° and would rise to 12·5° at three o'clock without managing to disperse the haze entirely. Rain was falling by the bucketful in Brittany and Normandy. There had been frosts in the centre and in the east. Sunshine on the Mediterranean coast and in Dauphiné. It was 'normal weather for Holy Week'. And all over France, torn between winter and spring, between the *ancien régime* and the new epoch, packed churches opened to the traditional procession, which had gone the round in the sharp scent of consecrated box. The door was closed, the nave empty, and the priest knocked three times with the base of his cross: 'Be ye lifted up, ye ever-lasting doors; and the King of glory shall come in . . . ' What strange distractions must have haunted the faithful at that moment! 'Jerusalem, let Him enter, Who is come unto thee!'

✳

As soon as it was light, at Auxerre, Napoleon set off again on the road to Paris. The vast military procession resumed its progress to force the gates of the capital. It now stretched from Montereau, where the advance guard had arrived, to Chalon, where some battalions originating from Lyons were ready to come in support at the least call. The Emperor travelled in the carriage drawn by six horses that belonged to the Prefect Gamot, in preference to the one he had used since March Lyons, the springs of which were thought to be 'tired'. Saint-Denis, or Ali, sat on the bench, beside the coachman. Marchand followed a little further off in a barouche with the portfolio and the baggage. Napoleon settled himself against the cold in a corner of the carriage: the banks of the Yonne were powdered with snow. The Mayor, the municipal council and the National Guard were to accompany him as far as the gates of the town. A large crowd, in spite of the early hour. '*Vive l'Empereur!*' echoing from all sides. At the beginning of the road to Paris the procession came to a halt before going through the massive pilasters of the 'Porte Saint-Siméon', a monumental construction of 1810 decided upon by the municipal council 'in honour of His Majesty the Emperor and King'. There, M. Robinet de Malleville offered Napoleon his good wishes one last time, the postilions whipped up briskly, and the two carriages disappeared in a cloud of dust, followed at the gallop by some Polish lancers and by two other carriages, less speedy vehicles, entrusted to Santini.

'Meanwhile, our death knell was sounding,' wrote Vitrolles. 'Our last moments had come, in the same indecision and the same inertia. The King, through his age and a lifetime's habit, conceived royalty as a principle, but he in no way considered himself charged with the exercise of power. Not one of his ministers was prepared to take that authority upon himself, not one was capable of it, and M. de Blacas, who enjoyed his master's particular favour, less than any other. The consequence of this situation was a sort of paralysis . . . It was only at the last moment, when our cause was morally lost, that appeal was made to those who might have been willing to shed their blood. There is a long way between liking a political order and deciding all of a sudden to get oneself killed in support of it.'

In a state of great nervous tension Vitrolles entered the King's room at eight in the morning. Louis XVIII never slept in the state bedroom, but in the little salon adjoining his study (one said at that time 'his cabinet'). Every evening, an extremely narrow iron bedstead was erected there, furnished with little curtains of green silk. 'The King's great corpulence not only filled the width of the bed, but even seemed to overflow it; a white cap covered his head and gave him the look of a vast and colossal child.'

Before this monstrous baby, Vitrolles put up his last fight for resistance. He went down on his knees, wept, shouted—everything necessary to cover himself with shame. Not one of those who surrounded Louis XVIII understood what formed the essence of his character: a constant anguish concealed by his indestructible serenity, by virtue of that psychological law which makes us show outwardly the opposite of our deepest impulses. He created his character of debonair old man. In fact, this character was one of the most uneasy, most ruthless, and most insensitive to the great world tragedy on which the curtain had risen in 1789. Besides his need for security, to which he sacrificed those who served him best, the other spring of his personality was the incoercible ambition of a younger brother which had gripped him since early childhood. With old age, he possessed at last what he had sought all his life: a position in which he was adored, not by virtue of what he did, but of what he claimed to be. And now here was this 'duffer Vitrolles' (the word is the King's own) carrying on a kind of St Vitus dance in order to bear him off to La Rochelle, at the risk of his being 'curtailed' like his poor brother!

'But you can see clearly that you are alone in your opinion!' he replied quietly.

'My voice had changed with emotion, and my eyes were moist,' continued Vitrolles, 'but the King met me with the calm of apparent indifference. He feared emotion and the effect it

215

might have on his own person. He saw his refuge in the towns of the north; up there, he relied on the frontier. The thought of exile did not trouble him. The course I tried to get him to accept was for him the beginning of an uncertain operation and of doubtful chances, which wearied his imagination.'

Vitrolles, by digging in his heels, managed to carry the day on one point only: the King gave up a flight in broad daylight and agreed to leave only during the night. 'I considered there was no need of sunshine to light up the shame of that flight.'

Hardly was he rid of Vitrolles, at nine o'clock, than the King sent for Marmont. 'Preserving the most profound secrecy towards him concerning the goal of his journey, with great composure His Majesty wrote on a little square of paper the order to the Marshal to convey the King to Saint-Denis,[1] waiting until later to give him other orders. The Marshal rightly observed that the King certainly did not imagine he would be able to stop at Saint-Denis and that consequently he should extend the services of his escort and the journey of his household beyond it. The King then took another little square of paper, which he dated from Saint-Denis, containing the order to convey him to Beauvais.'

Next, the King received Macdonald. Throughout the day he was to amuse himself in holding an even balance between him and Marmont: the two men hated each other, like all the marshals of the Empire. One can skim their biographies without finding in them a trace of sincere friendship. Napoleon used to like to cultivate their bickering. Louis XVIII had been delighted to inherit it.

'*Eh bien! duc de Tarente,* you know what course to take?'

'I suggested it to you yesterday, Sire: go to Lille. The majority of dangerous troops are, by my pains, at Essones. But one final precaution is necessary. Assemble your household troops on the Champ-de-Mars and review them, announcing that you will be going on to visit the troops towards Melun. Whatever happens,

---

[1] It was Vitrolles who brought out the unwitting element of black humour which the formula contained. Saint-Denis was where the Kings of France were buried.

this afternoon, you will be in safe keeping at the Military School. After the review, and if the population remains calm, return to the Tuileries. Your presence there will maintain confidence during the afternoon : after that, we shall see.'

So it was announced that the King would hold a review of the household troops towards midday.

'If the population remains calm . . . ' There, indeed, lay the great anxiety of *all* the leaders. The King, the Princes, the 'liberals', the ministers, the bankers, the generals, and Napoleon himself, who had just sent messages from Auxerre to his Parisian friends asking them to prevent 'any unrest among the populace' . . . What if Caliban should reawaken at last from that sleep imposed by the grape-shot since Prairial, Year III? It was important above all that March 20th should remain a quarrel between people of breeding, and that the lower classes should not begin to meddle in it, as they had done on a certain July 14, 1789. For this one could rely on the marshals. Whether they opted in the end for the fleur-de-lys or the violet was only a question of expediency. But that phantom in the red cap that was prowling about the Tuileries found himself up against a sacred union.

Far more than a disquieting phenomenon occurred on the morning of March 19th. *The cafés re-opened.* Timidly at first, then in unison after nine o'clock, the thousand or so 'coffee houses', where in addition to the new drink from the West Indies one could consume wines, liqueurs and lemonades, but above all where one could foregather and talk politics, broke the ordinance made the previous summer by Beugnot,[1] to please the Duchess d'Angoulême, which prohibited the opening of cafés and restaurants on Sundays and holidays. It had been a topic of general grumbling ever since. Ten thousand copies had been sold of a caricature which played on the fact that the apothecaries, for their part, could open shop at those times. (A hungry man, having presented himself fruitlessly at several restaurants and found them shut, is receiving an enema through the half-open door of an apothecary's; the print was entitled : 'Sunday dinner'.)

[1] At that time Director of the Police.

The insurrection of the coffee-house keepers: that was the first demonstration of the day. There was also a certain swarming activity, unusual among Parisians, who were fond of their lie-in. A lot of people on the streets by ten o'clock. Ten civilians to one soldier round the bivouacs. One rumour that was going around everywhere: 'Is it true that the King is about to leave?' The soldiers were questioned. Discipline was relaxed. The few regular-army men still at their posts laughed and winked: 'The pig is about to decamp, yes!' But a couple of yards away, the lifeguards were still braced up in their gleaming uniform, green dolman, yellow trousers and scarlet pelisse with black fur, under a bearskin with green and red plume and a golden tassel: 'The King is about to place himself at our head and lead us to Essones. And then the Usurper will find out who he's talking to! Keep your ears open: from this evening, you'll be hearing the guns rolling towards Villejuif.'

A little before midday, and in spite of the uncertain weather, the crowd thickened on the boulevards. But it was not ill-natured: just curious. March 19th was a gigantic bit of sightseeing. One did not have the chance every day of witnessing the downfall of a dynasty. And besides, it was not raining too hard.

Somewhat further east, however, matters took an ugly turn. Between Vincennes and Charenton the gatherings were more restless, the shouts louder and more frequent. Here was extreme poverty; cooped up beyond the decent part of Paris, a hundred thousand workers lived without water, without air, and three families to a hovel. The police—by a decision of Napoleon's in 1810—kept them in the locality and registered them like brothel-girls, thanks to the institution of the *livret*, which forbade them to leave their employers without permission. However, there was not a trace of hesitation about them: they had been champing at the bit for a week. Their brothers, their fathers, their friends, their 'native' folk, were in the regiments that had rallied to the Emperor *en masse* since March 5th. And the latter represented their one chance of freeing themselves somehow or other from the dominion of the nobles and curés. For want of being able to carry out the Revolution properly, with backs broken by the corrupt men of Thermidor, one outlet for ambition at least had remained to the people of the suburbs throughout the Consulate and the Empire: the army. The army, by which Lefebvre, Junot and Lannes had become noblemen, and in which everybody could go as far as his worth would take him. For a year that had been at an end.

Now a first procession formed at about eleven o'clock, under the impetus of leaders who have remained unknown, for want of documents, archives, memoirs, among these people who did not know how to write. They waved a tricolour flag. They paraded a bust of Napoleon. And they sang one of the numerous songs that were hatched in the streets during those days:

> Was he fit to reign over France,
> This King, who had the nerve to say,
> As bold as brass among the French:
> 'I owe my crown to Englishmen'?

> From that time on, says all of France,
> Smashing his sceptre to pieces,
> 'If you do have it from England,
> This won't matter!
> This won't matter!'

Near the Charenton ferry they collided with two or three hundred white-bobs, beside themselves with rage in their medieval disguise: the battalion of young volunteers from the Law School. Among them was a future advocate who would make his mark, Odilon Barrot. For a week their sole task had consisted of patrolling the suburbs to keep the savages in awe— and were they now coming to defy them to their faces? It was too much. No reading the Riot Act. No order even, it seems: a confused and panic-stricken volley. Of fear as much as hate. This lasted scarcely five minutes, and each group then retreated: the youngsters appalled by their crime, and the workers accustomed to such attacks. But the latter—who had no arms at all—bore away with them five dead. They would be, in Paris, the only victims of this Revolution.

From Auxerre to Joigny, eighteen miles. The Emperor's carriage covered them at full gallop. The more he had lingered at Auxerre, to make sound preparations for the final leap, the more rapidly this had to be carried out, the first part of it at the very least. The road lent itself to speed: wide, very flat, and edged with fine trees, which gave it the look of a promenade, it had been paved to a large extent under the Empire. Wherever this had not been done as yet, it was still necessary to slow down: certain parts were very muddy at the moment, before turning to sand all summer. To the right, the Yonne often drew near. On every side were rich meadows, in which the snow no longer lay.

A large crowd waited on the waterfront at Joigny, but would be disappointed. Napoleon had given orders to relay outside each town, so as to escape curiosity and to cut down the change of horses. So the postilions were waiting for him a little before the outskirts, near a modest little inn. He stopped there less than an hour, at the end of the morning, for a rapid light meal. This hardly allowed time for the carriages of his suite to catch up with him, and for the town authorities to arrive, all out of breath, to declaim their compliments. One could tell one was in Gamot's department: neither at Joigny nor at Sens were there to be any reservations or false notes. It was to be the pure and simple excitement of two fine towns visited by His Majesty. So the latter went dashing through, not the township, all in villainous streets, steep and winding in tiers over the hillside, but the great stone bridge thrown over the Yonne and the splendid waterfront, 'spacious and very elevated, adorned with a fine cavalry barracks', along the right bank. The inhabitants of Joigny hardly had time to notice 'the happy and festive air' which the procession of five vehicles, reformed in the meantime, derived from the tricolour ribbons that bedecked so abundantly the couriers, the postilions, and even the horses. It was July 14th going by! All this disappeared rapidly after passing through the great wrought-iron gateway, which made entering Joigny, when one came from Paris, like arriving in the courtyard of a chateau.

Louis XVIII no longer hid his fear. Haunted by the images of 1791, he trembled every time he was told of a gathering of ten harmless men in the suburbs. One memory obsessed him: that of the crowd bunched round the carriages of Louis XVI, to prevent him, one April morning, from leaving Saint-Cloud; the Count de Provence had concluded from this that all flight should take place in secret. That was why, three months later, he had succeeded in getting abroad, whereas the royal family had got themselves nabbed at Varennes. And that was why, that morning, Vitrolles had had no difficulty in persuading him to postpone his departure until nightfall. If he had agreed to lend himself to the masquerade of reviewing his Household troops, a thing he abhorred, it was so as to lay a false trail the better. While a few blusterers still besieged him, to get him to lend himself to a heroic resistance, the King had now but one desire, which was becoming an obsession: to depart in peace.

For this one prime precaution was necessary: to rid himself of the remnant of the French army that was still stationed in Paris. Since Ney's defection, every soldier was an armed stranger in the eyes of the Court. There was no longer any common language with these people. What if they were to proceed all of a sudden to take the King prisoner, in order to offer him to Bonaparte as an accession present? The rumours that were circulating in the city were so little reassuring that Louis XVIII sent for Macdonald again before midday, enjoining him once more 'to come without uniform, so as to be neither recognized nor noticed'. However, the continual bungling of the King's people was beginning to betray the secret of the flight. On arriving at the Chateau, Macdonald perceived

'the royal carriages horsed and ready, an enormous crowd milling round them, eager to know what was being planned, officers coming and going, saddled horses loaded with portmanteaux; everything indicated the idea of departure, although the carriages were arranged as for an ordinary outing. I mingled with the crowd and approached some of the groups; no unseemly words, but various opinions concerning the matters of the moment, on the effect of the King's presence before the troops, on the ridiculous idea of some fifty old men armed with muskets and halberds, the majority in general-officer's uniform and decorated with various orders on top of their coats, marching two by two and coming to offer their services. I must admit that anything like a martial air was missing and this set the crowd laughing, for the crowd always finds the amusing side of the most serious matters.'

M. de Gobineau, although he took part, himself admitted to his children that it was a matter of

'the most ridiculous and most non-military corps you could possibly conceive. Imagine old men, but also boys, rigged out in uniforms with epaulettes of every rank, hardly able to carry their knapsacks, rifles, and cartridge-pouches, and by an anomaly which the Restoration had hastened to revive, a guard with a colonel's epaulettes, led by a corporal with the epaulettes of a second-lieutenant!'

For his part, M. de Marsilly was not much more optimistic among the Hundred Swiss:

'Third guard. A day of sorrow and anguish. Rainy weather. The King was at mass. How fine the music was! Is this the last time I shall hear it? The King appeared on the balcony. What shouts of *"Vive le Roi!"* What signs of respect and affection! . . . But these are signs only. The army is abandoning the King. This good King has been deceived up to the last moment. At four o'clock, he went to review some combat units of his Household troops on the Champs-Élysées. During that time, his trunks were packed and vehicles were loaded. All the aides-de-camp to Monsieur and Monseigneur the Duke de Berry were ready to leave. *It was only at this moment that I opened my eyes.*[1] I thought the company was going to send a single detachment to fight and that I would remain with a picket by the King. I retired to my guard unit, given up to the most poignant grief.'

[1] In the same way as the majority of the poor 'knights of the dagger', 1815 version, who for a week had come flocking in from everywhere to prepare for a fresh August 10th, forgetting that before, on August 10th, the King had betrayed those loyal to him at the last minute by taking refuge in the Assembly without telling them.

During this time the King held his review . . . but did he go to the Champ-de-Mars, as had been announced, or to the Champs-Élysées, as M. de Marsilly has said?

To the Champs-Élysées. And for a not very glorious exhibition.

Macdonald had calmed him: 'The troops have obeyed and left Paris. But with not very reassuring intentions, it is true. In the end, I got rid of them as I could by sending them to Villejuif, Vincennes, Saint-Denis, how do I know? Your Majesty no longer has any but loyal men about him.'

So Louis XVIII had left for the Champ-de-Mars in his barouche, surrounded by a glittering staff, in which rode some of the most illustrious cavaliers of the Empire: Berthier, Marmont, Lauriston . . . But, Macdonald continues:

'it was scarcely half an hour after the King had left when I saw him coming back. Surprised at such a prompt return, I went up to the Chateau. The crowd was growing every moment; *the King was worried about it*; I told him that, from what I had seen and heard, there was nothing in it but a very natural curiosity; besides, it was Sunday, and the day was sufficiently fine to bring a lot of people to the Tuileries garden.'

So it was fear of the crowd that had made the King turn back when scarcely out of his palace. In order to disguise it, he had found a good excuse: he met some of the lifeguards crossing the Champs-Élysées, having come from the left bank. Misinterpreted, Macdonald's warning directing them to hold themselves ready to reach Saint-Denis had also provoked the departure of the King's household. Marmont fulminated, without hiding his dislike of Macdonald, and ordered a return to the Champ-de-Mars. Advantage was taken of this to have the detachments, which had just turned about and were completely in the dark, file past Louis XVIII. A few damp cheers hailed the enormous blue mass in the barouche, the white wig, and the still-slender hand that was indolently raised. And the crowd had swelled like a sea about this parade. What a sudden attraction for the bowls-players of the Champs-Élysées! Louis XVIII, hardly hoisted back to his study, asked Macdonald anxiously:

'How do you expect me to leave quietly just now?'

'The crowd will gather all the time your carriages are standing in the courtyard, Sire. Send them away openly, empty. Everyone will think you are cancelling the departure. The majority of the curious will go away. And you will be able to recall the carriages during the night, when everybody has dispersed.'

And so it was done. Macdonald was right: after five in the evening there were none but insignificant groups in the approaches to the Palace. Nothing in the world prevented the Parisian from dining early on Sunday.

＊

Now at the same hour, and sixty miles from there, Napoleon too was worried and did not conceal the fact, and for the same reasons as the King. The sovereign who was collapsing and the one who was returning both feared a rising in Paris more than anything, and it mattered little in the eyes of the latter that the former would be its victim. This was poor consolation. The evidence has been provided by Napoleon himself, who was to declare in his memoirs that he had refused to stop at Sens and had given the worthy people a pure lie by way of explanation:

'The Emperor went through Sens in the midst of a huge crowd, who begged him to stop for a few hours. He told them: "The advance-posts have come to blows. There is not a moment to lose to prevent blood from flowing, and my presence alone can rally everybody."'

Confound it! There was the Mayor of Sens, M. de Laurencin, completely stunned, hat in hand at the door of the carriage, while they were relaying in haste by the side of the street, magnificent and straight as a die, which crossed the town like the stroke of a sword. So there was a revolution in Paris? And where were the advance-posts fighting? Should ambulances be prepared? Since that morning, Napoleon had sent a further three emissaries to his friends hiding in Paris to order them to be prudent, and above all that the streets should not stir on any account. Between the Emperor and the King everything took place as though a third thief were suddenly thinking of inter-

vening: the people. And all those who were afraid of them, all
the 'proprietors' enriched by the Revolution of '89, but
threatened by that of '93, began to take charge of the dynastic
quarrel in order to settle it among themselves, before 1815
should really become a new revolution, directed this time against
Money. The ideal would be an almost official transfer of power:
Louis XVIII disappearing by one door of the Tuileries while
Napoleon came in by the other . . . So the former would be held
back until nightfall, and the latter should come on the scene in
the morning if possible. Above all, they would try to avoid that
vacuum at the summit which had previously frightened La
Fayette during the flight of Louis XVI, that vacuum into which
Bill Bloggs might slip, wearing a Phrygian cap.

In fact, the people of Paris made no real move. Since the morning, only the fusillade at Charenton had been reported, and the
general opening of the cafés. The considerable crowd that surrounded the King at that moment was one from the 'good'
quarters, rather sympathetic towards his misfortune and above
all curious. But the 'haves' were haunted by the phantoms that
had dusted down the salons of the Tuileries that night. It was
from the same circle, the same salons, that Louis XVIII and
Napoleon, since the day before, had received the same alarmist
rumours.

So Napoleon's carriage went dashing past Sens cathedral and
the town hall without his giving them a glance. And he left
behind him a proud but slightly disappointed city, whose
ancient walls 'gave it a Gothic and not very gracious air'. It was
five in the evening. The sun was already going down and peep-
ing through a tight pack of large white clouds.

The attention of Paris was not wholly centred on the Tuileries.
People of quality went in large numbers to regale themselves,
at Saint-Sulpice, with the last Lenten lecture by the Abbé
Freyssinous. A worldly chronicler, somewhat Voltairean in
spirit, was present at that meeting-point of the world of piety:

'The vast precincts of Saint-Sulpice were too confined to contain the crowd. One can have no idea of the eagerness of the

faithful. The curious had been besieging the doors of the church since midday, and the adjacent streets were full of the most glittering equipages. It was only with the greatest difficulty that I managed to secure a place among the audience. It is true, I was not known to any of the Swiss . . . To be observed in the assembly were a large number of women, sparkling with elegance and finery. It could be ascertained, near me, that the majority of them had been at the Opera the day before yesterday. The most lively and most sustained attention clung to every part of this discourse, in which the speaker treated of the existence of God. He concealed not one of the most insidious arguments for atheism, and annihilated them all successively. Sophists too often urge against the existence of the divinity the long horrors of the Revolution. M. Freyssinous turned this argument against its authors, by considering the Revolution as a necessary punishment merited by the disorders of the century and the corruption of the peoples. The individual injustices that it produced did not, according to him, in any way impair divine justice, which only encompassed generalities.'

Here was something to rejoice his audience, in spite of the difficulties of the hour. When the worthy ecclesiastic descended from the pulpit, from which he had sent forth, rolling out under the vault, 'that voice like a violoncello, indeed a double-bass, housed by a miracle in a slender reed', he too had every reason to be satisfied. The beautiful women, whose flood of yellow and green, the colour of the coats in fashion, suddenly inundated the parvis of Saint-Sulpice (while the choristers began to sing Vespers; it was customary to leave immediately after the sermon), no longer knew which sovereign would be lodged the next day on the other side of the Seine. Some said prayers for the Bourbon, others for Bonaparte. But what matter, the Abbé would reascend the pulpit the following Sunday to denounce the horror of the Revolution. He refrained from pronouncing for or against Napoleon. More adroit than provincial priests, the Paris clergy were quite ready to intone the *Domine, salvum fac imperatorem* again, provided they were left to control consciences.

✳

226

When evening fell, at the Tuileries, it was ruination. 'One needs to have been present during those last moments to understand the peculiarity of that situation in which, quite alive still, one knew one might be dead the next day', observed Vitrolles, who had returned from Blacas' house, where the favourite, showing foresight at last, had just paid out a hundred thousand francs[1] to each of the ministers prepared to follow the King. The whole of the afternoon had been spent 'in negotiations, personal arrangements, and the news which we were continually receiving of the approach of the enemy, who had got too close for us not to be informed of it every few minutes'. However, the magnificent style of the palace went on as though nothing had changed: the servants laid a 'cover' for thirty people in a room on the ground floor, in honour of the Spanish ambassador, who was to be 'entertained in the King's name' by his chief steward. On the first, just above the Baccarat crystal, the fine porcelain and damask cloths, the merry-go-round of panic-stricken courtiers quickened its course round the King, who had regained an Olympian calm the moment the crowd had more or less dispersed.

What was biting Macdonald suddenly? The man who the previous day had been the very first to recommend a northerly direction suggested, quite without thinking, a desperate adventure: 'Let the Hundred Swiss dress up as soldiers of the line. Disguised in this way, let them advance towards the Emperor as some detachment or other that has rallied! Let them surround him and take him prisoner, or even kill him on the spot . . .'

Well, well, Duke of Taranto! Could he be jealous of Marmont's frenzies? Had he been needled by Benjamin Constant's article, which everybody had been reading avidly since midday? Or, by proposing something that would obviously be rejected, did he simply want to do an easy bit of overbidding? Sensible for once, and rendered lucid by the disintegration of his 'army', it was the Duke de Berry who observed:

'How do you think our old men will get to Bonaparte unnoticed? Would you have them all massacred?'

At seven in the evening the King gave final orders:

[1] About 300,000 New Francs [about £25,000].

227

'I see that all is over. We shall not engage in useless resistance. I have decided to leave. Let us try to lead our partisans away into Flanders and to have ourselves followed by the regiments that left this morning.'

Upon this, Berry put a significant question: since the day before these people had been reliving 'the flight to Varennes' minute by minute:

'And what if the National Guard of Paris, on duty at the Château tonight, should resist the King's departure, as occurred in 1791? Should I have to rout them and would the noblemen and I have to pass over their bodies?'

'*Monsieur mon neveu,*' the King protested weakly, 'we must not alienate the Parisians from us for ever!'

Macdonald, in a vein of decidedly odd ideas, suggested that the carriages wait outside Paris, that the King be taken out clandestinely in a sedan-chair, and then in a coupé. This enabled Berry to relax the atmosphere with a sally that released uncontrollable nervous laughter, in which Louis XVIII did not disdain to join:

'Where the devil do you think we can find a chair large enough and two men strong enough to carry the King?'

So they were to leave, without concealment, in the large berlins from the royal stables, already loaded with baggage, towards midnight. The Duke de Berry was to accompany the King to Saint-Denis and Macdonald, at Villejuif, was to attempt to recover what he could of the regular troops. But till then, mum was the word! The greater the number of people to suspect a departure, the fewer they had to be who knew its precise hour.

'It was obvious that a bolt was being contemplated,' wrote Chateaubriand, who met Richelieu on the Champs-Élysées, where the two of them were wandering about during the afternoon in search of news, like any other subscriber to the *Moniteur.*

'We are being deceived, my friend,' said the Duke. 'I am mounting guard here, because I don't intend to wait all alone for the Emperor at the Tuileries.'

There were in fact, that evening, nearly a hundred important people who had burnt their boats in 1814, and believed them-

selves rightly or wrongly in grave danger. Louis XVIII was not
to send word to a single one of them.

✳

It was night when Napoleon arrived at Pont-sur-Yonne and
crossed the river there once more. It was a very small town, ill-
built and ill-provided with streets, of 1,200 inhabitants, packed
tight round a bulging church. But, just opposite the bridge, the
relaying of the post was made at the Auberge de l'Écu, where a
Pantagruelian meal had already been kept hot since midday.
Exhausted by this stage of forty-five miles, the Emperor agreed
to stop for a few hours, to take refreshment, to wait for the other
vehicles, and to receive intelligence from Montereau and Fontainebleau. He was to leave again in the middle of the night.

This was the scene of an obscure episode. Throughout the
day, the travellers had been working their way up the considerable traffic on the river, of boats of every calibre, which were
going down the Yonne carrying the soldiers loaded at Auxerre.
Several times, Napoleon had been impatient at their slowness
and had even put his head out of the window to shout at the
boatmen, who could do no more; this impatience, moreover, was
second nature with him. He had shown it during all his campaigns. His familiars took hardly any notice of it.

But is it true that on arriving at Pont-sur-Yonne the Emperor
really let fly at the master watermen, who had moored their
boats in order to spend the night there, not wishing to take any
chances without light on a river in spate, with overloaded boats?
It is possible. Nothing proves it.

'Are you afraid of getting wet?' he is even supposed to have
asked them, 'jokingly' according to his partisans, 'cruelly'
according to the royalists. Did he go further? Did he formally
order them to resume nocturnal navigation, before he entered
the inn or when he left it again? Sailors, even fresh-water ones,
had always exasperated him, and he had sacrificed a certain
number of them to his whims in the roads of Boulogne and
Anvers. The fact remains that he was absent at the moment of
the tragedy, and was to be 'keenly affected', according to
Marchand, when he learned of it.

The soldiers of the 76th of the Line, whether they had heard

his reproaches, or whether they wanted to show their enthusiasm when he passed, begged the watermen and then forced
them to set off again. Thick clouds prevented the first quarter of
the moon from giving even a feeble glimmer. From every boat
that cast off rose the fatidical *'Vive l'Empereur!'* So nobody paid
any particular attention to one of them. It was only the next
day, at dawn, that it would be remembered that one of those
outcries had been of 'an almost superhuman loudness and had
been accompanied by the sound of a mighty crack.' At that
moment, a large quantity of debris was recognized floating on
the current: the wreckage of a boat that had been dashed to
pieces against an arch of the bridge. Thirty-three brave men of
the 76th of the Line would be missing from roll-call for ever.

After supper on Sunday, Mme de Chateaubriand sent a servant to the Carrousel with orders not to come back until he
was sure of the King's flight. At midnight, the rogue still not
having returned, M. de Chateaubriand went to bed.

More prudent, Richelieu went to the Tuileries himself, where
the musketeers, confined to quarters with their horses saddled
and bridled, had been waiting since five o'clock for orders that
still had not come. At nine o'clock, Rochechouart saw the Duke
return 'half in anger and half in grief':

'There is not a moment to lose, *cher ami.* Let us mount horse
and be off. Would you believe it, the King, with whom I spoke
for half an hour, said not one word to me of his intentions, nor
of his decision. He apparently did not have sufficient confidence
in me for that, and I should have been caught, as everybody
probably will be tomorrow[1] on hearing of his departure from
Paris, if the Prince de Poix had not spoken these words in my ear
just now: "The King is leaving in an hour and retiring to
Lille".'

They both finished their preparations at once.

'In our haste to mount horse, the Duke de Richelieu, who had
bought a leather belt that morning in which to place his 10,000

---

[1] Yet Richelieu was first gentleman of the Bedchamber!

gold francs,[1] put the belt on the wrong way, that is to say, the openings of the little pockets which held the pieces of gold were placed at the bottom instead of at the top, so that the movement of the horse in trotting shook out a large number of these pieces, a few of which were lost, but the rest lodged in his pants, his trousers and even his boots; it was only on stopping at Beauvais, the following morning, that he could restore everything to its place, but one can readily imagine in what a state of abrasion and bruising the poor Duke's thighs and legs must have been.'

✳

When Macdonald returned to the Palace towards nine o'clock, he found, as he had foreseen, the customary peace in the almost deserted gardens. The apartments, on the other hand, were in distraction: Bedlam had broken loose and everybody was floundering in uncertainty and a panic all the greater since Napoleon was thought to be very near. So many lies had been told in connection with him (*La Quotidienne* that morning had still been announcing the recapture of Lyons), that it would have been no surprise to learn that he was at the gates of Paris, whereas he was still at Pont-sur-Yonne.

The Marshal had great difficulty in crossing the salons to reach the main study. At every step, courtiers plucked at him and plied him with questions. The King put in a majestic appearance and played his Louis XVI (still the same imitation of June 20, 1791), talking of this and that with the greatest apparent placidity. He finally withdrew to his private study and took leave of the Duke of Taranto, informing him that he was leaving in an hour. He pressed his hand 'affectionately':

'*Au revoir, mon cher maréchal*, I shall not forget either your zeal or your devotion.'

✳

At the same moment, Vitrolles was prey to a veritable fit of hysteria in an adjoining room. The Baron had packed his bags during the afternoon and ordered his carriage so as to follow the King, but he had been intercepted by Monsieur. Since his return

[1] 30,000 New Francs [about £2,500].

from Lyons, struck by a curious apathy, the Prince, so restless in quiet times, was floating like a cork on the waves.

'We were speaking of you, Vitrolles, and I told the Chancellor that I should consider it very fitting if the King were to send you to the Midi. If anyone can do anything there, it is certainly you.'

The Midi: that meant Bordeaux, where the Duchess d'Angoulême was still holding on, Toulouse and Nîmes, where her husband was raising an army 'against Napoleon's rear'. To land down there as royal proconsul involved a good chance of getting oneself shot, but what a slice of luck for the wounded vanity of the poor hatcher of schemes that were always mocked!

But all evening Vitrolles had been waiting in vain for express orders from the King, without which it was inconceivable that he should go. At first, he had been sent word, by Blacas, 'that he could do as he wished . . . ' Vitrolles had stamped his foot at this:

'With a reply like that, there is nothing to be done. One doesn't give oneself such a mission, when one is not called upon to! The King's reply drives me to despair, not so far as it concerns me personally, but as a fresh example of his disinterest and his inability to take a decision!'

Whereupon, he took it into his head to draw Monsieur into the adventure with him. He even dared exclaim in his presence:

'I wish so many devoted men were not being abandoned by the very Princes to whom they have devoted themselves! In short, I wish that if we must go down, it could be in blood rather than mud . . . '

And he said this to the man who, twenty years earlier, had sent the leaders of the Vendée to the slaughter-house, to the one who had been awaited for more than a year every morning on the cliffs, and of whom Cadoudal had ended by saying: 'Oh, the coward! the coward! . . . '

Highly embarrassed, Monsieur was saved by the irruption of the Duke de Maillé:

'The King is asking for M. de Vitrolles immediately.'

It was after 11.30 when Vitrolles found the King 'in the calm and routine of his everyday life. Between the first two fingers of his hand he held a little letter, like a visiting card.'

Fossard

'You will leave for Bordeaux, for Toulouse. You will do there whatever you judge to be necessary in my service. You will deliver this letter to my niece. You will tell her to hold Bordeaux for as long as she can. And when she can do no more, she is to act like me . . .'

'The allocution was no more heroic than that.'[1]

Vitrolles bowed, pointed out that it might at least have been possible to inform him twenty-four hours earlier, that he would, in that event, have arranged with the ministers to receive instructions . . . And he craved at least a mission in due and proper form, some powers! . . .

'Powers? You have no need of them. You are my minister: you have full powers. Besides, the presence of my nephew and niece will give you authority.'

'After these words, the King held out his hand to me, which I kissed, more moved for sure than he was himself.'

Are we already at March 20th, or still at the 19th? For the two episodes that follow witnesses are unable to give an exact timetable. In the darkest hour of the night, Louis XVIII abandoned Paris and Napoleon left Pont-sur-Yonne. Low clouds, intense darkness, sudden squalls of soft rain: tomorrow was the equinox. In Paris, as on the banks of the Yonne, everything took place by torchlight, among men already tired by the long previous day and who on the next would be reeling with exhaustion.

So, round about midnight the Emperor's carriages left the Auberge de l'Écu and took the road to Fossard. There Napoleon caught sight of confused shadows enveloped in the night, who were waiting for him by the side of the road, 'like a resurrection of men and horses'. These were the dragoons of the 'King's Regiment'. He alighted, 'saluted them with that military gravity that became him so well', and questioned them:

'But where are your officers?'

No officers! These had elected to follow the King while the troops had preferred to rally to the Emperor without them. That

[1] It is impossible, in *all* the memoirs of Louis XVIII's familiars, to find a sentiment other than hatred and contempt with regard to their King.

233

same night, at Essonnes, the 3rd Hussars adopted a different solution; their Colonel, the son of Marshal Moncey, was fond of Napoleon 'but believed it was his duty to flee'. So he set off towards Saint-Denis, exhorting his men to follow him. The latter idolized Napoleon, but believed it was their duty to obey their Colonel, whom they worshipped. And this they did, yelling '*Vive l'Empereur!*' Such was the kind of regular soldier still available to the King.

At Fossard[1] the Emperor decided to make the detour through Fontainebleau, rather than advance on Melun, where he believed the Duke de Berry to be, at the head of an army whose importance he was still overestimating. He relied on the brave Colonel Galbois' lancers to cover his right by holding the bridge at Montereau. The aim of his move was to avoid an encounter with the royalist forces and to slip into Paris 'through the half-open door'. Besides, near at hand, in the heart of the forest, was the château of his death-throes the previous year, which was about to become the château of his incredible revenge. How could Napoleon resist the temptation? To Fontainebleau! But all about him were filled with dismay: another fifteen miles of roads to cover without taking off one's boots? And were they about to plunge into the forest in the middle of the night, when there was a Chouan, perhaps, behind every tree-trunk?

Napoleon shrugged his shoulders.

'We shall be stopping for a couple of hours at Moret, time to receive intelligence. Those who want will be able to sleep there.'

At the top of the Château des Tuileries, the white flag no longer flew on the clock-house. The official explanation: a gust of wind had carried it away during the evening, and it was considered no use hoisting a new one. It is more probable that no one wanted to leave the trophy for Napoleon. All the windows of the Palace were lit up. But nobody, or hardly anybody, was standing about in the vicinity. The Parisians had not stayed for the wake.

Midnight, undoubtedly. A grinding of iron gates. Brief orders to the guards. A dozen carriages entered the courtyard of the

[1] See the map.

234

Tuileries. Two of them took up a position by the vestibule to the state staircase. A brisk movement then took place: it was the end. All those in the precincts who had been waiting, weeping, praying and watching since the morning came hurrying to witness the incredible: France, your Monarchy is stealing away. It was not possible! It was not possible! Why, less than a year had passed since the triumphal return, Paris hung with white, Cossacks and Uhlans presenting arms to the King, smiling paternally in his carriage. Twenty nightmare years had vanished and everything had resumed its place: the people in their gutter, the soldiers in their barracks, the squire in his churchwarden's pew, and a cipher on the throne. It had taken only eight months of accumulated errors of judgment, a sort of digest of all the follies of the *ancien régime*, to arrive at this night worthy of *Macbeth* or *King Lear*.

An invisible signal ran through the whole Château. The National Guards on duty abandoned their posts and came to mingle in the vestibule with the courtiers, the attendants and the lifeguards. The two or three hundred loyal to the last ranged themselves on the steps of the grand staircase, in the hall and around the carriages. They were silent. They spoke in low tones. Oppression was general. A sort of refusal and bewilderment was on every face. A feast of bags under the eyes and wrinkles, shown up by the wavering lamps. Three hundred years of uniforms were at the tryst. For a few unbearable minutes, each of those men felt his life falling apart. Not one witness allows the least hope of revenge to penetrate his account. They knew nevertheless that Europe was arming, but not one of them really dared have any presentiment of Waterloo. They honestly felt they were dying.

At last the doors opened to the Hall of the Marshals. First came four lackeys bearing wax torches, then the ushers, a herald of arms in Merovingian style, two or three dignitaries, and finally Louis XVIII, supported by Blacas and Duras, or rather almost carried by them. His gout had grown much worse during the past month. He could scarcely walk and was concentrating his efforts on a dignified ascent into the carriage. He had about a dozen yards to cover, and that was to be his torment: nothing upset him more than emotion. So he had directed that the curious were to be dispersed. But no one obeyed him any more. A confused murmur rose from the crowd. Everyone took off their hats. Some fell to their knees. A few shouts of 'Vive le Roi!', but above all a lot of stifled sobs, and this cry from an old man: 'He wears a crown of thorns!'

In fact, the King had on a three-cornered hat of hardened calf and was warmly wrapped in a large cloak. Hue, his valet de chambre, had smothered him in a large number of underpants and leather waistcoats so that he should not take cold: it was his first journey by night for seven years, he who was usually in bed every evening by nine o'clock! A few worshippers crawled up to him on their knees and tried to kiss his garments. He reproached Blacas:

'I knew this would happen! I didn't want to see them! I should have been spared this emotion . . .'

He really had to raise his voice, to improvise a few words. So he turned that noble and impassive face to the public, which with the Bourbons was the great-actor's tradition in all great crises. To be a prince, before all, was to master oneself. The fine deep voice rose and went out to the far corners of the courtyard: 'My children! . . . Your attachment touches me. But I have need of strength . . . In the name of mercy, spare me! Go back to your families . . . I shall see you again before long.'

Beneath his elephantine feet they unfolded the 'footboard with six treads', which enabled him to climb into the carriage without too much difficulty, with Monsieur, Berthier in full-dress uniform, who was biting his nails 'and bore death on his face',[1] and the eternal Blacas. The Duke de Berry caracoled at the door. A strong group of lifeguards rode behind. And the carriages moved off heavily towards Saint-Denis, while the servants hastily went back in to blow out the lamps. Closing time!

Such was the disappearance to fresh exile of Louis XVIII, King of France and Navarre, ex-Count of Provence, the assassin of Favras, the persistent calumniator of Marie-Antoinette, the patient detractor of his brother Louis XVI, the pretender maintained by the courts of Europe for fifteen years in war against France, 'the fat Pig'. In seeing him go, nobody, even among those

[1] He was to throw himself from a window in Bamberg, Bavaria, in three months.

who were weeping, doubted that he was disappearing along with history, and that this was justice. M. de Marsilly concluded:

'At about one o'clock, M. le duc de Mortemart ordered me to assemble the guard and lead them to the house. The company (of Hundred Swiss) was already assembled and prepared to leave. M. le Duc enjoined me to save the four big drums. He said good-bye to me, as also to my comrades. I was the last to leave the Château, where there were still some tired lifeguards who were asleep and some old corporals who did not know whom to join. I told them the route which the troops had taken by the Saint-Denis road.'

Two o'clock in the morning. The little town of Moret was not sleeping well. That afternoon, it had received two regiments one after the other, the 14th Hussars and the 13th Dragoons, who bivouacked on the spot and threw out what were called 'outpost pickets', that is to say, cavalry patrols radiating from there out into Fontainebleau Forest. Others kept watch nearby on the old Roman bridge over the Loing, still shattered by the mines of 1814, with one arch spanned by a footway only. Here was the ancient frontier between the 'Estates of France' and those of the Dukes of Burgundy, and the transition now from the department of the Yonne into Seine-et-Marne.

Orders were so strict, because of the threat of a surprise royalist attack, that not one soldier was billeted with the inhabitants; instead they were lodged in the inns or public buildings.

All day long, and up to midnight, the inhabitants and soldiers had been waiting for 'Père la Violette'. The Mayor and his municipal council had stayed permanently in the town hall bedecked in tricolour. A fine speech had been prepared, and as it was Sunday, God how they had drunk! So much that they could take no more, and everyone went to bed when rumour had it that Napoleon was stopping at Pont-sur-Yonne. As a precaution, the civic dignitaries remained at the town hall, where in no time at all they were snoring in their armchairs. So it was minus trumpet and drum, and taking everybody by surprise, that the Emperor came to rest at Moret. He stopped before the posting-house, the relay 'La Belle Image', and irrupted there 'like a cannon-ball'. Some citizens, running up in haste, informed him that the Mayor and councillors were waiting for him opposite, at the town hall:

'Eh bien! Let them sleep to their heart's content! That suits me!'

One can understand it! The landlady was seventeen, with a ravishing smile, and did the honours of the house with the authority of a little queen. This was Mme Clément, the Mayor's own wife, who had just brought her notary husband by way of dowry the inn which she held from her father. In no way intimidated, she noticed that the Emperor 'wore an old cloak, with a leather waistcoat containing a large pocket full of snuff'. She thought he was disguising himself in this way to escape assassins but soon saw, when he opened his coat, the famous red-white-and-green uniform that had made Europe tremble.

Napoleon wanted to rest for a few moments. He was conducted up a little stairway to a room on the first floor lovingly adorned for him. On the mantelshelf Mme Clément had placed the most beautiful object in her house: a vase of fine porcelain. The Emperor refused the bed, well-warmed though it was, and threw himself into an armchair. He was hardly to close an eye: he was to be disturbed a score of times in two hours, for he demanded to see for himself all the couriers arriving from Paris. Not to mention the hubbub occasioned by Drouot, who surprised an urchin of ten with his eye glued to the keyhole; the great artilleryman did not miss to speed the unwary boy to the foot of the stairs with a kick. Meanwhile, the population had aroused itself, the soldiers who had hurried along presented arms, and a veritable torchlight tattoo was held round the Emperor and his suite, amid delirious cheering, when he went on his way again at four o'clock, having learned that his advance guard was in possession of Fontainebleau Château, and that the road was clear up to there.

He scarcely bowed or waved 'and proved rather ungracious', still preoccupied by two contradictory anxieties: he thought Louis XVIII was lying low in Paris, and he still dreaded a popular rising.

Mme Clément, so very young, went back upstairs to the room

hallowed by the idol, and her petrified parents then heard her emit an historic exclamation:

'Oh! The duffer!'[1]

A dozen people rushed into the room and verified that the epithet really had been applied to the Emperor, but that Mme Clément had certain extenuating circumstances for her *lèse-majesté*: her porcelain vase, taken down from the mantelshelf, stood by the bed, but it was no longer empty. Napoleon had put it to very personal use.

From midnight to dawn there began for the Royal Household the horror of desolation. In the collapse, the King, the ministers, the Princes had literally vanished. A general rendezvous had been vaguely indicated (by whom?) 'outside the Étoile gate'— that is to say, where the fields began. It was thereabouts that the 'four red companies' were supposed to meet. Richelieu and Rochechouart went there at all events, 'but a great disappointment awaited us there, for the number of officers and corporals or sergeants exceeded by far that of simple guardsmen, the majority of whom had returned to their homes, or even to quarters, crossing the streets of Paris by night.' Rochechouart did not consider his presence indispensible among the depleted ranks of his brigade. Having only seven or eight musketeers under his orders, he handed over command of them . . . to three officers and four N.C.O.s. 'I continued on my way with the Duke de Richelieu, following the road which the King had taken as far as Beauvais, where we arrived all at one stretch, at about seven o'clock in the morning, on March 20th.'

Poor M. de Gobineau, for his part, followed the movement:

'At about eight o'clock in the evening, Count Jules (de Polignac) said to me: "Are your preparations all made? We are leaving tonight." "For where?" I said to him. "Wherever Providence shall lead us; the King is leaving for Lille, and beyond that

[1] The historian must be forgiven: he can only set down the facts avouched by M. Déborde de Montcorin in the *Études napoléoniennes* of 1923. The utensil was to be religiously preserved from mother to daughter in the Clément family, but there are still plenty of gaps in history: it is impossible for us to know the use that was made of its contents.

I know nothing." Such was his reply. At ten o'clock in the evening, I was at the Tuileries with my modest accoutrements. We resorted to the Champs-Élysées, where we found the Royal Household, and then set off for Saint-Denis, leaving by the Maillot Gate and taking the road of the Revolt.[1] Along the way, I learned that Louis XVIII had left two hours before us. That night march was deplorable, through the confusion that reigned in every corps.'

✳

Chateaubriand was asleep, or at least so he claims, when a messenger from Chancellor Dambray came to drag him from his bed. It was M. Clausel de Coussergues, who told him of the King's departure.

'The Chancellor, knowing I was in danger, violated the secrecy for me, and sent me 12,000 francs,[2] recoverable from my salary as minister to Sweden.[3]

'I obstinately decided to stay on, not wanting to leave Paris until I were physically sure of the royal removal. The servant sent to reconnoitre came back: he had seen the carriages of the Court file past. Mme de Chateaubriand thrust me into her carriage, on March 20th, at four o'clock in the morning. I was in such an access of rage that I had no idea where I was going, or what I was doing.

'We left by the Saint-Martin gate. At dawn, I saw some crows descend peacefully from the elms along the highway in which they had spent the night, to take their first meal in the fields, without a care for Louis XVIII and Napoleon: they were not obliged to leave their country, not they, and thanks to their wings, they laughed at the bad road over which I was jolting. Old friends of Combourg! we resembled each other more when of old, at break of day, we broke our fast on blackberries in our thickets of Brittany!

[1] The direct route from Saint-Germain to Saint-Denis, so called after a rising in 1750.
[2] About 40,000 New Francs [about £3,300].
[3] Appointed the King's ambassador in Stockholm, whereas he had expected so much more, Chateaubriand had carefully refrained from actually going to take up that post, having been far too anxious to intrigue at Court.

'The road was full of holes, the weather rainy, Mme de Chateaubriand unwell; she kept looking through the little window of the carriage every minute to see if we were being followed.'

A text that offers the advantage, rare, alas! coming from this great man, of being at once splendid and sincere. Everything really did happen in this way that night for François-René. Borne along in the muddy ebb of the Monarchy in rout, there was this unnoticed barouche in which a woman, still young, still pretty, but with eyes wild from constant disappointment, overwhelmed with her bitter contempt a man choking with rage. 'Why did I come at a period in which I was so badly situated? Why was I a royalist against my instinct at a time when a miserable breed at Court could neither hear nor understand me? Why was I thrown among this crew of mediocrities who took me for a scatterbrain when I spoke of courage, and for a revolutionary when I spoke of liberty?'

At Villejuif, Macdonald wandered from barracks to town hall in search of a general staff that had already dispersed. He received again the same impressions as at Lyons ten days earlier, but worse: of soldiers already wearing tricolour cockades in their caps, of officers who showed him respect but did not hide their hesitation. There was no longer anything solid between Paris and the Emperor's army. At Lyons, Macdonald had argued, waxed indignant, and agitated almost to the end. At Villejuif, gloomy, he went slowly, silently, at the pace of his horse, along the muddy streets, accompanied by Generals Haxo and Ruty, in search of a single detachment, a single battalion, that might still shout 'Vive le Roi!' that night. A leader in quest of men, too dignified to beg. Were these the troops from Paris, which Maison swore could still be relied upon? Maison himself had disappeared. One of his aides-de-camp ended by emerging from the night, soaked to the skin, to hand Macdonald a letter from the Governor of the capital. 'I will join you at Saint-Denis' . . . and without troops, he too.

Saint-Denis let it be then! His friends pulled Macdonald by the bridle :

'The head of a Bonapartist column is approaching Villejuif . . . ' The little group of vanquished men set off again for Bicêtre and were to cross Paris without being recognized.

❋

The Mameluke Saint-Denis was still to remember it twenty years later as though he were there : 'The Emperor set out (from Moret) for Fontainebleau, where he arrived at about four o'clock. By the sides of the road, through the darkness, grenadiers and light infantry of the Guard could be seen, who hastened their step by running, like tired men. Shadows, one might have said. If they did not arrive at the Château at the same time as the Emperor, they reached it quarter of an hour after.'

Nearly a hundred cavalrymen, armed to the teeth, accompanied Napoleon's carriage at that moment, so sharp was the fear of an attempt on his life. The town was asleep, but the Château pierced the night with a hundred lighted windows, as in a fairy-tale. Then came the tumultuous entry into the huge square of the Cheval Blanc courtyard, scene of the tearful farewells of April 20th, through the great new iron gateway. Some officers and all the little staff of the Palace yelled their joy. But everyone noticed the Emperor's exhaustion, as he slowly climbed the steps of the famous horseshoe stairway, leaning on Bertrand's arm. He went to his room at once, where a fine log-fire was burning. The concierge, one of his former servants, in tears, pointed out that he had managed to preserve the crowned Ns, still carved in the gilded wood of the bed. Napoleon congratulated him, had his boots pulled off, and lay down at last, half-dressed. He wanted to wait for the various bodies of troops to whom he had designated Fontainebleau as the place of general rendezvous.

❋

And the sun rose on March 20, 1815, at 5.59, an hour after Napoleon had gone to bed. The temperature was 8·2° and a thick mist enveloped the full-grown trees of Fontainebleau, in which a whole population of birds hailed the spring day. It was the moment chosen at Tréguier, a little Breton town, by four ex-sailors, one of whom was called Philibert Renan, to climb briskly up the steeple of the cathedral and attach an enormous tricolour flag. Not far from there, the National Guard of Saint-Brieuc took up arms for the Emperor. At Orléans the soldiers revolted in the night and drove out General Dupont. At Épernay the whole town awoke at the sound of the tocsin: the troops, led away by their regular commander, General Rigau, filed past amid bravos 'to go and join the Emperor'. A shower of similar revolutions were sparked off at Strasbourg, Rouen, Cherbourg, Troyes, Bourges and Brest: these towns, and a hundred others, bubbled all day under the shaky lid of the civil and military authorities, who were only waiting for the official news of Napoleon's entry into Paris to declare themselves. They were thus to proclaim the Empire on the following day.

France at that time numbered 25,000,000 souls, which can be divided roughly into half a million nobles and landed proprietors; half a million 'bourgeois', people of private means, officials, businessmen, priests, students; half a million soldiers under arms or on half pay; and all the rest in peasant masses, a fringe of which, still weak, was on the way to proletarianisation in the towns, wherever factories had been set up. Save in the west and the Midi, where the influence of the clergy kept even the people royalist in sentiment, the great majority of the 'poor' were about to vote, out of enthusiasm and fervour, the overthrow of the regime, sparked off under the impulse of the army. These were the people whose 'annual income', as it would now be called, did not even amount to the equivalent of 400 new francs per person per year,[1] and whose expectation of life did not exceed thirty-three years.

Eight o'clock in the morning at Villejuif. Indescribable military confusion. Regiments of infantry and cavalry stamping about waiting for food and orders. Until then they had flowed back from Melun and Essonnes as slowly as possible, in the hope of being overtaken by le Tondu. Now, they refused to go further. The officers and men stared at each other with hostility,

[1] About £33 [trs.].

the former still considering themselves part of the 'royal army' and keeping the white cockade, while no order to change it came from higher up.

Salvation arrived from Paris in the shape of a general at the gallop, brandishing his sabre, who charged at the head of the column of the 2nd Regiment of the Line shouting:

'The King is saved, my lads! It's all over! *Vive l'Empereur!'*

It was Sébastiani, who was known to all the men. One of the most brilliant *sabreurs* — one of the most brutal, too — in the whole army. Where had he sprung from? Was he one of those who, in the background and very mysteriously in Paris, had prepared that day's events, in secret liaison with Elba? He acted as though he had authority and was obeying an order, received perhaps from Auxerre. His appearance 'catalysed' the process of dissolution in the last regular armed force in the region of Paris. The soldiers put the butts of their muskets to the ground and took out their tricolour cockades. Shouts of *'Vive l'Empereur!'* ran through Villejuif and decked the houses in flags. Philosophically, the men awaited the outcome of the discussion around Sébastiani, who had made the officers form a square. The latter for the most part required no more than to be convinced, but the occasion did not lack the inevitable hysterics of a young lieutenant, M. Negré de Massals, who tore off his epaulettes, jumped on them, and threw them at the head of his men. By nine o'clock all the troops at Villejuif had rallied to Napoleon and formed a sort of little military republic, for each regiment, indeed each battalion, was discussing what course to take. The current was drawing the men rather to Fontainebleau, to see HIM again more quickly. Sébastiani, on the other hand, insisted vigorously that they continue the withdrawal to Paris, but this time in the name of the Emperor, to maintain order there. So the ranks were wavering. Finally, about half the troops returned to Paris, a quarter filed off for Fontainebleau, and a quarter chose a solution of discretion: to stay at Villejuif, where the men took the one bad inn by storm. There they would wait quietly. They were the only ones who had any chance, that day, of getting anything solid between their teeth.

Between seven and eight o'clock Napoleon awoke and called his servants. Quick, a bath, a massage for his whole body! Saint-Denis noticed that he had not 'recuperated' as he used to on the morning of battles, a few months earlier. 'Although he had travelled by carriage from Grenoble, he appeared tired.' Marchand brought him some hot tea, served on the magnificent salver of the Imperial plate, recovered intact in the cellars of the Palace, thanks again to the brave concierge. His familiars shaved and spruced themselves up as they could. Already, the Cheval Blanc courtyard was too small to hold the lancers, hussars and light infantry who had arrived to draw up there haphazardly. The Emperor came down to review them as early as nine o'clock, and was to do so again two or three times during the morning, though this was only to help out Bertrand, who was at his wit's end. A poor major-general, he had neither Berthier's endurance nor Soult's authority, and overwork drove him to distraction: he had not closed an eye, for his part, and was lost between the battalions that were appearing from Paris and those that were catching up from Auxerre. How were they all to be fed? How provide for a proper battle order, in the event of a clash with the 'Army of Melun', which constituted for him a real bogy to the east? The Mayor of Fontainebleau and the Prefect of Seine-et-Marne, both present at the Emperor's rising, were put to a rude test. To crown all, along came the grenadiers from Elba suddenly, having reached Montereau early in the day.

Unruffled, Napoleon made his calculations. He could dispose from there that evening of 20,000 men and fifty cannon. (He was later to exaggerate these figures twofold; it was an old habit of his.) But all this was in great disorder for want of senior officers and a general staff. He had not wished to have himself accompanied by Ney, who, moreover, was only good for leading men into battle. Bertrand was out of his depth, Drouot without initiative. Thus the Emperor had not a single really great leader to help him discipline that mob. And at his beck and call he had not even that team of clerks, with no personality, but methodical and zealous, which he had formed to spare himself vexations. The familiars who gathered about him that morning, in a touching mixture of cheerfulness and incapacity, were still with very minor exceptions those of the little Court on the island of Elba, about which Pons de l'Hérault more than anyone has provided some notes of a very shrewd psychology, which show them to us, there at Fontainebleau, just as they were on that last day. That evening, the winds of History would scatter them.

'Except for General Bertrand and General Drouot, the Emperor personally had made no appeal to anyone's devotion to have himself followed into exile, and nothing is so astonishing as that he did not even concern himself in the choice. Thus, the Emperor's companions were not all equally devoted friends in life and in death. Nevertheless, they were all fond of him, and the Emperor asked no more of them. In that chance collection, in which nothing, so to speak, was homogeneous, each had had some advancement. A few individuals, because they had followed the Emperor Napoleon, thought themselves at least little Napoleons, and their conviction, which manifested itself in ridiculous pretensions, often made them a laughing-stock.

'General Bertrand was a right-thinking man in every sense of the word. The events that had shattered the Imperial throne had also shattered the soul of General Bertrand. Ceaselessly a prey to the distressing memories of that immense catastrophe, he was no longer a man of work, he was a man of repose. His heart was completely with his family; his wife and children absorbed all his thoughts. If I were required to give a rigorous opinion on the essence of the bonds that had attached Napoleon to General Bertrand, I would say that, from all I have seen, the two natures, that of the Emperor Napoleon and that of General Bertrand, were not sympathetic,[1] and the tightening of their union, more apparent than real, was rather a matter of habit than a matter of sentiment. Their initial opinions were never the same: these always began by clashing, and General Bertrand did not give in easily. I have seen the Emperor Napoleon give up in disputes more than once. As for Drouot, read Plutarch, behold the finest character of his great men; this was his character. General Drouot was the perfection of the moral man. He had followed the Emperor on condition that he would not pay him any salary. He was the only one of Napoleon's companions to make this reservation. There were two men in him: the public man and

[1] To be understood as 'were not disposed to get on well together'.

246

the private man. The private man was too good, the public man was too severe.

'Monsieur Peyrusse, pay-master to the Crown, was a young man from the Midi, full of spirit, vivacity and frankness, always gay, always obliging, and strongly attached to his duties. M. Peyrusse did not parade his devotion to the Emperor, for he used to say to whoever would listen, laughingly, however: "I didn't follow the Emperor Napoleon, I followed my cash-box." And this was true. The military men were not always kind with regard to him, which did not prevent him from rendering them all the services that went with his functions.

'Doctor Foureau de Beauregard, in whom medical science had disclosed no merit, was, in Paris, physician to the Imperial stables, and on the island of Elba, physician in chief to the Emperor. He was what is vulgarly known as 'an old woman', and to please the Emperor he retailed him exactly all the tittle-tattle good or bad, which had ended by rendering him suspect. He was, moreover, too obsequious with the Emperor. This obsequiousness formed a contrast with his vanity towards people who were subordinate to him.'

Added to which were the pharmacist Gatti, 'a good fellow', the palace quartermaster Deschamps, 'an old gendarme in officer's uniform who always kept apart', and Baillou, another quartermaster, 'who had in him something soldierly and good', the valets de chambre Marchand and Saint-Denis, both of them lively and sly, but the former very conceited, occasionally playing the confidant, and the Corsican or Elban 'grooms'.

There were also the secretaries: Rathery, insignificant, and Fleury de Chaboulon, vain, foppish and inclined to romanticize, whom Napoleon regretted having engaged at Lyons. But he had wanted to show his gratitude to the young man for having come to bring him news, a month earlier, from Paris to Elba, with an introduction from Maret.[1]

In brief, Napoleon was alone, as he had never been at the

[1] Later, Fleury was to claim in all seriousness in his *Mémoires* to have been the determining agent in the decision to return, although he had been only one of the elements in it and certainly not the most important. Napoleon was to do justice to all this on St Helena by a few brisk comments in the margin of his gossip.

start of a great encounter. And he would have been badly hampered by such an entourage if he had really had to give battle. That morning, he had the choice of two solutions: to rush haphazardly towards Paris (which he thought to be still in the hands of the King), in the midst of a veritable horde, or to install himself at Fontainebleau for a few hours, for time to get everything organized. Aided by fatigue, he seems to have chosen the second solution at first, and took time at all events, before midday, to look over the Château and the gardens. He wandered through that confused mass of buildings of different styles (there are supposed to be four chateaux collected into one) 'with as much pleasure and curiosity as though he were taking possession of it for the first time'. Fleury de Chaboulon, naturally, clung to his heels, observed him closely, and was astonished not to see him show any emotion. Yet here he had despaired; there he had taken poison when all was collapsing. Here he had waited in vain for Marie-Louise, submitted to the Marshals' reproaches, had seen the courtiers leave for ever, one after the other . . . But it was not to this booby that he would allow what he was feeling to appear. He had taken his measure. In reascending to the library, he hardly accorded him a 'word':

'We shall be comfortable here . . . '

'Yes, Sire,' Fleury hastened to reply, 'one is always comfortable where you are.'

And the poor man added: 'He smiled and was grateful to me, I believe, for my flattery at his remark.'

It was eleven o'clock. Installed in the library, Napoleon dictated a provisional order of the day in which he anticipated sleeping that night at Essonnes. Manifestly, something between Moret and Fontainebleau had 'braked' him in his rapid dash to Paris, and this could only have been to ascertain at what point his army lacked order. His fear of popular riots was still as great as ever and he did not want to expose undisciplined soldiers to infection from these. Nothing seemed to him more urgent than a resumption into hierarchic hands of his own forces first, and of France afterwards.

But around the Palace, and along the route from Fontainebleau to Paris, one same phrase was running from mouth to mouth among the soldiers: 'Of course he'll be back home

tonight, for the little Napoleon's birthday . . . He's foreseen
this all along, just imagine!'

Four years earlier, to the very day, the cannon of the
Invalides, by its twenty-second report, had announced to the
world the birth of the heir to the western Empire.

On the morning of Easter Monday the King of Rome entered
upon his fifth year. He had slept that night in surroundings new
to him : a cold and dismal room in the Hofburg, the palace of
his grandfather the Emperor of Austria, in Vienna. The day
before, on the entreaties of the 'president of Police', who since
March 7th could not sleep for fear of a kidnapping, he had had
to leave Schönbrunn and its fine park, where he had played at
looking for the first violets. It was a week since the guards in
the Austrian Versailles had been doubled, and the small army
of servant-policemen reinforced, with orders to keep an eye above
all on the three French people who in fact made up the little
prisoner's family : Méneval, de Bausset, and especially Mme de
Montesquiou, 'governess to the Children of France', who had
been appointed by Napoleon, and whom the child called 'Maman
Quiou'.

If the boy had a mother in his life, it was she. A woman of
duty, she had been able to let such a tenderness with regard to
him emerge under her apparent severity, that the character and
nervous system of the little Napoleon had, up to that time,
escaped the tragic consequences of events. He had passed almost
unconcerned through the departure from the Tuileries, the disappearance of his father, and the comfortable deportation to
Schönbrunn. Nothing of all this had left any mark on him,
since he had not lacked for a single day the essential for a child
of that age : the soft warmth of a nest in which he always found
the same habits and an ever-attentive maternal face : Maman
Quiou. It is true, he was also told to address as 'maman' that
pleasant person, pink and blooming, with eyes of china, who
came from time to time to play with him at dolls and who
murmured in his ear interminable German words constructed
like cakes. This lady was still called 'Your Majesty'. But why did
this Mama-Empress call him Franz? Maman Quiou for her part,

for want of the right, addressed him as 'Sire', as she had done for the past six months, even when she was giving him three strokes of the whip, and merely refused to give him a 'Highness' as the Austrians did—but her *vous* was wonderfully coaxing, with her good-night kiss, without which he would not go to sleep. Napoleon's son had thus been a happy child until that day.

. . . Until that day of March 20, 1815, an account of which has been left to us by Mme de Montesquiou. Already on the previous day, anguish had seized her. Why this sort of kidnapping from Schönbrunn, at the very moment when the spring air would be beneficial for the child? Why these two hundred men, disguised as flunkeys, scheming all round her? Her correspondence gone through, her movements spied upon? And Marie-Louise, who no longer even said good-day to her?

'If this child had a mother, for goodness' sake, I would give him over into her hands, I should be at ease; but she is as far from that as she could be, she is a person more indifferent to his fate than the least foreigner in his service . . . We are a band who often weep around the cradle.' [1]

So the governess had spent the whole night 'in that agitation caused by anxiety'. She felt a ring of iron tightening about her. It was not only against the Father that Europe was mobilizing, but against the little child whom the good nurse, Mme Marchand, led in to her at his awakening, because she had wanted to be with him again 'the moment he opened his eyes'. We have the sad opportunity to 'see' him exactly as he was that morning, thanks to the particulars sent out, precisely on March 20th, to all frontier-posts by the 'president of Police' Hager, and spread also among the headquarters of the troops that encircled Vienna and searched every suspicious vehicle to avoid the 'kidnapping'.

Napoleon II: a child tall for his age, with a very sweet appearance, full cheeks, blue eyes, a small upturned nose with the nostrils well exposed, small mouth, the slightly protrusive lips divided by a dimple, long golden-blond hair falling in large ringlets to the shoulders. He was usually dressed in a white jacket, trimmed with gold buttons, and expressed himself with animation accompanied by large gestures of the hands, and

[1] From a letter to her husband, who was urging her to return to Paris and put an end to their separation.

always in French, though he was beginning to gabble a few words of German.

'You are four years old this morning. For how long have you loved me?'

'For four years, madame. And I shall love you all my life.'

'Kneel down, and say your big prayers with me . . . '

But they would not have time to reach the part where he asked God every morning to 'watch over the soul and health of my dear father', which Mme de Montesquiou made him say more slowly, more solemnly, since she had known of the return from Elba, *of which, however, she had revealed nothing to him.* A valet de chambre interrupted them:

'His Excellency Count d'Urban, Grand Chamberlain to His Majesty the Emperor.'

No doubt the grandfather had sent him to congratulate the child on his birthday? But Mme de Montesquiou quickly realized that it was a matter of a dramatic message, of personal embarrassment.

'Madame, I wish to speak with you in private.'

So the child and the women were removed. Fortunately! They were not to know until the next day what was now about to be said.

'Madame, the Emperor, my master, has charged me to tell you that political circumstances force him to make some changes in the education of his grandson. He thanks you for the cares which you have bestowed upon him and . . . requests you to leave at once for Paris.'

She had been expecting it. But it was a thunderclap all the same. Oh! it was not, indeed, for herself that she suffered. But in a flash, the Eaglet's destiny pierced her heart. Now, the child would be alone for ever. Does a Montesquiou weep, however? She scarcely batted an eyelid:

'Monsieur, be so kind as to tell the Emperor that, accustomed as I have been for a year to depend upon no one but him, I wish at least to deliver into his hands the sacred trust that has been confided to me.'

Hardly had the old gentleman left when the King of Rome came back to throw himself into Maman Quiou's arms, 'as he had a habit of doing whenever he lost sight of her for an instant'.

And then, the prompt return of Count d'Urban: naturally, Francis II refused to talk to her face to face. A large part of the life of sovereigns consists of running away from emotion. Mme de Montesquiou found herself favoured, however, with a letter:

'Madame la comtesse de Montesquiou, the circumstances of the moment forcing me to make a change in the persons charged with the education of my grandson, I do not wish to miss this opportunity to express all my gratitude to you for the care with which you have ministered to him since his birth. Pray accept the expression of this sentiment and the token of remembrance which I have charged my Grand Chamberlain to deliver to you on my behalf.

'Your affectionate
'Francis'   Vienna, 20th March, 1815.

The 'token of remembrance' . . . ? Nothing was spared the noble woman by these people, not even the offer of a tip. 'It was a most beautiful set of sapphires.' Nothing could have been more calculated to make her fly off the handle. She restrained herself from hurling the present at the messenger's face; she drily requested him to take it back to the Emperor, forthwith. But how could a courtier understand? 'He told me in reply that presents from the Emperor could not be refused, and then he began to make excuses for not having been able to offer me the jewellery in a case, the choice having been made too suddenly. This stupid remark was for me the supreme added woe, for I then saw clearly that nothing of what I had been saying could have been understood by this imbecile intermediary. It was a desolating thought, and one that disheartened me.'

From now on, one idea haunted her: poison. There had been precedents among the Hapsburgs. Whether Napoleon reigned again in France or disappeared, his son, tomorrow, would be the most inconvenient in History. And he would be in the hands of these servile Germans . . .

While this was going on, Marie-Louise appeared. She had been sleeping with Neipperg since September 27, 1814. On March 12th she had signed a public letter to her father, drafted by her lover, in which she formally abjured her husband and craved, for herself and her son, 'the protection of Your paternal tenderness. We shall acknowledge no other will but yours . . . ', that is to say, Metternich's, to whom she had handed over, without reading them, all the letters that Napoleon had just written to her.

Between these two women who had always detested each other, the duel was brief. Marie-Louise, with 'a cold air and an embarrassed attitude' before the stiff *grande dame*, a living statue of France's reproach with regard to her ephemeral first lady. Mme de Montesquiou treated her haughtily and laid down express demands:

'I declared that I wanted a consultation between the chief physicians to the Emperor of Austria, the child's usual physician, and the surgeon to the Empress, in order that my pupil (*sic*) be carefully examined, and that I be issued with a certificate which would testify to the perfect health to which my cares had brought him.'

So that at least, later on, everyone would be able to say : she had left *them* a splendid infant.

Marie-Louise had to obey to get any peace, and she arranged the convening of the medical corps. She hesitated and blushed before asking:

'Do you expect to see the Emperor Napoleon?'

'Wherever he may be, I shall go and render him an account of my conduct.'

And Mme de Montesquiou still managed to spend that last day with the child and to leave him during the night, without his suspecting anything.

'I wanted to ensure him twelve more hours of peace and happiness.'

'At 6.30, I rose,' wrote M. de Marsilly. 'Wearing neither fleur-de-lys nor cross, I went to the Château to hand over the key to the cupboard where the cartridges had been which I distributed to the King's Swiss guards. In the courtyard I met the adjutant of the Château, M. Auger. He no longer had a cross; he had a sad air. I said nothing to him, but handed him the key. I raised my eyes and I saw that the white flag was no longer flying on the dome of the Palace. I hastened to leave that place . . . I met Riquebourg, superintendent of the King's Victuals, and M. de Chamilly, chief valet de chambre. At the gate was the Major of the lifeguards, M. d'Albignac. We looked as though we had never known each other. I crossed the most frequented quarters of Paris. Everything was quiet, the respectable people seemed sad; the rabble and the children were already shouting "Vive l'Empereur!" occasionally . . . '

For his part, Count de Lamothe-Langon descended to the street at seven o'clock, wrapped in his carrick, that great cloak which had come over from England with the Princes, and which covered its wearer in a vast cylindrical sheath that fell to the ground. 'It was cold, but dry, and the unsettled weather ceased to be rainy from that moment: Napoleon's sun had reappeared with him.' Quite as upset as Marsilly at the resurrection of Satan, Lamothe-Langon was of that irreplaceable species of men in whom curiosity prevails over every other sentiment. They would console themselves on dying, if they could relate how. So he was to record faithfully the thousand details of that day, which cut him to the quick, but greatly excited him. 'On leaving home, my first excursion was to the Carrousel square, where I took up my abode until Napoleon's arrival; I even dined there,[1] so as to miss nothing in the least scene of that curious drama . . . '

With him, and from seven o'clock in the morning in fact, the Tuileries saw the arrival of the first spectators. But it was merely a matter of inhabitants from the neighbourhood, 'drawn by simple curiosity, and more disposed to regret the King's departure than to aid in the Restoration of the Empire.' Still the same 'gilded sections' of Paris, who were cast down at seeing the return of 'General Vendémiaire'. The iron gates to the courtyard of the Tuileries were closed, and the National Guard remained there to some extent prisoner; this was a measure of prudence to prevent the pillaging of the apartments. As it was a matter of the National Guard of the quarter, the Palace at that moment

[1] Meaning 'I lunched there'; that is to say, he took the main meal of the day there, at about five o'clock.

254

could be considered as still belonging to the royalists, even if it
no longer belonged to the King. And the first Bonapartists to
venture into the vicinity made proof of this; the tricolour
cockades which they believed they could, at last, put up freely
earned them boos, stones and, before long, punches. Two of
them, under serious attack, took refuge near the gates . . . but
the National Guard made only feeble efforts to protect them
and treated them with suspicion. It was the moment when the
last members of the Royal Household left the Tuileries, like
M. de Marsilly, and delivered into the armed hands of the
Parisian bourgeoisie the Palace of the sovereign, which had
known that situation once before: when Louis XVI did a flit in
the direction of Varennes.

The rest of Paris, up to nine o'clock, was relatively quiet.
Many people still refused to believe that the King had left. To
be convinced of it, they had to read the proclamation, hastily
printed during the night on the presses of the *Moniteur*, which
was posted at a hundred or so places:

'Louis, by the grace of God, King of France and of Navarre, to
our trusty and well-beloved friends, the Peers of France, and the
deputies of the departments:

'Divine Providence, which recalled us to the throne of our
fathers, today suffers that throne to be shaken by the defection
of a part of the armed forces which had sworn to defend it; we
could have profited from the loyal and patriotic disposition of
the vast majority of the inhabitants of Paris to challenge their
entry, but we shudder at the misfortunes of every kind that a
struggle within her walls would have brought down upon the
inhabitants. *We are withdrawing with some brave men* (sic)
whom intrigue and perfidy will never succeed in detaching from
their duty, and since we can in no way defend our capital, we
shall go further afield, to gather strength and seek in another
part of the realm, not subjects more loving and more loyal than
our good Parisians, but Frenchmen more advantageously placed
to declare themselves for the good cause. The present crisis will
abate. We have the quiet presentiment that the misguided
soldiers, whose defection abandons our subjects to so many
dangers, will not be slow to acknowledge their errors, and will

find in our leniency and in our bounties the reward for their return.

'We shall come back before long into the midst of this good people, to whom we shall once again restore peace and happiness.'

And so the King passed an ordinance declaring the session of the Chambers closed, and adjourning them to a later convocation.

Le Moniteur, moreover, was about to leave the presses at the usual hour and would slip this embarrassed text in at the end of one of its last columns; the others were still filled with addresses of loyalty to the King, emanating from the departments. This number was the work of the worthy M. Sauvo, the perfect pattern of an official journalist and precise executive who had taken orders the previous evening from M. de Vitrolles and would take them that evening from the Emperor.

But the ancestor of the *Journal Officiel* was the only one to appear in Paris that morning. The five or six other papers that had constituted the Restoration press had shut up shop, and their editors had gone to ground.

An end to the *Journal des Débats*, which had declined in six months from 28,000 to 15,000 subscribers, when its vaguely liberal ideas had melted in the fire of criticism, so that it had begun to attack the men and the deeds of the Revolution with ferocity; Benjamin Constant's philippic enabled it to die in comely style. An end to the *Journal royal*, that 'diary of monarchic Europe'. An end to the *Gazette de France*, 'that decrepit old jade in court dress', the child of Théophraste Renaudot. An end to the *Quotidienne*, nicknamed 'the bloody Nun', each issue of which had demanded the gallows for republicans and spewed forth a torrent of denunciations. Prudently, the *Journal de Paris* and the *Journal général de la France* likewise gave up appearing, in spite of their relative moderation as compared with the frenzy of their colleagues. By no means disposed to break lances, these two sheets had none the less taken up certain attitudes, and the *Journal général* had got itself called Harlequin by reason of 'the motley of its opinions'.

Paris

Since the morning, a little group of men wild with delight had been meeting again in the printing office of M. Fain, 'Rue de Racine, near the Odéon'. It was a matter of the mysterious editors of the *Nain Jaune*,[1] that savoury little review which had been appearing every five days in book format, and saved the honour of the Parisian press. Strictly anonymous, its short paragraphs of a few lines, crammed with loaded words and veiled impertinences, had riddled with its arrows the clergy, the émigrés, the notables of the Empire who had rallied to the King and, above all, the other papers. When one runs through the complete collection of this glorious elder among satirical journals, one has difficulty in understanding how M. d'André's police could have allowed it to appear. On January 6th, among a hundred examples, the following lines could be found there:

'M. l'abbé Gallais has published a long article in the *Quotidienne* in which he endeavours to prove that Bonaparte was a bad commander. We know a lieutenant of hussars who is busy with an article in which he will prove that M. l'abbé Gallais is a bad theologian.'

A large number of similar allusions made it look as if the *Nain Jaune* was committing the supreme offence against opinion: not only did it refer to liberalism, but it defended Napoleon. The royalists, maddened by its harrying, accused it of being written by Queen Hortense and the frequenters of her salon, indeed, even of publishing notes 'from Buonaparte's own hand'.[2]

Be that as it may, until March 20th it had been tolerated, probably because the journal had amused the King, delighted to find in it gibes about his entourage and his ministers. Week by

[1] Literally 'Yellow Dwarf'; also the name of a card-game known to us as 'Pope Joan' [trs.].

[2] The truth was simpler: it was a matter of seven brave men, full of humour, Bonapartists, it is true, but whose names need to be rescued from the unjust oblivion into which they have fallen, while certain muck-heaps of that era have not ceased to infect our nostrils ever since. Talleyrand, Fouché, Barras and others will continue to lumber our libraries, whereas Cauchois, Lemaire, Bory-Saint-Vincent, Arnault, Étienne, Jouy, Harel and Merle were to know, after Waterloo, all the horrors of the white terror, a ban on writing, police surveillance, poverty for all and exile for some, without their being accorded even a mention by historians, except for Henry Houssaye.

week the *Nain Jaune* had inveighed increasingly against established ideas, even to the founding of the *Order of the Extinguisher* in the name of Misophane,

'Sovereign of the Obscure Islands, of the Kingdom of Moles, of the Lake of Crabs and other places,[1] for all our loyal subjects, people wearing hats, turbans, birettas, amices,[2] soutanes and in livery, for all the blind, one-eyed and myopic, born or to be born.'

In expounding the statutes of the Order, the number for January 6th had 'King Misophane' proclaim:

'The glare of daylight, which has found its way into our Estates, having wearied our eyes and injured the sight of the people of our vast moledom, we wish, as far as it lies in us, to arrest the progress afflicting the lights and maintain our subjects in that sweet darkness, those palpable shades, in which our fathers lived with so much glory and happiness.'

The Knights of the Extinguisher had to 'give proof of four generations of ignorance, paternal and maternal,' and to 'take a vow of ignorance, impudence and bad faith.' They were never to lose sight of the following fundamental principles: brutalize to govern, persecute to persuade, grovel to succeed. They took an oath to hatred of philosophy, liberal ideas, and the constitutional charter.

To crown their temerity, the formula that ended this ordinance insolently parodied the one that wound up royal ordinances: 'Enacted and given at Obscuropolis, the first year of the discovery of cold storage, and the 2734th night of our reign. Signed: Misophane.'

After March 5th, the *Nain Jaune* had been accused of being in the front rank of 'the great conspiracy of the return'. It is true that three lines in their number for that very day turned up there like hairs in a bowl of soup:

[1] In the French idioms, 'to go to the kingdom of the moles' means 'to die', and 'to walk like a crab' means 'to go backwards' [trs.].
[2] 'The fur of the marten or miniver which canons and choristers wear on their arms when proceeding to office' (Littré's dictionary).

'The following letter has been communicated to us from M. X. to M. X.: "I have worn out ten goose-quills in writing to you, without being able to obtain a reply, perhaps I should have better luck with a duck-quill (*plume de canne* [*sic*]): I shall try it." '

... *Canne? Plume de canne?* And Buonaparte had landed near Cannes! This number had been printed before the arrival of the dispatches. No more had been needed for the men of the *Nain Jaune* to be suspected of high treason.[1] Luckily the police had other fish to fry. They had confined themselves to imposing upon them the watchful presence of a censor from the royal bookseller's, who had made them transform their paper into a supplement of the *Moniteur*: all the anti-Bonapartist proclamations had passed through it, but the editors, true to themselves, had added not a single line of their own.

From the morning of March 20th, at the Fain printing office, they were preparing their number for the following Friday with relish, and were vowing to 'place a huge extinguisher over the men and affairs of the Restoration'.

At eleven o'clock, the sun became stronger, but only for an instant, between clouds that grew blacker as the day advanced, and a few of which burst in brief showers. Some spring songs, of which Paris had lost the habit, began to be heard in the north-east and the south-east: the *Marseillaise*, the *Ça ira*, and the *Carmagnole*. Gatherings of fairly minor importance formed in the popular quarters, bordering on the Faubourgs Saint-Antoine and Saint-Marceau. There, where the Parisian '*sans-culotterie*' of 1793 had changed the prime mover of History for ever, by delivering the levers of France into the hands of industry rather

---

[1] The editors, in the number for March 25th, formally denied this complicity, after the return of Napoleon, and at a time when they might have boasted of it to advantage: 'We resolutely declare that we did not have any knowledge of the events that were being prepared. The coincidence that occurred between our anecdote about the duck-quill (*plume de cane*) and the Emperor's landing was a simple freak of chance . . . But the historian is obliged to point out the faltering in the typography: CANNE in the issue for March 5th, CANE in that for the 25th . . .

than those of commerce, something stirred, timidly, confusedly. The revolutionary spirit was not altogether dead in those vast collections of dark hovels where the bourgeoisie were beginning to build the great nineteenth-century concentration camp in which to pen the workers, without water and without light, in a paradise of rickets, tuberculosis and smallpox. But any movement there, in 1815, could only be instinctive and formless: all structure was lacking. The purges of Germinal, Year II, against the *hébertistes* and the *cordeliers*, the ferocious persecution of Prairial, Year III, led by the Thermidorians, the deportations ordained by the First Consul, especially after the outrage in the Rue Saint-Nicaise, and ten years of nibbling by the police, of Fouché and then of Savary, had reduced to nothing the communal organization that had waged the people's war. However, it was a fact that a few weak cells did still exist among the veterans of the 'sections' Popincourt, Temple, Montreuil, Quinze-Vingts, Observatoire, Jardin des Plantes and Gobelins. They remembered the time when they had been King. And their sons' generation, artisans, proletarians (the word had just been invented), journeymen of the twelve-hour day, paid less than forty sous [about 3s 6d], had regrouped themselves in those new associations, in which the romance of secrecy and craftsman's pride appreciably tempered the spirit of revolt: the *Compagnie des Bons Enfants*, the *Compagnons du Devoir*, the *Enfants de Salomon*, which had inspired the first strikes ever held in France, those of 1808 and 1811, when the price of bread rose beyond endurance. But it was not this heterogeneous combination of survivors from the great days with seeds of *carbonari* that could seriously improvise an insurrection, on March 20, 1815, in a Paris where there were still only 90,000 workers to 714,000 inhabitants, and they divided up, we learn from recent work on the archives, among 27,330 dwellings.[1]

So the popular movement of March 20th was restricted to two or three processions of demonstrators, in which there was more singing than shouting, and each of which amounted to no more than two or three hundred people. They came down the Rue Saint-Antoine, followed the boulevard to the Seine, and

[1] The city numbered 96 squares, 1,094 streets, 27 alleys, 166 passages and 133 culs-de-sac.

there grew a little excited on meeting those who had come from Glacière and Gobelins. They waved a few tricolour flags. They surrounded a few of the oldest veterans, symbolically wearing red caps.

And they had sufficed to make Paris tremble. We shall never know whose voice it was that Lamothe-Langon heard being raised at the corner of the Rue Sainte-Anne and the Rue Chabanais. But how carefully he noted what was said!

'Frenchmen, the Bourbons have left Paris! Bonaparte hasn't entered as yet. No armed troops, no henchmen of tyranny are oppressing us. The moment is propitious; let the Republic rise again from the tomb to which two despots had confined it! . . . '

No more was needed for nearby shops to close, and for strollers to go home.

'Oh! This time, we said, it's Marat, it's his tail!¹ These are Fouché's one-time friends, who are taking over the street again! . . . '

The little death of the 'haves' of Paris was to last no longer than this shudder, before midday. What frightened them above all was the appalling void: no army any more in the capital.

'Thus Paris was no longer defended, served and protected except by her own citizens. That decision of Macdonald's forestalled all rivalry, all struggle, averted a collision, and prevented any shedding of blood among French soldiers; but, from another side, it was to be feared that brigands, convicts, who had little respect for the armed bourgeoisie, might decide to fight them, if they saw any chance of pillage and arson . . . This did not happen, however.'²

No, indeed! For Napoleon arrived. In the space of a morning, under the pressure of that mere shadow of popular menace, the bourgeoisie of Paris, abandoned by the King, were about to rally to him, not because they wanted to, but because he would save public order.

'There were still not many people at about ten o'clock in the

¹ An expression current at the time, even if it makes us smile now. Napoleon himself said of the last Jacobins that they were 'Robespierre's tail'.
² Lamothe-Langon.

Carrousel square, but imperceptibly the onlookers, the populace and the actors each gathered at a separate post, and as if places had been designated for them in advance. The onlookers, well-dressed people for the most part, occupied the superior regions, the entrance to the Rue Napoléon, the bottom of the Rue du Musée, and, in general, *access to the walls*, so that they could withdraw if the public peace were momentarily disturbed . . . The populace, that is to say a considerable gathering of petits bourgeois, workers and loiterers, to whom were added a considerable number of pickpockets, sharpers and dissolute women, clung to the railings of the courtyard and filled the vast extent of the square, coming and going, laughing and singing and beginning rounds, which were no sooner formed than broken off, about the first officer with big epaulettes they could see.'[1]

There would be two alarms. The first at about nine o'clock: thick black smoke suddenly rose from the finely-wrought chimneys of the Pavillon de Flore. No more was needed 'to send the onlookers within walls' and to cause an outbreak of panic:

'The Tuileries are on fire! Fire! Fire! The Château is ruined!'

The ebb of the crowd went as far as the Palais-Royal. It quickly subsided when some National Guards appeared at the windows and made reassuring signs. The 'fire' was only a chimney-fire in a flue choked with the winter's soot, brought about when the King's last secretaries, just before leaving, had maladroitly set light to a great pile of compromising papers.

Towards ten o'clock it was more serious: a column of people ended by emerging on to the square shouting at the tops of their voices:

'Down with the priests!'

And, what was more formidable:

'Down with the National Guard!'

A few of them made so bold as to rattle the railings, while the people of the quarter scattered again like a flight of sparrows.

The civil guards took up their arms and set about their duty of reducing this tiny riot. Would it come to a scuffle, even a fusillade? This was the moment dreaded for a week both by those who had left and by those who were arriving. But some

[1] Lamothe-Langon.

262

officers of the National Guard were to calm everything rapidly with the all-powerful cry: 'Vive *l'Empereur!*'

And that did the trick. Started by the 'armed proprietors' and taken up by the poor, who charged it with a sort of Messianic hope in the revolution reincarnate, this cry became the cement of the day. The little band of men and women, who had come to the foot of the Palace to express the slight touch of fever in the poor quarters, retreated, not without grumbling their way along the Rue de Rivoli and the Rue Saint-Honoré. But not one broken pane was reported, nor one ravaged shop. March 20th, decidedly, was to be no August 10th, nor even a June 20th.[1]

The idlers emerged afresh from every hole. But the crowd remained undecided and quick to change direction, for want of information and precise instructions. It was now that two men, more determined than the rest, would assert themselves and virtually take possession of Paris in the Emperor's name: a civilian, La Valette, and a soldier, Exelmans; while for his part, at Villejuif, Sébastiani was rallying the capital's troops.

Since the morning, Bonapartists of note had felt the police surveillance relaxing and had gone back, one to his town-house, another to his apartment. But the first to go a step further and resume his former office was La Valette, director of Posts under the Empire.

Elegant, amiable and zealous without genius, La Valette was of the breed of the Narbonnes and the Ségurs, that is to say, of the nobles of the *ancien régime* who had rallied to Napoleon, and who retained with regard to him the feelings of liegemen. They were not obeying precise orders, but rather the general instruction sent to the faithful from Auxerre:

'Show yourselves only when there is no danger, and then only if it is to avoid any disorder.'

So towards ten o'clock La Valette entered the Hôtel des Postes, that is to say the point of contact through which the whole nervous system of France communicated with the power of Paris. From there the *Moniteur* and the couriers, public or

---

[1] Feeble though the spasm had been, to be noted is this: it was the only movement of the people of Paris between 1795 and 1830.

private, went out each day. There, for ten years, M. de La Valette had held the pulse of the Empire in his hand. He was liked by the staff, and hardly had he appeared than a cheerful revolt of the clerks reinstalled him in his former office, which its royalist occupant, Count Ferrand, was delighted to surrender: here the transfer of power for the maintenance of good order was made quasi-officially, between men of the world.

'Gentlemen, in the name of the Emperor, I assume possession of the Post!'

Immediately after pronouncing these words, the first to re-establish the Imperial regime in Paris, La Valette stopped the dispatch of everything emanating from the government in flight, especially that of the *Moniteur*, which contained Louis XVIII's last proclamation, and he sent the fastest available courier to Napoleon, to tell him the wonderful news:

'Make haste, Sire! The King has left; the Tuileries are yours.'

This last point was not true yet, but the gallant General Exelmans was in the midst of attending to it.

✳

Fontainebleau, midday. The Emperor summoned Fleury de Chaboulon.

'You will go on ahead. You will have everything prepared.'

'At Essonnes, Sire?'

'In Paris. The King and the Princes are in flight. I shall be at the Tuileries tonight.'

La Valette's courier had arrived. At the same time as he, other messengers, sent by Savary, Maret, Queen Hortense, and perhaps Fouché, had come rushing along at top speed. The news, for once, had not been kept back at first, for the Master: they were dancing with joy in the Palace courtyards, vast slaps on the back were being exchanged in the antechambers. Horses were saddled, carriages harnessed, without even waiting for orders. From that moment on, Napoleon himself would be overtaken by the human tidal-wave which, with its final surge, would lift him up and hurl him into Paris. Caught in the cogs of what he himself had set going, he was about to become hostage to a second 18th Brumaire, the idol borne on its shield by a brute procession. No doubt he would have been carried off by sheer force, if he had decided to linger at Fontainebleau. Of course, he decided to rush on: his face, its pallor emphasized by exhaustion, was lit with a faint smile. Now, he would have liked to go very quickly, to arrive in daylight. But he was to come up against the contrary tide of those who were on their way to form a procession for him—and so, caught between two pressures, he could only submit to events without being able to impose on them his usual rhythm. During the final hours of the return from Elba, the Eagle hovered on the crest of whirlwinds.

At least he managed to get rid of Fleury de Chaboulon: 'The Emperor gave me secret orders; I left Fontainebleau with my heart full of joy and happiness.' In truth, Napoleon could stand him no longer, and as soon as he got to the Tuileries he chose to have back his usual secretaries and office organization.[1]

Later, in dictating his account of the day, Napoleon would try to give this moment the greatest possible solemnity:

'At midday His Majesty received the news that the Court had left Paris, that the troops of the camp at Villejuif were on the march, part to rejoin the Emperor, part to return to barracks (their commanders having given this last order so as to prevent complete disbandment); that Count de La Valette had assumed control of the Posts and Duke de Rovigo control of the Police,[2] that the Emperor was awaited with the keenest impatience and that the tricolour cockade was already being displayed. The Emperor then boarded a posting carriage with Grand Marshal Bertrand and General Drouot.'

In fact, this took place amid a certain confusion. It was in order to make quicker progress that Napoleon refused a coach

---

[1] After Waterloo, Fleury de Chaboulon, like so many others, was to sing a different tune, on family pretexts, so as not to follow the Emperor into exile. But it is probable that the Emperor hardly insisted. Thank God! One shudders to think what sort of *Mémorial* might have been written by this character. The thought is almost enough to reconcile us to Las Cases.

[2] A point expressly denied by Savary in his *Mémoires*, where he states, on the other hand, that he rushed to Cambacérès on the morning of March 20th to beg him to tell the Emperor, as soon as he arrived, that he did not want to resume the portfolio of Police. Duke de Rovigo was not anxious to be compelled to persecute the royalists. But it is probable that he nevertheless took a stroll to the Ministry building and wrote to the Emperor in the morning, if only to counter Fouché.

from the Château stables and preferred to return to the Prefect Gamot's barouche. He tried not to admit to his train any but a few platoons of lancers, and gave orders that would cause a lot of teeth-grinding: the soldiers of the Old Guard were to proceed to Montereau to re-embark for Paris, where they were not to arrive until the following day. Contrary to Cambronne's fears, himself furious, the grenadiers from Elba did not protest too much: they were drunk with fatigue . . . and with the good wine that had been lavished on them by the barrelful. Thus Napoleon was not to have with him, for his re-entry into Paris, a single one of the private soldiers that had embarked at Porto Ferraio.

From midday on, Paris was no longer afraid. The funds rose from 68 to 73 francs. It mattered little that the weather was less fine, that the sky was clouding, and a chill wind raising coat-collars. The little revolution was turning into a fair. There would be no disorder. The workers had gone back home, or were heading for the boulevards to the south, in the hope of catching sight of *Père la Violette* on his arrival. In the rest of the city, an air of Sunday descended on that Monday: traffic was almost non-existent. 'A universal decision had sent home the chaises, the hire-cabs, the livery carriages, the diligences, the carts. This was done without orders.' M. de Marsilly went to lunch at the *Rocher de Cancale*, where the oysters were bigger than anywhere else in Paris. 'I saw a young artillery officer arrive with a young lady on his arm, who said to Mlles Baleine (the *patronnes* of the famous restaurant): "Allow me to present to you one of the belles from Elba!"', which showed that the Paris braggarts were beginning to cash in. After that, poor Marsilly went gloomily to the police, to have his passport endorsed for Reims. He had nothing to do any more in Babylon, and would not stay there a day longer. On the Pont-Neuf he met 'a carriage drawn by four horses, taking the Rue Dauphine. It was said that this was the Emperor's carriage; some people had recognized his coachman . . . ' There he is! There he is! It was the cry that would be heard a hundred times, spurting along the embankments of the Seine, from two o'clock onwards. At that moment, all that was idle and unoccupied in Paris began to slide in one same movement towards the expected scene of the last act: the neighbourhood of the Tuileries. There, they were about to see Napoleon arrive, as if it had been by arrangement. The cast-off rags of the abortive monarchy were already far away to the north, carried off by the equinoctial winds. People no longer felt anything but a vague confusion at having pretended to believe in the solidity of those phantoms. With Napoleon, it was good sense, reason, logic that were returning to power that day. And it was also for these that in twenty years nearly a million Frenchmen had died.

'Half the shops in the vicinity of the Carrousel square, in the Palais-Royal, on the embankments, and in the Rues du Bac, de Thionville, de la Monnaie, du Roule, de l'Arbre-Sec, des Poulies, Saint-Honoré and Croix-des-Petits-Champs, stayed shut, as on holidays. Their proprietors were mounting guard at their respective town-halls, or else, without leaving their families, had sent their chief assistants on reconnaissance, who, swept away by curiosity like the raven in the Flood, failed to return to the Ark. Everyone wanted to see Napoleon, which did not prevent people from seeking to satisfy their appetites, at the improvised open-air restaurants. Coconut-vendors, *vivandières* of the Grand Army, with their little horses, barrels of brandy and three or four children, as dirty as they were handsome, pedlars of fried potatoes, of wafers, saveloys, cracknels and brioches completed the picture. Café-waiters moved about the square, distributing glasses of beer and drinking with the customers, to redoubled cries of *"Vive l'Empereur!"* '

What square? Above all, the Carrousel, opposite the Tuileries gardens, which ran up to the great edifice,[1] shutting off the vista from the Palais-Royal to the embankment, where the Pont-Royal began. On the other side, where the Palace turned its hundred windows to the east, was

[1] Partly burnt down by the Communards in 1871, later completely demolished [trs.].

'a wide paved area between the Arc de Triomphe[1] and that half-ruined quarter . . . with the Chapelle du Doyenné and the former Hôtel de Longueville, which no longer had a roof. From there — from those streets that began at the Palais-Royal, or thereabouts, to reach by devious ways the great gallery of the Museum, separating the Tuileries from the old Louvre, which was hard to imagine behind the hovels, sheds and squalid houses —had come the attacks of August 10th against the Tuileries; and whatever Napoleon had knocked down, to have more room at his back . . . had still left intact behind the Rue Saint-Nicaise, where the infernal machine had exploded, a whole baroque quarter of junk-dealers, courtesans and servants.'[2]

More than a thousand passive witnesses were gathered there when Napoleon's advance guard arrived from a direction in which it had certainly not been expected: the north! The advance guard, it is true, was an improvised one.

'A clinking of arms, a din of horses on the *pavé*, a rumble of artillery-pieces, sabres and bayonettes that glittered, resounding cries of *Vive l'Empereur!*, an eddy in the crowd under the powerful pressure of men of war. It was the half-pay officers whom General Exelmans had led from Saint-Denis, with a squadron of cuirassiers and some gunners dragging two cannon.'[3]

Exelmans — like Grouchy, Sébastiani, Labédoyère, Brayer, Girard, Ameil, Drouot, Cambronne, Drouet d'Erlon, Lefebvre-Desnoëttes — represented a new generation of Bonapartist officers, those who tomorrow hoped to become the Marshals of the restored Empire. Taken prisoner by the English in Spain, he had escaped from the hell of the hulks by crossing the Channel in a small boat. Appointed General by Napoleon on the field of the Battle of the Moskwa, resisting the Restoration fiercely, he had been arraigned before a court-martial for having corresponded with Murat, and his triumphal acquittal, on January 25th, had sounded the knell of a certain royal tranquillity; if the

[1] The little arch, quite recent, by Fontaine and Percier, still capped at that time by the four winged horses of St Mark's, Venice.
[2] Aragon, *La Semaine Sainte*, p. 64. The poet's vision, here, achieves an impressive accuracy that exceeds that of the historian.
[3] Henry Houssaye.

senior officers had acquitted Exelmans, it was because there was still something rotten in the French army. Since then the gallant General had kept quiet. That morning, obeying the same half-controlled impulse as La Valette or Sébastiani, he had given himself the mission of rallying all the troops more or less left in confusion to the north of Paris, along the road to Saint-Denis. All night two sorts of assemblies had been reported from there: the forces of the Royal Household, dejected and still disciplined, who were in retreat towards Beauvais, and a whole lot of infantry and cavalry regiments strung out in echelon that had already risen, who allowed the debris of the Monarchy to pass with some muttering, but found themselves at a loose end. With them, some bands of half-pay officers, which Soult and Clark had been unwise enough to organize, thinking to neutralize them in this way, became the leaven of the agitation. Since dawn certain of them had been stopping carriages and, sabre in hand, forcing travellers to shout 'Vive l'Empereur!' It was to all these good men that General Exelmans had come to give a lead in the morning. Setting out from Saint-Denis, where he had discreetly betaken himself, and where the royalist troops held the town too firmly for it to be possible to intercept the Princes (he had undoubtedly thought of this at first), Exelmans had returned to Paris, draining every available corps, group and band as he went.

There he was, passing the Quai Voltaire towards two o'clock, riding proudly at the head of his little troop, 'holding a magnificent tricolour flag wound round his gigantic body', made with this in mind several days before by an obliging Bonapartist *comtesse*.

The final suspense: the National Guards seemed disinclined at first to open to him, and Exelmans had to parley with Adjutant-Major de Laborde, when he presented himself at the gate on the Seine side. Hard discussion went on for ten minutes between bourgeois and praetorians, more on a question of form than about essentials. Finally, it was decided that Exelmans and the Bonapartist officers would occupy the Palace, but that the National Guard would continue to hold the gates, with the concurrence of the soldiers. This would allow a few stalwarts one last flirtation; they were to stand by the entries till evening, still with white cockades. By nightfall they would have vanished. At 2.22 p.m. the tricolour flag brought by Exelmans was floating over the Tuileries on the dome of the clock-house. At 2.30 it was on the dome of the Invalides; prior to this some of the disabled had got hold of the cannon and haphazardly fired a few salvoes of artillery, which made all the Parisians believe that the Emperor was already there. At 2.45 the tricolour was hoisted on the Vendôme column. At the Lycée Louis-le-Grand, Carnot's son followed events from a window and passed them on to his comrades, who had already broken off their studies. A happy crocodile of students formed spontaneously and invaded the street. In the space of an hour, more than a thousand tricolour flags flowered on public buildings and at private windows, while the officers inside the Tuileries threw down to the crowd, over the platform of the Hall of Marshals, the white flags and other royalist insignia that remained in the Palace.

At that same moment, in Vienna, the three doctors demanded by Mme de Montesquiou were drafting an official report, specifying that she was delivering into the hands of the Austrians an infant in perfect health. They had abundantly palpated and manipulated the frightened King of Rome, who had understood none of it, but *Maman Quiou* had reassured him calmly, without letting him see anything of her inner agony. All this had taken place in the presence of General Neipperg, whom Marie-Louise had shamelessly delegated to represent her.

Neipperg was in a hurry; he was leaving that night for Piedmont, to take command of one of the armies that were being prepared to repulse Murat's offensive. It was now understood in Vienna that the war would begin with this Italian hors-d'oeuvre, the prospect of which, moreover, was making the Aulic Council grimace. Certainly, they were glad to be freed of all circumspection with regard to the King of Naples, who was heedlessly putting himself in the wrong by starting hostilities. But his army was known to be numerous, well-armed and well-commanded, and Italy simmering, poorly held by scattered occupation troops; to concentrate them would require another ten days . . .

However, this was only a minor worry compared to what was brewing: each day, the ministers of England, Austria, Prussia and Russia pushed forward the drafting of the treaty of alliance, which was to be signed in four days *in the name of the Most Holy and Indivisible Trinity,* and by which each of the high contracting parties undertook, 'for the preservation of peace' (*sic*), to maintain 150,000 men constantly in the field so long as Buonaparte shall not be placed completely beyond the possibility of exciting disorders, of renewing any attempts to seize supreme power in France, and of threatening the security of Europe. It is true that England, by a secret article, obtained permission to 'pay' thirty pounds for every soldier she might be unable to provide, up to the amount of the number imposed.

. . . That anaemic England, uneasy and shaken with suppressed shudders, where precisely on March 20th, in the afternoon, a man rose from the benches of the House of Commons to put some impertinent questions to the noble Lord Castlereagh, the Prime Minister, back from Vienna. The man in question was Whitbread, one of the most eloquent leaders of the little band of Whigs opposing the ferocious domination of the Tories, who for fifteen years had kept England at war and her people in misery. Since the beginning of March, London had been in a state of latent insurrection,[1] because of the Corn Bill, which further starved the half-million poor of London. A mad King, a cynical and debauched Regent, a stupid aristocracy hanging on to power and refusing all reform, a nation of weavers and miners reduced to unemployment, that is to say a slow death, by the new machines—what more was needed to create an explosive situation? People were beginning to prophesy that a British Republic would be proclaimed before 1820. And a chronicler has given a singular picture of London in that month of March, when finally Revolution was closer to breaking out there than in Paris:

[1] 'What stability is there with these enormous cities? A serious insurrection in London, and all is lost,' Lord Liverpool was to say to Chateaubriand.

'Every man who has passed through the streets of London a week since will have seen the inscriptions placed on walls with the intention of inflaming minds and exciting disorder and tumult. "There's Lord Grenville, that's Lord Stanhope; here's the Chancellor of the Exchequer"; and he was cheered or booed according to whether the member going by was known to support or oppose the Bill. From time to time, there were shouts of "No Corn Bill". Everything was broken at Lord Elldon's house, windows and furnishings. Armed forces did not arrive until after the havoc. It was the same at Mr Robinson's house, where everything was devastated in less than an hour. At Lord Darnley's they were only able to break the windows, because military forces arrived. It was the same at Mr Yorke's, Lord Harwick's and Lord Ellenborough's. At the Lord Chancellor's, the mob appeared at about ten o'clock, when His Lordship was ready to go to bed. He left by a back door and returned with some troops, who advanced with bayonets before them, which put the mob to flight, though two or three of them were arrested. After nightfall, two successive attacks were made on Lord Castlereagh's house, but the crowd was repulsed each time by the cavalry, which watched its every move. A man and a woman were killed.'

Is this then the moment, asked Whitbread, to launch England once more into a war on the Continent, which would complete her exhaustion? After lashing in scathing terms the free-for-all of the Congress of Vienna, to which Lord Castlereagh had pledged himself, that auction-sale of populations, Saxons, Poles and Italians, as if it were a question of Indians, the Whig orator went on to say that the Congress of Vienna had only resulted in bringing Bonaparte back on to the political scene; it had brought him back invested with fresh moral force, which had been lent him by the injustices committed by his adversaries. Whitbread wanted to know whether the Powers themselves had not furnished Bonaparte with legitimate grounds for complaint? Has the Treaty of Fontainebleau been broken? Had they refused to pay the pension which had been promised to him? Had they tried to take the Duchies of Parma and Piacenza away from Napoleon's young son? If the Bourbons held out, they would undoubtedly learn moderation. If Bonaparte should triumph, it was not unlikely that great reverses would teach him to estimate his true interests better, and that, as a consequence, England might well be able to rest at peace with him.

To the honour of Great Britain—and of Europe—these words were pronounced in London at the very moment when the tricolour flag was being raised once more over Paris. In a London, we learn from another dispatch, which for several days had been completely surrounded by cavalry, infantry and artillery. 'The rabble that is still giving itself up to excesses is composed of children and young people, who are acting without a plan and according to the whim of the moment. Have they not attacked the offices of the *Morning Chronicle?*'

As for the Italians, were they about to draw breath? A voice was raised—a French one—on March 20th at Ancona:

Italians! The hour has come when the destiny of Italy shall be realized. When all foreign dominion shall vanish from Italian soil! When a truly national representation, a Constitution worthy of this century and of you, shall guarantee your liberty, your internal prosperity, as soon as you shall, by your courage, have secured your independence. I summon all brave men about me to fight. I summon equally all those who have given profound thought to the Constitution and the laws that shall govern an Italy happy, an Italy independent.'

It was the King of Naples, Joachim Murat, who read these ardent phrases in the afternoon, at the secret council which he held beside the Adriatic, with his ministers and military commanders. The official purpose of the meeting: to decide whether the Neapolitans were to stay on the defensive, to choose a good fortified position and wait for Austria's attack—or whether they were to dash across the Roman Marches and States to try and rally the whole peninsula, before Vienna had time to reinforce its occupation troops. The ministers and high officers were unanimous in begging the King to temporize. Without the least outburst, Murat, smiling, relaxed, unruffled, seemed to accept their point of view, and read them the text of his proclamation to the Italians 'merely to submit the text to them, as a rough draft, without knowing whether any use would be made of it'. But those who knew him well were not deceived and knew what was burning inside him under that appalling calm. Having arrived at Ancona the day before, acclaimed by the common people and flattered by the notables, Murat felt himself twenty years younger and believed he had found his historic vocation at last: to give life and liberty to the whole of Italy; to make the French Revolution assimilable for the whole Latin world; to have done with that feudal patchwork, which drew lots for this people, proud and poor, as for the outraged garments of Christ— Austria, the Kings of Sardinia and Sicily, the Dukes of Tuscany and the Princes of Parma, the Pope and the senators of Venice. One single Italy, from the Alps to Calabria! Under Murat's sceptre, no doubt? That was a mere detail. Was not Napoleon in the process of restoring equality to power in France? Whatever might be said or written later, it now appeared that the two men found themselves fleetingly fraternal again in that month of March.[1]

The war they had waged with one another in 1814 was already far away in 1815. But the essential difference between them lay in the fact that if Napoleon sincerely desired peace, Murat's whole future was in the coming war. He believed he would be the more certain of winning it the more quickly he started it.

King Murat dismissed his council in a good mood and quietly went for a long ride on horseback by the seashore. He was not

---

[1] 'There were more than twenty couriers between the Island of Elba and Murat,' Napoleon was to write on St Helena. It is true, he was to accuse Joachim, when everything went wrong, of precipitancy. But he would nevertheless send him a letter, in a few days, which breathed 'the spirit of Vendémiaire': 'I have arrived. I have crossed France . . . Until this moment, I am at peace with everyone. I shall support you with all my forces.' (A phrase with which Napoleon was to be bitterly reproached later by Murat.) 'I am relying on you. As soon as Marseilles has put up the tricolour cockade, send me some of your vessels so that we can correspond, for I much fear that correspondence through Italy may become difficult. Send me a minister: I will send you one on a frigate shortly.'

to return to the Governor's Palace until about midnight. His decision was taken: in a week he was to give orders to move forward and would date the proclamation he had in his pocket from the first town to be taken. It would enter history, therefore, under the name of the *Proclamation of Rimini* and would be the first swallow, quickly brought down, quickly forgotten, of the Italian spring.

That same night, Cardinal Pacca, Secretary of State, ordered the Pontifical gendarmerie to take the necessary measures, in the greatest secrecy, to station along the road from Rome to Viterbo the cavalry pickets needed to serve as escort to Pius VII, whose departure, absolutely secret, was fixed for March 22nd, in the afternoon. Napoleon in Paris, Murat at Ancona, the Pope leaving Rome: signs of a break-up in the European ice, which everyone thought had set too quickly.

All that afternoon Napoleon advanced at walking-pace only. In Paris, there was already some anxiety at his lateness—and for a long time historians would try to find the mysterious reasons for this slowness. This is indeed the way to create sham enigmas. Everything is so clear when one sees this triumphal march through the eyes of Saint-Denis, known as Ali:

'Part of the cavalry, which had been reviewed during the morning, served as escort. The whole army preceded or followed the Emperor's procession. It went at walking-pace or a jog-trot, so that everyone could follow. The cavalrymen of the escort advanced one by one, lining the two sides of the road; a multitude of inhabitants from the villages accompanied the Emperor, either inside or outside the hedge of cavalry. Every moment saw the arrival of senior officers and many other personages, who came to greet the Emperor and swell his already very considerable staff.'

The whole of this expansible and improvised little court had packed themselves as they could into posting barouches, in the retinue. At the entrance to Essonnes, carriages from the King's stables were found with six or eight horses 'driven by coachmen, postilions and grooms, dressed in civilian clothes,[1] who had all been part of the Emperor's Household'. La Valette had sent them haphazardly that morning, and they were in the hands of worthy people who had been scraping the paintwork since midday, to bring out the eagles overlaid with royalist emblems. But they were to remain empty: Napoleon kept to his barouches.

He had arrived at one of the finest moments a man could ever have desired.

'What we had seen up to that time held nothing to compare with the sight that met our eyes when the Emperor reached Essonnes: it was nothing but carriages, saddle-horses, officers of every rank, of all ages, peasants, bourgeois, women, children, soldiers of every corps, of every branch; it was an enormous rendezvous, in which everything was jumbled together. Never can greater diversity have been seen, and the whole multitude, radiant with joy, happiness and enthusiasm, made the welkin ring with their *"Vive l'Empereur! Vive Napoleon!"* '

This roisterous scene unfolded in a setting that was made for it: at a spot where the Essonne, branching into several arms, watered a land that resembled 'a vast garden, English, Chinese or natural, interspersed with ruins and the most picturesque buildings'. Here was a dense swarm of uniforms, red, white and green, of helmets and lances, of caps raised on the points of bayonets. Cheers, drums and bugles. At one stroke, it was brutal spring for France, who had thought herself old and led on the leash by senile idiots. Napoleon alighted and advanced to review the 2nd Regiment of the Line, which he was to send off again at once for Paris.

He was forty-six. He was in the midst of regaining a throne *merely by showing his cap. It was the greatest miracle God had performed!*, Balzac was to make a grenadier exclaim. 'He resembled no one. His physiognomy could belong only to him.

---

[1] They had not dared as yet to resume the Imperial livery, green and gold.

His look was calm. His eyes were bright, his gaze seemed marked by benevolence, and a dignified smile touched his lips.'[1] He stood on an improvised platform while the men filed before him, thinking they were living a dream. A sketch of him to the life, which the Englishman Hobhouse was to make a few days later in similar circumstances, enables him to be seen with precision, just as he was at that moment, the true culminating point of the return from Elba:

'His face was of a deadly pale; his jaws overhung, but not as much as I had heard; his lips thin, but partially curled, so as to give to his mouth an inexpressible sweetness. He had the habit of retracting the lips, and apparently chewing, in the manner observed and objected to in our great actor, Mr Kean. His hair was of a dark dusky brown, scattered thinly over his temples: the crown of his head was bald. One of the names of affection given him of late by his soldiers is *"notre petit tondu"*. He was not fat in the upper part of his body, but projected considerably in the abdomen, so much so, that his linen appeared beneath his waistcoat. He generally stood with his hands knit behind or folded before him, but sometimes unfolded them: played with his nose; took snuff three or four times, and looked at his watch. He seemed to have a labouring in his chest, sighing or swallowing his spittle. He very seldom spoke, but when he did, smiled, in some sort, agreeably. He looked about him, not knitting but joining his eyebrows as if to see more minutely . . . '

He was wearing, and had been wearing since Porto Ferraio, the green coat of a Colonel of the *chasseurs* of the Imperial Guard, with epaulettes. Attached to his buttonhole was the star of the Légion d'Honneur.

The stop at Essonnes was further prolonged by the arrival of a group of men in full-dress uniform, moved beyond all expression, who rushed towards him. He saw them coming and clasped them in his arms: at last, his *true* familiars! The human background that he had constructed for himself in ten years of the Empire: Caulaincourt, Master of the Horse, whom he made get into his carriage; Mouton, the hero of the Island of Lobau;

[1] Pons de l'Hérault.

277

Flahaut, 'the most handsome man in the Grand Army'; and Durosnel, Dejean and Planat, his three favourite aides-de-camp. They had left Paris together at about eleven o'clock, when high-ranking Bonapartists had split into three groups: those who, like La Valette, took possession of Paris; those who flew to meet him, the youngest, the most impatient and—save for Caulaincourt—the most sincere; and finally, the 'torpid old crabs', who continued to lie low at home and foresaw no good coming of it all, Cambacérès, Mollien, Lebrun, etc.

The Emperor asked Mouton to mount horse and hurry to the Tuileries to confirm his imminent arrival. And he turned affectionately to a worthy man, all white and wrinkled, with a body like a dried-up vine-shoot: a veteran who had come with all those 'young ones', and whose great plumed hat the soldiers cheered with redoubled enthusiasm: at last, a Marshal of France —no! a Marshal of the Empire, as they were beginning to say once more. It was Lefebvre.

. . . Marmont, Berthier, Macdonald, Mortier, Oudinot and Gouvion-Saint-Cyr were following the King, or still trying to fight for him wherever they were. Augereau, Jourdan, Suchet, Masséna, Soult and Victor, after fulminating abusive proclamations against Napoleon, had adopted a prudent neutrality in those last days, and were looking for a way to change cockades. Brune was silent in his country property. Lannes, Duroc, Bessières and Poniatowski were dead. Kellermann, Sérurier and Pérignon were 'out of the race'.

Of all the great soldiers of the Empire, covered in titles and honours, only two Marshals went over to Napoleon's side in that month of March: Ney, shortly before—and we have seen with what reservations. Now Lefebvre, who was recovering his fervour of '89, when he had been a sergeant in the French Guards. In a few hours Davout would bring him his rallying, at a moment when this would no longer present the least danger. It is true that Lefebvre and Ney had been in little greater hurry.

Forward! The loaded procession moved off on the last stage: the paved highway was growing wider and already opening the arms of the great city. It was at Essonnes, indeed, that Napoleon regained his own men: those who loved him without trickery, at least on that day.

Saint-Denis

The sun went down; it was two minutes past six.

That was how things went to the south of Paris. But when one turns to the north, at the same hour, one might think one were entering Lapland. The Bourbon monarchy and its moth-eaten trappings seemed to be foundering quite as much under the pressure of the elements as under that of the people. Fifty miles away the rain has changed its nature. Paris observatory, however, gives us unbiased information: at three o'clock that afternoon it was 12·7°, and the weather 'cloudy and changeable'. But nothing shows better how much it is our opinion that makes rain and fine weather than the different estimates of the weather of March 20th in the *Mémoires* of the royalists and those of the Bonapartists. At Essonnes, as we have seen, it was spring: the occasional rain was almost enjoyed, nice showers to make the weapons gleam. At Saint-Denis it was winter: squalls and an ocean of mud. Everyone groped and floundered.

They had lost the King. The main occupation of his people throughout the day seems to have been to look for him. How could a sovereign as encumbered as he have vanished into thin air? One forgets that Louis XVI's brother, for his part, had always succeeded in his *'escampatives'*, his flittings, and that this victim of gout possessed a remarkable gift for effective flight. While his family, his ministers and his guards were roaming in sinister fashion across the great plains of beetroot, Louis XVIII was fleeing towards the sea with a start of two stages, thanks to a rapid vehicle and a series of excellent relays well anticipated by Blacas and Berthier. He dozed on the shoulder of one or the other, at least so long as it was not on Duras', and displayed a perfect calm, except on arriving at Beauvais, where he was anxious about lunch. But a fricassée of chicken, of which he devoured 'an admirable quantity', restored to his person the noble bearing from which he would lapse no more. He insisted, nevertheless, that speed should be further increased. What had seized him? Wherever he passed the people were peaceable, the troops respectful, he was pitied, he was admired. Only one thing might have alarmed him: the slenderness of his escort, which melted in proportion to the speed imposed. The same sacrifices could not be imposed upon horses as upon men. In that case, why not stop, to regain breath, wait for the rest of the House-hold, and set off again amid the imposing pomp of a sovereign?

The answer came at Amiens, at the end of the day, when the King gave the order to leave the direct road for Lille to turn off to the left, and announced that he wanted to sleep at Abbeville. It was not so much before Bonaparte that he was quickening his pace; it was to escape from his own people. He was tired of all those great souls who had been recommending him martyrdom for a fortnight. Lille? It is true, Mortier was still in command there and had just given proof of his loyalty . . . but since the Ney affair, could these people be trusted even for twenty-four hours? And under Mortier there was a whole garrison of those savages, the French soldiers. What if they went and caught Louis XVIII in a trap? From Abbeville, on the other hand, it was possible to reach Dieppe or Boulogne, and embark at once for England, to know again the beloved life of Hartwell, a large park, a good fire, peace. Twenty years in exile had anchored the King in the conviction that there existed but one valid fortress for not falling into the hands of Bonaparte: Britain.

During this time, Macdonald, at Saint-Denis, had been able to savour all the bitterness of the disaster. He had not found the headquarters of the Paris troops there any more than at Villejuif, 'but all these officers had not failed to draw the allowance for going on campaign, and some good gratuities on account of their future services . . . '. The Marshal was to await the arrival of General Maison's troops until one o'clock. Finally, one of Rapp's aides-de-camp came to inform him that the defection was general. Already, Exelmans had headed off the majority of those on half pay. But there were still too many of them in Saint-Denis.

'I was then told that a detachment of artillery was entering the town (on its way to rally to the Emperor). I sent General Ruty to head them off, but the half-pay officers, no longer observing any propriety, threw themselves on this artillery, and General Ruty, in trying to carry out my orders, nearly became their victim. I was informed at the same time that General Maison, being pursued, had been obliged to save himself. Shortly after, another scene took place before my eyes: the carriages of the Duke de Berry were passing through Saint-Denis, having come from Villejuif; the rebels seized them, made the drivers get down, with violence, and mounted the horses in their place; I was ashamed to see French officers behave in this way, all in uniform, epaulettes on their coats, fatigue-caps on their heads, but the majority drunk and disorderly. If anything can excuse their conduct, it is drunkenness and excitement: it still makes me blush for them.

'Tired of waiting uselessly at Saint-Denis, I left there at one o'clock for Beaumont, which I provisionally named as head-quarters. A large number of half-pay officers had collected in front of the inn where I was, the first on the left after the square; I expected some opposition from them, fully resolved not to let myself be insulted with impunity, if I had to compromise myself, but they kept quiet, even polite, and respectful. At Beaumont I found the tail-end of the Royal Household, a number of dismounted lifeguards, some leading their horses by the tether, others lying in carts, others on foot, portmanteau under the arm; all this had the air of a rout after a defeat. As I did not stop at Beaumont, I found the route marked out in this way as far as Noailles. At Beaumont I left the same orders as at Saint-Denis, and I took the post in order to rejoin the Princes, with the van of the Royal Household.'

Rochechouart, who that afternoon worked his way on horse-back up that mess sprawled over twenty-five miles, while chatting to the Duke de Richelieu, states that:

'the King's military household was composed of some lifeguards, gendarmes, light horse and musketeers, grey and black; for infantry it had the Hundred Swiss with four pieces of cannon, commanded by the Duke de Mortemart, and finally some hundreds of volunteers, called royal, alongside which marched Louis de la Rochejaquelein, with part of his company of horse grenadiers; the whole under the orders of T.R.H. Monsieur, the King's brother, and the Duke de Berry. The total of this little army might have amounted to 4,000 men: infantry, cavalry or artillery. They had left Paris very late, in great disorder and precipitately, without even knowing too well what road was supposed to be followed. Also the number of stragglers was considerable.'

At the Tuileries, on which night was falling, the rising of the curtain would appear interminable to spectators of the last act, ill-informed of the reasons that were delaying the Emperor. Minds were haunted by fear of an attempt on his life. Besides, by a very understandable reaction, those who had nothing else to do but wait had time to consider the improbability of the event. Napoleon revived? They would not be sure of it till they touched him.

In the steps of Exelmans, the Imperial staff had rushed in through the open breach, from chamberlains to scullions. When Savary appeared in his turn,

'everything had already been re-installed, each had resumed his post at the Château. The Emperor dined there, found his apartment ready, one would have said he was simply returning from a journey. The officers of the honorary service, employees of every kind, had resumed their functions, nothing was lacking to the reception. There are some awkward souls (*sic*) who have tried to see in the resumption of this routine the consequences of a conspiracy, whereas each of us only did what he had seen done to employees of the Court at Versailles, at the time of the King's return.'

While the staff were busy tidying up and making everything function normally, the salons were filling with councillors of State, ministers and equerries, all in full dress, on which the red blob of the Légion d'Honneur was prominent. They had brought their wives, in Court dress, who revenged themselves that night for the vexations endured at the hands of the King's dowagers. In the Throne Room and the Diana Gallery, where the chandeliers blazed as for a ball, it was a feast of fashion in the style of the day, in which amaranth was gaining on the colour *Jean de Paris*, which had been the rage the previous summer. Marten and blue fox decorated the Capuchins, with a preference for miniver and ermine; but Capuchins were diminishing in number compared with pelerines, 'which at this time have gained two inches, some *couturières* make them fall to the waist, others allow the belt to be seen'. Beneath them, the enchantment of bare shoulders, and already the adornment of the year: a mixture of violets and immortelles on the bodice. The few stray men in civilian dress in the midst of the braided uniforms had, by a similar reaction, rejected the English fashion: the cut-away frock-coat, pale butter-coloured breeches of kerseymere, pearl-white stockings and white quilted waistcoat brought back the masculine fashion of 1811.

Everyone of this fashionable world was embracing and questioning each other and talking loudly. Fleury de Chaboulon, who arrived very intimidated, observed that 'the rooms of the Palace seemed transformed into a battlefield, where friends and brothers, having escaped death unexpectedly, were finding one another again and embracing after the victory'. They surrounded the important people, who were the more anxious to prove that they had done nothing, positively nothing, to bring about the return of the Emperor — except perhaps for Maret, Duke de Bassano, the entirely devoted Secretary of State, who for his part had at least corresponded regularly with the Island of Elba. But also present were Gaudin, Arrighi, Admiral Decrès, Daru, Ségur, Regnault de Saint-Jean-d'Angély and, of course, La Valette. Two women were much courted: Queen Hortense and Julie, the wife of Joseph Bonaparte, ex-Queen of Spain, a country in which she had never wanted to set foot. Both of them were in mourning for their mothers: Josephine had died less than a year before and Mme Clary a few weeks. In high spirits, the ladies were busy ripping off the fleurs-de-lys, merely stitched on to the covers, beneath which the Imperial bees were reappearing. In the courtyard a strong battalion of the National Guard was ready to present arms, and above all, a profusion of officers without troops, who would rather have died than miss this moment, were bubbling with noisy excitement.

By contrast, outside, in the Place de Carrousel and in the gardens, the crowd had dispersed; only a few rather sparse groups remained. As we have seen, the influx of the day had been formed rather of onlookers, and the inhabitants of the neighbouring quarter were relatively hostile. A cold little drizzle was falling on the banks of the Seine; those who stayed on the spot had to stamp their feet to keep warm. Uncertain weather has always discouraged the Parisian sightseer, and he is not one to like waiting. Now, since midday not a quarter of an hour had gone by without an outcry suggesting the arrival of the Emperor. There would remain, therefore, for the great moment, only about 2,000 spectators, concentrated for the most part within the Tuileries, but these, all devotees. The rest of Paris, apart from some workers gathered in coffee-houses on the boulevards to the south, had gone to bed—or else to the theatre, why not? There was no lack of diversions for the night-birds, whom politics did not impassion. If the Théâtre-Français had suspended performances, they were playing that night at the Opéra-Comique *Félicie ou la fille romanesque*; at the Odéon, *La Griselda*; at the Vaudeville, *La Petite Intrigue épistolaire, Une soirée des boulevards* and *Gaspard l'avisé*; at the Variétés, *Jocrisse corrigé, La Noce interrompue, Le Savetier et le financier* and *Je fais mes farces*; at the Théâtre de la Gaîté, *Le Chien de Montargis* and *Les Chevaliers de Malte*; at the Ambigu-Comique, *Palmerin et Cælina*; at the Porte-Saint-Martin Theatre, *Le Tanneur de Lesseville, Le Berger de la Sierra Morena* and *Le Sergent polonais* . . . And there was also the instructive spectacle of M. Robertson, Boulevard Montmartre (every day at seven o'clock), before the *Panoramas of Boulogne*, and the Picturesque and Mechanical Light Theatre of M. Pierre (continued by his pupils), Rue de la Fontaine-Michaudière, Carrefour Gaillon (every day at 7.30). This last show had just been enriched by six new scenes; among others, *The Straits of the Dardanelles* and *The Fort at Porto-Ferraio*.

At eight in the evening Napoleon's son was put to bed in his room at the Hofburg, which was already more familiar to him. He went to sleep peacefully. Mme de Montesquiou then approached the bed: 'I went down on my knees. I commended him to Heaven. I asked above all that his name should never be abused to cause disorders.[1] I embraced him several times, and I

---

[1] A bitter destiny was that of this child, betrayed even in the prayer of the one who loved him most: but no force in the world could do anything against the spirit of the aristocratic class.

tore myself from his side, after fixing to the curtains of his bed a little crucifix that he had often asked me to give him.'

With 'Maman Quiou' it was France, and above all worship of his father, that was being effaced for ever that night, from the life of the nameless child who was soon to be called the Duke de Reichstadt.

The same evening, Talleyrand wrote to Louis XVIII:

'The Emperor Francis has just ordered Mme de Montesquiou to hand over to him the child with which she had been charged. Her language in the present circumstances was so contrary to the resolutions laid down by Austria and the other Powers that the Emperor did not wish to allow her to remain by his grandson any longer. Tomorrow she is to receive the order to return to France. The child is going to be established in Vienna, at the Palace. In this way, no one will be able to kidnap him, as several circumstances might let it be supposed.'

It was nearly nine o'clock when Napoleon re-entered Paris. After so many glorious scenes there was something of an anticlimax about the end of the event. Fleury de Chaboulon admits it:

'We had been so spoiled along the way that the welcome given the Emperor by the Parisians by no means came up to our expectation. Repeated cries greeted him as he passed, but they did not present the character of the acclamations that had accompanied him from Golfe-Juan to the gates of Paris. One would be mistaken, nevertheless, if one were to infer from this that the Parisians did not look upon his return with pleasure. Because the people were for him, and the cries came from the people. One must simply conclude that Napoleon missed his entrance.'

The royalists, indeed, would not fail to compare 'that almost clandestine arrival, like that of a thief', with the solemn procession which had installed Louis XVIII in Paris. To which Napoleon himself was to reply very sensibly:

'The Emperor entered Paris, as he did Grenoble and Lyons, at the end of a full day's march, and at the head of armies that had been set against him. He entered Paris as on his return from Marengo, Austerlitz, Tilsit, etc. He had plenty of other things to do than waste two days in order to prepare a ceremonial entry. He did not give up a quarter of an hour for that.'[1]

However, it is true that the mental temperature of Paris remained cold that evening. He had never been very well liked by the capital, and he fully reciprocated. Was it true, moreover, that, as Planat asserts: 'the old police of the Empire had already resumed its customary operations and persuaded the Grand Marshal that His Majesty would have run great risks by following the most direct way, via the Austerlitz bridge, where an immense crowd was waiting for him'? It is possible, but certain it is that even around the 'Jardin du Roi', which was about to become the 'Jardin des Plantes' again, the crowd was not 'immense'.

Be that as it may, relates Saint-Denis, 'at last we arrived at the Villejuif *barrière*; we followed the Boulevard and reached the Invalides; we crossed the Louis XVI bridge and entered the courtyard of the Tuileries by the Pont-Royal gate'. It is still a matter of Gamot's barouche, which had again outrun the other carriages, and was surrounded only by a few cavalrymen with drawn sabres and loud of voice. It penetrated the courtyard 'without anyone knowing at first who was inside', but then a sort of explosion occurred among the crowd, overheated from waiting. A shock that convulsed and shook a thousand people in one spasm of joy. All those who lived through it could no more contain their emotion in recounting it.

And first, the Mameluke and the coachman had their work cut out:

'Up to the gates, there being plenty of room, we travelled freely. But once inside the courtyard, it was no longer possible

[1] However, during the Hundred Days he would try to give provincial opinion quite another idea of his entry into Paris, and was to favour the diffusion of a very strange print, which gave an idea of things very different from the reality.

for us to move. The whole of the part on the Pavillon de Flore side, near which is the usual entrance to the Palace, was filled with such a dense mass of generals, officers, National Guards, and a large number of distinguished persons, that it was impossible for me to drive the carriage up to the steps. The Emperor, seeing he could go no further, got out in the middle of the huge crowd which pressed round him.'

He was not even able to set foot to the ground. No presentations, no speeches. Those nearest to the barouche tore the Emperor from the hands of Bertrand, Drouot and Caulaincourt, and bore him off on their shoulders across the courtyard, up the steps, up the grand staircase. Others in their turn wanted to take up the relay, and there was almost a quarrel over it. At that moment he was in serious danger, for the flood coming from the outside met the stream of those who were jostling their way down. A sort of whirlpool occurred on the stairs, and a mild protest was heard from Napoleon:

'*Mes enfants!* You are suffocating me!'

'In the name of God, put yourself in front of him!' shouted Caulaincourt to La Valette.

The latter, supported by the banisters, went up backwards in front of the Emperor, making a shield for him with his body, and repeating, 'It's you! It's you!' in a sort of hypnosis. Ghastly pale, Napoleon shut his eyes, abandoned his hands to the kisses, seemed not to recognize anyone, and staggered into his apartment, the doors of which closed on him at last.

He had recaptured Paris. It was his greatest victory.

Marchand had difficulty in getting a quiet moment to change his clothes. He observed:

'Everyone seemed drunk with happiness and hope. The Emperor himself was unable to hide his delight; I have never seen him so wild with glee, so lavish with pats on the cheek. His speech showed the agitation in his heart; the same words came ceaselessly from his mouth, and it must be acknowledged that they were by no means flattering for the crowd of courtiers and important men who were already assailing him; he repeated ceaselessly: "It's the unselfish people who have brought me back to Paris; it's the second lieutenants and the soldiers who have done everything; it's the people, it's the army, to whom I owe everything".'

Fleury de Chaboulon was there when he recovered his workroom:

'He found his writing-table covered with mystical books; he had them replaced by maps and military plans. "The cabinet of a French monarch," he said, "should not resemble an oratory, but a general's tent." His eyes dwelt on the map of France. After contemplating her new boundaries, he exclaimed in a tone of deep sadness: "Poor France!" He remained silent for a few moments, and after that started to sing one of his habitual refrains between his teeth:

> *S'il est un temps pour la folie*
> *Il en est un pour la raison.*

'The King left so suddenly that he did not have time to remove his personal papers. In his writing-table we found his family portfolio; it included a very large number of letters from the Duchess d'Angoulême, and some from the Princes. Napoleon glanced through several of them and handed me the portfolio, ordering me to have it preserved religiously. Napoleon wanted one to have some respect for royal Majesty, and for everything to do with the person of kings.

'The King had made habitual use of a little table that he had brought back from Hartwell: Napoleon took pleasure in working at it for a few hours; he had it taken away after that, and prescribed that the greatest care was to be taken of it.

'The King's wheel-chair, which could not suit Napoleon, whose body and health were full of strength and vigour, was relegated to the back closet. Someone happened to be sitting in it at a moment when the Emperor was passing without being expected. He threw him a furious glance, and the chair was removed.

'One of his valets de chambre, thinking to gain his favour, dared to put some caricatures offensive to the Bourbons on his mantelshelf; he threw them scornfully on the fire, and ordered him sternly not to permit himself such impertinences any more in the future.'

Shortly before midnight, Louis XVIII went to bed at Abbeville and would sleep for twelve hours on end. It was there that Macdonald would find him again the next day and would get him to resume the road to Lille. It is true that the King was experiencing cares far more serious than the collapse of his throne. In the panic of the flight the portmanteau containing his baggage had been lost, and especially the two enormous leather bags which, for some years, had been used to enshroud his bad feet.

'They've taken my shirts; I had none too many before! But it's my slippers I regret more; you'll know one day, my dear Marshal, what it is to lose slippers that have taken on the shape of the foot!'

So he took the road to Belgium, accompanied by two or three hundred waifs from a past that seemed, at last, to be finished for ever. But already some were raising their heads again. The Duke of Wellington's troops were arriving in Brussels. Nothing is more significant of the mentality of the vanquished of March 20th, who tomorrow would again become the vanquishers of the French people, than an unacknowledged little masterpiece, *Le Catéchisme à l'usage des royalistes*, which the team of editors of the *Nain Jaune* were in the process of writing, in the euphoria of victory, and which begins with a sufficiently terrible response:

Question: Are you French?

Answer: No, I'm a royalist.[1]

After dinner, 'served as if the Emperor had never left the Tuileries', Napoleon overcame an immeasurable weariness, expressed in alternations of excitement and prostration, to pass rapidly into the salons. He spoke severely to Hortense about her compromises with the King and greeted Julie absent-mindedly. Not one member of his true family was there to savour this

[1] We publish the full text in an Appendix.

triumph with him. Joseph had fled that morning from Prangins to rejoin him, escaping just in time from the Swiss gendarmes, who had been on their way to arrest him at Talleyrand's request. Jerome was in Italy. Louis, vexed, was in Austria. Lucien was preparing to leave Rome to come and make things up with him. Madame Mère and Pauline were still on the island of Elba. Élisa was a prisoner of the Austrians in Tuscany. Caroline reigned in Naples against him, and was trying to resume relations with the English.

He was incredibly isolated that night, in the midst of the general intoxication. His wife was deceiving him and he suspected as much. His son was in captivity. The crowd that had carried him thus far had gone back to their houses. The cavalrymen of the escort were encamped on the spot, in the gardens and in the Carrousel, 'transformed into a sort of Tartar encampment', and were awaiting the order to move into Belgium tomorrow, if he made a sign. That sign which he was not to give, because he sincerely wanted at first to try the chances of peace, and at any rate to reorganize the army.

Above all, he could do no more. He had dominated events for as long as he could: at Porto Ferraio, when he had taken the decision to set out, under the threat of a deportation resolution by the Congress of Vienna, under the pressure of lack of money, and because he realized that if he were not to come, others would drive out the King. At Laffrey, when he had advanced towards the battalion of the 5th of the Line, at the moment when everything could still have gone wrong, and had cried: 'Soldiers, do you recognize me? If there is one among you who wishes to kill his Emperor, here I am!' At Lyons still, when he had made the revolutionary decrees and convoked the people of France in a Champ de Mai. At Chalon, at Autun even, when he had threatened to 'string up' the nobles and the priests . . . but already the tone was dropping. And then there was the mounting exhaustion, the onslaught of the flatterers who had been liming him for fifteen years. There were the Palaces: Fontainebleau, the Tuileries, the crowd of valets, and Fleury de Chaboulon, insinuating in his ear: 'How comfortable it is at home with you . . .'

At home . . . He was indeed about to find himself at home

again, by forming that very night, through lassitude, through habit, and through snobbery, still, a not very homogeneous government of liberals and imperialists who had but one idea: to prevent him from 'donning the red cap'. Even Carnot? Even Carnot, who again found himself before all, in 1815, the enemy of Robespierre. Even Davout, 'the most Jacobin of the Marshals', but who refused to believe in the war, and was to wait several precious days before mobilizing all the country's resources. At midnight on March 20th Napoleon strangled with his own hands the unprecedented opportunity that destiny had just given him by agreeing to give audience to Fouché, who presented himself audaciously and arrogantly, as if he had been the author of the return. Although Savary had just warned him, although other loyal followers had already told Napoleon all. Although he knew, from sure intuition and from experience, what the man was worth and where he was going. It made no difference: he heard the general cry of the salons:

'Bring in M. Fouché!'

And he no longer heard 'the clamour of the street'.

Fouché, appointed Minister of Police, was to say to his friend Gaillard the following morning:

'Within three months I shall be more powerful than he; and if he doesn't have me killed, he'll be at my knees.'

We are already, it is true, at March 21st. No! at June 18th.

It remains, however, that those days—and that day—were lived. And that this makes it worth the trouble of reliving them. In one of the water-coaches that brought the battalion from Elba to Paris there was that corporal from Marseilles who was known as the 'scholar', because he 'talked better than the others', and whose great speech had been overheard by Pons de l'Hérault on the ramparts of Porto Ferraio, at the time when everyone on the island of Elba was beginning to live the return in his imagination, before it had become reality. Across a hundred and fifty years this striking text shows that something of the people's spring was beginning to break through confusedly in 1815, in that popular consciousness which already presaged a Europe, and—why not?—a mankind, united in justice:

'The Emperor is spreading the idea that he wants to take Egypt again. The people at the Tuileries are glad we'll be out of the way; they laugh about it: all right. The signal to leave is given; we set sail: all right. The Emperor hasn't been sleeping, everything is ready to receive us, to back us up: all right. We revictual at Malta; we take some galleys there, if we need them: all right. We land on the banks of the Danube, a little higher or a little lower: all right. Constantinople is in the secret, it shuts its eyes, one would think it sees nothing, knows nothing: all right. Then we march forward with flag unfurled, in close columns: all right. The Greeks come and join us, the Moldavians and the Servians too: all right. We take Belgrade. If necessary, we rest there: all right. The Hungarians have been expecting us, so as to rise against the Austrians; they've risen; they march under our flags, because the Hungarians and the Austrians, they're like water and fire: all right. Our army has grown; we go up the Danube: all right. But that's not all. A Polish army has set out from Warsaw to come and help us; this army is the twin of our army, you see, and at the signal we all find ourselves in the walls of Vienna: all right. Vienna is surrounded: she gives in, and there she is, ours again: all right. From the capital of Austria to our capital we know the way and can do it blind-fold: all right. There we are, in Paris; the Tuileries people have cleared off, and the Parisians shout *"Vive l'Empereur!"* All right.'

Pons de l'Hérault had transcribed this text word for word, in order to take it to the Emperor the next day.

Napoleon had read it 'with avidity' and had exclaimed:
'*All right!*'

Malmaison. March 20, 1965.
The 150th anniversary.

Appendix I

FROM THE *Journal des Débats*, MARCH 19TH.

COMPLETE TEXT OF BENJAMIN CONSTANT'S ARTICLE

The representatives of the nation have carried to the foot of the throne the expression of their devotion and their gratitude. They have at the same time expressed the admiration of the people for the courage of their monarch, and the wish to see associated with the destiny of France the men who, for twenty-five years, have at various times defended the motherland, glory and liberty of France, a salutary association which brings together all opinions, wipes out the last vestiges of the opposition parties and surrounds the constitutional King with his true supports, those who in 1789 wanted to have liberty flourish under the Monarchy and who in 1815 want to consolidate the Monarchy through liberty. They are indeed the bulwark of governments, those who comprehend the grounds upon which they defend them. When a man asks no more than to serve despotism, he passes with indifference from one government to another, quite sure that he will regain his place as instrument under the new despotism. But when he cherishes liberty he risks his life about the throne that protects liberty.

So now, reassured about all our anxieties, happy and proud of the dignity, the courage, the sincerity of our Monarch, let us redouble our efforts against the enemy of France, against the enemy of mankind. Louis XVIII, out of a confidence worthy of a King of France towards the French, far from surrounding himself with suspicious precautions, seizes the moment of danger to make the constitution that governs us more liberal still. Supported on this unshakable foundation, the only one that in these times can give governments strength and continuance, he is relying on our zeal, our patriotism, and on that courage which was tried by Europe, and which will ever arouse his undying admiration. It is a matter of all our interests, our wives, our children, our properties, of liberty, of our industry, our opinions, our words and our thoughts. The man who threatens us had encroached upon everything. He abducted labour from agriculture, he made grass grow in our commercial cities, he drew away to the ends of the world the élite of the nation, to abandon it then to the horrors of famine and the rigours of frost; by his will, twelve hundred thousand brave men perished on foreign soil,[1] without succour, without maintenance, without solace, deserted by him after defending him with their dying hands. He is coming back today, poor and greedy, to wrest from us what still remains to us. The riches of the world are his no more; it is ours that he seeks to devour. His appearance, which for us is a renewal of all the misfortunes, is for Europe a sign of war. The peoples are alarmed, the Powers astonished. The sovereigns, who by his abdication had become our allies, feel with sorrow the need to become our enemies again. No nation can depend upon his word; not one, if he rules us, can remain at peace with us.[2]

On the King's side is constitutional liberty, security, peace; on Buonaparte's side, servitude, anarchy and war. Under Louis XVIII, we enjoy a representative government; we are governing ourselves.[3] Under Buonaparte we should suffer a government of Mamelukes; his sword alone would govern us. And if I may be allowed to take up a delusion which no doubt would not have weakened stout hearts and brave resolves, but which might have shaken wavering spirits and common souls. There has been talk in these times of the clemency which Buonaparte has promised, and there has been indignation at this clemency. But this promise does not exist. I have read these proclamations of a fallen tyrant who is trying to seize the sceptre again. The words 'clemency' and 'amnesty' are not to be found in them any more than the words 'constitution' and 'liberty'. A few phrases, thrown scornfully into the texts that have appeared since March 31st seem, it is true, to offer those who attacked the overthrown tyranny the guarantee of contempt, but these phrases contain not one commitment, they leave the field open to every revenge.

[1] This is a long way from the 'three millions' of Mme de Staël. The truth is that nobody, in 1815, could make an exact estimate of the number of soldiers who died in the Napoleonic wars, which borders on a million.
[2] These last lines would have been enough to get Benjamin Constant shot by any *'tribunal d'épuration'*.
[3] The property qualification for the vote reduced the number of electors to about thirty thousand, for a population of twenty-five million souls.

Buonaparte's proclamations are in no way those of a prince who believes in his right to the throne, they are not even those of a sedition-monger exerting himself to tempt the people with the bait of liberty: they are the proclamations of an armed leader who flourishes his sword to excite the greed of his satellites, and throws them upon the citizens as on a prey. It is Attila, it is Genghis Khan, more terrible and more odious, because the resources of civilization are his to use; one can see him preparing them to regularize massacre and to administer pillage; he does not disguise his schemes; he scorns us too much to deign to beguile us.

And what people, indeed, would be more worthy to be scorned than us, if we held out our arms for his shackles? After being the terror of Europe we should become its laughing-stock; we should regain a master whom we ourselves had covered with opprobrium. A year ago we could say we had been carried away by enthusiasm or deceived by guile. Today we have proclaimed that our eyes are open, that we detest this man's yoke. It would be contrary to our vow, known, declared, repeated a thousand times, that we should resume this dreadful yoke; we should acknowledge ourselves a nation of slaves, our slavery would no longer have any excuse, our abjection no bounds.

And from the depths of this profound abjection, what should we dare to say to this King whom we need not have recalled, for the Powers sought to respect the independence of the national desire, to this King whom we have enticed by spontaneous resolutions[1] back to the land in which his family had already suffered so much? We should say to him: 'You believed in the French, we surrounded you with homage and reassured you with our oaths. You left your asylum, you came into our midst, alone and unarmed. So long as there was no danger, so long as you disposed of favours and power, a vast multitude deafened you with noisy cheers. You did not abuse its enthusiasm. If your ministers made many mistakes you were noble, good, responsive. One year of your reign did not cause so many tears to be shed as a single day of Buonaparte's. But he reappears at the far corner of our territory, he reappears, this man stained with our blood, and but lately followed by our unanimous maledictions. He

[1] The vote of the 'Sénat Conservateur', under pressure from Talleyrand.

shows himself, he threatens, and neither oaths restrain us, nor your virtues impress us, nor your confidence touches us, nor your old age moves us to respect. You thought to find one nation, you found nothing but a herd of perjured slaves.' No, such will not be our language. Such at least will not be mine. I say it today without fear of being disregarded. I have sought liberty in various shapes, I have seen that it is possible under the Monarchy, I have seen the King rally to the nation; I am not going to crawl, a miserable turncoat, from one power to the other, to cover infamy with sophism and mumble desecrated words to buy back a life of shame. But this is by no means the fate that awaits us. These warriors, who for twenty-five years covered France with boundless glory, will not be the instruments of the national shame. They will not sell their country, which has admired them and which cherishes them. Deluded for an instant, they will return to the French flags.[1] Afflicted by a few errors, to which they fell victim, they are seeing these errors rectified. They have as guides their former commanders, their brothers in arms, those who led them so often to victory, those who, knowing their services, will help the Monarch to reward them. The aberration of a day must be forgotten. They were ignorant perhaps of their own mistakes. Like them, the nation will ignore them, in order to recall their admirable valour and their immortal renown.

[1] The white flag with the fleur-de-lys.

Appendix II

Question: Are you French?
Answer: No, I'm a royalist.
Q. What is a king?
A. He is a being of a nature more elevated than other men, who is accountable to no one for his conduct, who can do all, who sees through the eyes of his ministers, and who is supposed to know all.
Q. Who is King?
A. Louis XVIII by the grace of God.
Q. Where is the seat of his power.
A. In different places, according to the circumstances. He has reigned for nineteen years successively in Germany, Russia and England, and wherever he may be he will reign in spite of evil-doers until the good Lord takes him back unto himself.
Q. Why is he King?
A. Because he is the grandson of Louis XV and the brother of Louis XVI.
Q. Who will be king after Louis XVIII?
A. Count d'Artois, and after him all the Bourbons one after the other, not excepting the House of Sicily, until the extinction of the line. Rather than remain without a master, we should suspend the Salic Law, if there were a shortage of men.
Q. Why have we been created and put into the world?
A. To regret the past, to disparage what the French call the glory of their country, to obtain decorations and rewards, and to declaim in distress.
Q. What must we do to be saved?
A. The indispensible qualifications are to be a Knight of the Extinguisher and of the Lily and to be ready to fight against France in foreign armies.
Q. What must a good royalist do?
A. First, he must be prudent, for fear of compromising the

safety of the good cause, denigrate all that is French, shun the scandalous joy of Bonapartists and constitutionalists; shut himself up in a select little society, imbued with sound principles; have a mysterious air; spread false social gossip on the quiet; make a Novena to St Roch that it may please God to speed the progress of Louis XVIII; and for the rest, have confidence in the wise bounty of Providence, who will permit the return of Buonaparte only to render his punishment the more terrible, and the return of the Bourbons more complete.

Q. What are the theological virtues of the royalist?

A. Faith and hope; he must keep these in spite of experience. In order that he may practise them in comfort, he is dispensed from charity.

Q. What must be the state of the soul of a good royalist?

A. His soul must be divided between two well-pronounced sentiments, in which all other thoughts come to be lost and annihilated : hatred of Buonaparte and liberal ideas, infinite love for the Bourbons and their doctrine.

Q. Hatred, then, is not a sin in a royalist?

A. No, certainly not; Bonapartists are not our fellow-creatures. It is even a laudable and meritorious action for him to detest his parents when they are infected by this abominable error.

Q. Anger, then, is not a sin in a royalist?

A. No, because it is hallowed by passing through his mouth. The more anger approaches fury and rage, the more holy it is.

Q. Is pride permitted to a royalist?

A. It is the very human attribute that is wanted; however, it must be used with moderation, while awaiting the events that will put each in his place.

Q. Repeat the secret *Confiteor* of the royalist.

A. I repent for having aided the revolutionaries of '89, by inflaming an argumentative people; for having in the States General prepared our private disasters and the fall of the throne, our ancient safeguard, by refusals and just persecutions, which should, however, have been kept for a better time; for having then surrendered to a little gang of scoundrels. I bite my lips for having let myself be deprived so easily of my château, my coach, my cross of St Louis and my seigneurial pew : far from repenting for not having defended Louis XVIII, I congratulate myself on having preserved a loyal subject for him, by staying quietly at home, while he was losing his provinces, on not having squandered a useless courage, seeing that everyone was for Buonaparte; but what I sincerely regret is not having profited more from the King's good disposition towards us; if it please God, and the Allies, he will return, this good Monarch, and we shall make up for lost time.

Q. Repeat the royalist *Our Father.*

A. Louis-the-longed-for, who art in Ghent, resounded be thy proclamations from one end of Europe to the other, thy will be done in the Congress and in the camps of the Allies, as it was done in the Chamber of Deputies; thy kingdom come to us in Paris; come to give us our privileges and our *Quotidienne;* come very quickly, for fear we should succumb to the temptation of accepting something from Buonaparte; and deliver us from that evil Corsican. Amen.

Q. Repeat the Royalist Salutation.

A. Hail brave Amazon,[1] whose name is beatified by the ladies of Bordeaux; see that the fruit of thy bowels be blessed. Holy Daughter of kings, pray for us in our hour of trial; pray for the sins of France, that she may acknowledge her blindness and return to her legitimate king. Amen.

Q. Say the Act of Faith of royalists.

A. At the risk of falling out with all so-called reasonable men, I believe in the imprescriptible rights of the House of Bourbon to the throne of France, I believe as much in the *Moniteur de Gand* as in the evangelical saints, I believe in the miracle of a second coalition, which will bring us back our beloved Bourbons, across fields of carnage and cities laid waste. Amen.

Q. Say the royalist Act of Love.

A. I love Louis XVIII, although he was weak enough to concede a constitutional charter to unworthy subjects, which I forgive him, nonetheless, since he has not observed it; I love Count d'Artois, because if he had been allowed the time, he would have restored the sacred privileges of the nobility and the clergy, given the Cross of the Lily to the whole world, and handed back to their legitimate owners the goods of which a rebellious nation had despoiled them; I love the Duchess d'Angoulême, because

[1] The Duchess d'Angoulême.

she was disagreeable to everyone, except the heroes of Koblenz and Quiberon, and because, at last, conjointly with her august spouse, she promised us a wholly spiritual reign; I love the Duke de Berry, because he treated those military brigands properly, and because under him we should have seen flower once more the amiable good breeding, the magnificent elegance of Versailles and the Palais Royal.

Q. Say the Act of Hope of a good royalist.

A. I hope to see the defeat of the rebellious army and people; I hope to see the Russians, Prussians, Austrians, English, Spaniards, Cossacks, Bashkirs, Tartars and others occupy Paris and the strongholds, in order to keep dutiful this insolent nation that would think itself free; I hope to see the lifeguards resume their splendid service at the Tuileries, and the French, vassals to the foreigner and humbled by us, become more docile than Turks; finally, I hope to recover, at the cost of their shame and their despair, honours, decorations, privileges, goods and power. Amen.

Bibliography

I should like to express my special thanks to M. Fleuriot de Langle, Conservateur of the Bibliothèque Marmottan, for having eased my access to a large number of documents and books very hard to find, especially the precious collection of the *Nain Jaune*.

My bibliographical researches, conducted for ten years on the Hundred Days, have lain mainly in eight different sectors:

1. *General histories* of the Empire: Thiers, Masson, Tarlé, Lefebvre, etc.;

2. *Synthesizing books on 1815*: especially the incomparable *1815* by Henry Houssaye, *Le Vol de l'Aigle* by Jean Thiry, *Napoléon* by Friedrich Sieburg, *La Dernière Année de Murat*, by Major Weil, etc.;

3. *Works by contemporary writers*, which have brought a series of fresh insights into the question: Henri Lachouque, Henri Guillemin, Émile Tersen, André Maurois, etc.;

4. *Documents of the period and regional monographs*: the complete collections of the *Moniteur*, the *Journal de Paris* and the *Journal des Débats* for March 1815, the correspondence of the prefects in the National Archives, the irreplaceable *Nain Jaune*, and witnesses on Napoleon's halts at Mâcon, Chalon, Autun, Auxerre and Fontainebleau;

5. The *reports of the trials* of Ney, Cambronne and Drouot;

6. The *Descriptions géographiques et routières de l'Empire français*, which appeared between 1810 and 1815, and the delightful little book by Monier, *Les Bords de la Seine*;

7. The *Correspondance* and the *Oeuvres complètes* of Napoleon, and at the same time the *Mémoires* of Las Cases, Montholon, Bertrand and Gourgaud, in which the testimony of the main person concerned reaches us in attenuated and garbled form, but is still occasionally striking;

8. Finally, and above all, the *Mémoires* of contemporaries from all camps: Chateaubriand, Fleury de Chaboulon (with the terrible marginal notes by Napoleon), Planat de la Faye, Marchand, Saint-Denis, known as Ali, Macdonald, Marmont, Vitrolles, Marsilly, Gobineau, Gaillard, La Mothe-Langon, Beugnot, Fouché, Rochechouart, Talleyrand, Captain Coignet, Benjamin Constant, La Fayette, Mme de Staël . . . and so many others! . . .

Index

Abbeville, 280, 289
abdication, 19, 26f., 59, 76, 88, 90, 134, 173, 248
Aboville, General d', 52
Albignac, 254
'Ali', see Saint-Denis, Louis-Etienne
Alexander I, Czar, 39f., 84, 103, 173, 185, 198, 208
Allied Powers, 20, 41ff., 55, 76, 80, 159, 164, 203, 285, 294; see also Holy Alliance
Allix, General, 69, 164, 195-6
Ambrosio, General d', 188
Ameil, General, 109-11, 123, 141f., 182-3, 268
anarchy, 26, 37, 51
Ancona, 188, 273-5
André, 83, 208, 257
Angoulême, Duke of, 35, 105-6
Angoulême, Duchess of, 23, 105, 160, 163, 217, 232, 288, 299
Anjou, 68, 157
army, 19ff., 29-38, 43-5, 48-51, 52, 56, 61ff., 69ff., 75, 109f., 126-8, 132ff., 141, 167, 175-81, 190, 219, 221ff., 228ff., 233-4, 237, 241, 261, 266, 268ff., 275ff., 288, 290
army, royalist, 86, 104f., 107-8, 141, 143-8, 157, 181, 201, 203, 227, 233f., 244, 269, 281
Artois, Count d' (Monsieur), 25, 34, 56, 73, 84f., 87, 92-6, 99, 102ff., 110, 112-19, 143, 163, 193, 201f., 222, 231-2, 236, 281, 297, 299
Audibert, sub-prefect, 149, 189
Auger, 253
Augereau, Marshal, 61, 107-8, 278
Augier, General, 184
Augustin, 110
Austria, 39-43, 64, 89, 185, 187-8, 271, 273, 285
Autun, 26, 37, 38-9, 57, 67, 73f., 88-92, 129, 290
Auxerre, 19, 26f., 67-8, 90, 108-11, 123-8, 134, 141-3, 144f., 148-54, 158-67, 178, 183, 189ff., 200, 214, 219-20, 229, 244f., 263

Auxonne, 33, 56, 68
Avallon, 26, 37, 120, 123, 127, 128-35, 142, 145
Azaïs, Madame, 36

Baillou, quarter-master, 247
Barrot, Odilon, 219
Beaumont, 281
Beaune, 37, 68
Beauvais, 216, 239, 269, 279
Belgium, 36, 186, 197, 289f.
Berry, Duke de, 84, 86, 110, 114-19, 144-8, 157, 181, 200f., 203, 222, 227-8, 234, 236, 281, 300
Berthier, Marshal, 84, 223, 236, 245, 279
Bertrand, Marshal, 57, 60, 70, 76, 90, 131, 149, 154, 164, 166, 174, 189, 191, 193, 242, 245f., 265, 287
Besançon, 26f., 32f., 59, 91, 166
Beugnot, Claude, 83, 132, 182, 217
Beurnonville, Count de, 84
Bidot, Jean-Louis, 45
Blacas d'Aulps, Count de, 84-5, 95, 102-3, 114, 117, 135-7, 155-8, 168, 197, 214, 227, 232, 235f., 279
Blois, 30, 157
Bonaparte, Joseph, 208, 283, 290
Bonaparte, Lucien, 188, 208, 290
Bonne, Louis, Mayor of Mâcon, 23f.
Bordeaux, 105-6, 232f.
Boudin de Roville, General, 68, 108-111, 123-5, 127, 141, 161
Boulongue, 61
Bourbon, House of, 25, 31, 44, 48, 58, 64, 68, 83, 85, 89, 93ff., 109, 115, 134, 143, 151, 158, 160ff., 165, 173, 175, 192, 204f., 210, 236, 261, 273, 279, 288, 299
Bourbon, Duke de, 107
Bourcia, 33
Bourg, 32, 34
bourgeoisie, 105, 243, 260ff., 276
Bourmont, 177
Bourmont, General, 32-5, 44, 50, 63-4, 175
Bourrienne, Louis-Antoine Fauvelet de Charbonnière de, 77-8, 87, 99-103

302

Index

Louis, Baron, 198
Lyons, 19, 21ff., 28ff., 32, 34, 36f., 52, 55f., 61, 74f., 85f., 88, 90f., 103f., 110, 129, 133f., 142, 145, 149, 161, 164f., 183, 185, 190, 202, 214, 231, 241, 247, 286, 290

Macdonald, Marshal, 73, 85-7, 174, 201-3, 216, 221-4, 227-8, 231, 241-2, 261, 278, 280, 289
Mâcon, 19, 20-6, 33f., 36f., 45, 57, 75, 104, 129, 190
Maillé, Duke de, 232
Maison, General, 144, 155-6, 241, 280
Malartic, 92f., 102
Marchand, General, 182f., 195
Marchand, valet de chambre, 150, 173, 214, 229, 245, 247, 287
Maret, Hugues-Bernard, Duke de Bassano, 95, 247, 264, 283
Marie Louise, Empress, 23, 94, 161, 190, 248ff., 270, 290
Marin, Colonel, 189
Marmont, General, 61, 84, 107, 134, 167-9, 206, 216, 223, 278
Marsilly, 80-2, 222-3, 237, 253-4, 266
Masséna, Marshal, 35, 105, 154, 183, 278
Maubreuil, 192-3
Melun, 125, 144-8, 156, 200, 216, 234, 243
Mermet, General, 59, 63
Metternich, Prince, 40, 187, 253
Metz, 30, 177
Mézières, 36, 52
Michel, General, 178
Mier, Count, 188
Moncey, Marshal, 44, 234
Moniteur, 28, 79, 104, 128, 141, 256, 263f.
Montereau, 148, 200-1, 214, 229, 234, 245, 266
Montesquiou, Abbé de, 29, 84, 124, 135-7, 158, 177, 205
Montesquiou, Madame de, 249-53, 270, 284-5
Montigny, 177
Montpellier, 106
Moret, 234, 237-9, 242, 248
Mortemart, Duke de, 81, 237, 281
Mortier, Marshal, 52, 77, 179-81, 278, 280
Morvan, 121-3, 142

Mouton, Marshal, 277f.
Murat, Joachim, King of Naples, 186-8, 208, 268, 270, 273-5

Nain Jaune, 257-9, 289, 297-300
Nancy, 36, 177
Napoleon, abdication of, 19, 26f., 59, 76, 88, 90, 134, 173, 248; and 'the people', 19, 47, 57, 122, 129-30, 132f., 154-5, 176, 190, 248, 288; and the priests, 88, 162-4; attitude to Ney, 166-7, 173-6, 245; explains himself to Raudot, 132-4; fear of riots, 26, 70, 141, 195, 217, 224, 248; opinion of Louis XVIII, 132, 165, 183; proclamation to the army, 61-3, 69, 107
National Guard, 24, 37f., 50, 55, 57, 69ff., 74f., 81f., 84, 133, 136, 243; of Paris, 25, 100, 112-15, 144, 155, 194, 228, 235, 254-5, 262-3, 269, 283
Neufchâteau, 177
Negré de Massals, Lieut., 244
Neipperg, General, 252, 270
Nevers, 26, 69
Ney, Marshal, 20, 26, 29-35, 43-5, 48, 57-64, 74f., 78, 86f., 90, 104f., 109, 126, 142, 156, 161, 164, 166, 173-6, 181, 183f., 187, 221, 245, 278
Nîmes, 106, 232
Normandy, 68, 107, 157
Noverraz, 150
Noyon, 52

Old Guard, 30, 74, 142, 165, 176-9, 181, 190, 194, 266
Orléans, 27, 126, 157, 159, 243
Orléans, Duke d', 28, 94, 114-19, 179-81
Oudinot, Marshal, 30, 58, 176-9, 278
Ouvrard, Gabriel-Julien, 199f., 208

Pacca, Cardinal, 275
Pailhès, 81
Paradis, Boniface, 68, 151, 160
Passinges, Baron, 90
'people, the', 19, 22, 27, 34, 37, 47, 49, 57, 70, 79, 120ff., 129, 133, 154-5, 176, 190, 200, 218-19, 225, 243, 260-3, 266, 276, 288
Périgord, Countess Edmond de, 42-3
Peyrusse, 120, 247
Pignot, 38
Pius VII, Pope, 19, 188, 274f.

305